# THE WOMAN WHO
# MURDERED BABIES
# FOR MONEY

# THE WOMAN WHO
# MURDERED BABIES
# FOR MONEY THE STORY OF AMELIA DYER

Alison Rattle & Allison Vale

André Deutsch

This edition published in 2011 by

André Deutsch
an imprint of the
Carlton Publishing Group
20 Mortimer Street
London W1T 3JW

First published in Great Britain in 2007 as *Amelia Dyer: Angel Maker*

2 4 6 8 10 9 7 5 3 1

Plate-section picture credits: National Archives, Kew: page 2; Oxfordshire
County Council: page 1; Scotland Yard Crime Museum: pages 6 *top*, 8;
Thames Valley Police Museum: pages 3, 4, 5, 6 *bottom*, 7.

A catalogue record for this book is available from the British Library

ISBN 978 0 233 00316 0

Typeset by E-Type, Liverpool
Printed and bound in the UK by CPI Mackays, Chatham ME5 8TD

# Authors' Note

The texts of several letters written by Amelia Dyer have been included in this book. Rather than correct her spelling and punctuation or pepper the text with [sic] throughout, we have transcribed the letters as they originally appeared.

# Contents

# 1 *What the River Revealed*

On the Monday morning of 30 March 1896, local bargeman Charles Humphreys was leisurely navigating a cargo of ballast up the River Thames at Reading. He had passed the untidy belchings of the gasworks at the mouth of the River Kennet and was making his way in the direction of the tranquil expanse of the Thames which flowed past the broken teeth of the eel-bucks toward Caversham Lock, the foaming cascades of the weir and the wooden footbridge known as the Clappers. It was a bitterly cold day. Poplars and limes, just coming into bud, stood stark against the open scenery, and willows overhung the water's edge. To one side of the river were long views stretching toward the town of Reading, and to the other the outspread country-side of peaceful fields and farmland. The well-trodden towpath which ran alongside the river was pitted with horses' hoof prints and lined with fat tufts of coarse grass.

As the barge came within a few hundred yards of the main railway station, the left bank of the river ran away into King's Meadow, a green sweep of public recreation grounds, and the Huntley & Palmers cricket club, fenced off from the towpath. In the river, lying in the shallow water several feet from the bank, was a lumpy, brown paper parcel. Humphreys reached for the parcel with a punt hook and dragged it out of the water on to the boat. Curious, and expecting to find at least a cache of linen or some other goods of value, he began to pull open one end of the half-sodden parcel. Beneath the paper, however, there was only a layer of thick flannel fabric which, when pulled to one side, revealed, to his horror, part of a leg and a tiny human foot.

⚔️

Earlier the same day, retired ironmonger William Povey had been walking up by the river from the direction of the picturesque village

of Sonning, to the east of Reading. He had just crossed the GWR
footbridge over the Kennet into King's Meadow when he noticed
the tall, ample figure of a middle-aged woman coming toward him
along the towpath. She was dressed warmly, a dark cloak reaching
down to and almost covering her brown booted feet, and, while he
watched, she moved away from the fence at the side of the towpath
and approached the river a number of times, glancing down nervously
at the water. He was struck by the height of the woman and by the
peculiarity of her manner, and for a moment was afraid she might be
about to jump into the water. As their paths crossed her cloak swung
open, and he noticed she was carrying a brown paper parcel tucked
under her right arm. Povey continued on unhurried and a while later
the woman passed him again on her way back. This time he saw no
parcel.

⊰⊱

Charles Humphreys wasted no time in running for the police. At the
station, the unfortunate officer on duty was PC Barnett, who immediately accompanied the breathless and shaken Humphreys back to
the site of the grim discovery. A sack was fetched; PC Barnett placed
the sad little parcel inside it and carried it on his back to the police
station.

Detective Constable James Anderson, a member of the detective
branch of the Reading Borough Police and an officer of more than
fifteen years standing, had just entered the station when PC Barnett
arrived with his morbid load. Both officers took the parcel to the
mortuary and watched while local surgeon Dr William Maurice
cautiously pulled it open. Underneath layers of flannel, newspaper,
a quantity of napkins (nappies) and a child's cloak (known at that
time as a pelisse), the tiny body of a female infant, about six to
twelve months old, was finally revealed. A length of macramé string
had been used to tie the parcel together and wrapped up with the
body was an ordinary household brick. Most disturbing of all was
the piece of white tape wrapped twice around the child's neck and
tied with a knot under her left ear. The position and tightness of the
tape and the protuberance of her eyes suggested without doubt that
death had been caused by strangulation.

DC Anderson was convinced that the parcel had been thrown into
the water from the towpath, doubtless with the expectation that it

would sink in the deep channel. However, the parcel had landed in the shallows and was then too far from the towpath to be retrieved in order to be thrown further out.

A detailed inspection of the wrappings around the child revealed no clues as to its identity; until the very last piece of paper swaddling the body was removed. This crumpled, pale, brown paper shroud had upon it the faint outline of handwriting and a Midland Railways label bearing the address "*Temple Meads Station, Bristol*".

As the parcel had only been partially submerged in the water, the handwriting had not entirely smudged, and, after close examination, DC Anderson was able to make out another address and a name. *Mrs Thomas, 26 Piggotts Road, Lower Caversham, Reading, Oxon.*

# 2 Suffer Little Children

Toward the end of the nineteenth century Reading was an expanding and prosperous town, owing much to the world-famous Huntley & Palmers biscuit factory which employed almost five thousand local workers. In addition, other burgeoning industries – breweries, seed merchants, ironworks and brickmakers – encouraged new workers from outlying rural areas to move to the town for employment. Rows of distinctive red- and grey-brick terraced houses – built from locally produced bricks – soon began to spring up to accommodate the growing population.

It was to these busy streets, filled with bicycles, hand carts and horse-drawn trams, that NSPCC inspector Charles Thomas Bennett moved with his family, in the mid-1890s, to take up his first official posting. His house at 11 London Road was a short distance from the crowded pavements of Broad Street with its profusion of chimneys and shop awnings shading the wide pavements. The muddy road was crisscrossed by carriage tracks and churned up by horses' hooves; small islands of manure dotted its length. The grocers', cigar and tobacco shops, the shoemakers and the linen and wool drapers all jostled for space among the oversize advertisements for India Pale Ale, Reading Sauce and the ubiquitous Huntley & Palmers biscuits. London Road itself was quieter, a mixture of fine mansions and large red-brick houses with towering chimneys, majestic gables and ornate brickwork.

The Bennetts' home was a more modest affair. It had once been a shop, and Charles Bennett made use of the large bay window at the front of the house to display photographs of abused children while using the room behind as his office. The photographs on display were not for the faint-hearted and would have presented a shocking sight to the casual passer-by. This was no place to window-shop. Many of the children were victims of violence and neglect from within their own homes, but many more had been born illegitimate and had been sent out into the care of "nurses".

In Victorian England single mothers were judged harshly. They were left unable to find any form of employment, save that of prostitution. Shame and poverty condemned many of them, and their children, to lives of destitution and starvation. An unmarried mother's only alternative was either to abandon her child or foster it out into the care of a "nurse" or "baby farmer" for a weekly fee, or to have it adopted permanently for a one-off payment, or "premium". Anyone fostering or adopting more than one child under the age of twelve months was required by law to register with the local authorities. It was a shoddy system, rarely policed and widely abused. Many children were sent to an early grave by unscrupulous "nurses" out to make a quick profit. They were often starved or drugged to death; some met a speedier end and were murdered outright.

The images in Charles Bennett's window showed children and babies in distressing conditions: naked, skeletal, barely human figures with huge, haunted eyes, twisted limbs and swollen bruises; bones protruding from paper-thin skin which in some cases hung off their frail frames like hand-me-down clothes. Then there were photographs of the same children, the rescued ones, taken months later: plump-cheeked and smiling, dressed in clean, stiff jackets and sitting straight-backed on the photographer's chair. Those found alive, in whatever deplorable condition, were the lucky ones. The systematic mistreatment and murder of children was commonplace in Victorian England and the NSPCC was one of a number of organizations leading a vigorous crusade to help prevent it.

## NATIONAL SOCIETY FOR THE PREVENTION OF CRUELTY TO CHILDREN
### INCORPORATED BY ROYAL CHARTER.
### PATRON – THE QUEEN

*The sole object of this Society is to secure to every child in the land that its life shall be at least endurable. It does this with great success by enforcing and encouraging the reasonable treatment of Children by their Parents.*

*The following is a Record of the Numbers of the Children in the Nation on whose behalf it has employed its objects.*

*166,161– SUFFERERS from NEGLECT and STARVATION*
*41,226 – SUFFERERS from VIOLENCE*

*21,916 – LITTLE THINGS EXPOSED to SUFFERING to draw
the lazy and cruel charity of the street
7,053 – Pitiable GIRL-CHILD VICTIMS of Horrible Sensuality
3,897 – LITTLE SLAVES of Improper and Hurtful
EMPLOYMENT and DANGEROUS PERFORMANCES
1,067 – WHERE ILL-TREATMENT ENDED FATALLY*

The hordes of illegitimate children born each year had prompted one government report of the time to state:

> Their births are not registered, nor are their deaths; some are buried as still-born children, some are secretly disposed of, many are dropped about the streets.

It was impossible for the newspapers of the day to keep count of the numbers of bodies found strewn about the towns and cities. Scarcely a day passed without yet another report of the corpse of some young innocent being found abandoned beneath the seat of a railway carriage, under an archway, in a sewer grating or just care-lessly dumped in one of the open spaces of a city suburb. Many cases were not even reported, such incidents being so commonplace as to be denied column space in favour of the latest gossip from the Royal Circle or the House of Lords. In almost every case the inquest into the death would return a verdict of "found dead" or "murdered by some person unknown".

**Return showing the number of infants (under one year) found within the Metropolitan Police District of "k" division during the year 1895.**

| Month | Male | Female | Total | Remarks |
|---|---|---|---|---|
| January | | 1 | 1 | Found in a railway carriage at Bow works. Verdict "Inattention at birth" |
| February | | 2 | 2 | 1 found in cemetery passage. Verdict "Stillborn" 1 found in Whitehorn Street. Verdict "Accidental causes" |
| March | | 1 | 1 | Found on bank of Regents Canal. Verdict "Wilful murder" |

| Month | Male | Female | Total | Remarks |
|---|---|---|---|---|
| April | – | – | – | |
| May | 1 | | 1 | Found in sewer grating in Abbey Lane. Verdict "Stillborn" |
| June | – | – | – | |
| July | 1 | | 1 | Verdict "Supposed deceased died from inattention at birth" |
| August | 2 | | 2 | 1 found in a railway carriage. Verdict "Stillborn" 1 found on line of Great Eastern Railway. Verdict "Wilful murder" |
| September | – | – | – | |
| October | 1 | | 1 | Found on the green, Stratford. Verdict "Exhaustion from inattention at birth" |
| November | 2 | | 2 | 1 found in Regents Canal. Verdict "Stillborn" 1 found in River Lee. Verdict "Wilful Murder" |
| December | | 2 | 2 | 1 found in a barge in Royal Albert Works. Verdict "Inattention at birth" 1 found in a railway carriage. Verdict "Found dead being born dead" |
| Total | 7 | 6 | 13 | |

*One of many statistical returns for a Metropolitan Police survey conducted in 1895 to establish the extent of infanticide in the capital.*

# 3  A Casual Informer

Suspicions surrounding the illegal fostering of children in Reading had already been aroused two months before the discovery of the macabre parcel in the Thames. In January 1896, an elderly, benevolent-looking woman, broad-bosomed in a buttoned-to-the-neck dress and thick shawl, had stood gazing into the window of the NSPCC office for such a long time that Charles Bennett's wife had felt compelled to step outside to see if the woman was quite well. She had been moved to discover the old lady in tears, clearly most upset at the state of the children in the photographs. Pointing to the pictures, the woman had wondered how people could be so cruel to "the little mites". Mrs Bennett had ushered her inside and put the kettle on to boil. Once seated in the parlour with a cup of tea in front of her and a comforting hand upon her arm, the old woman had calmed down. She seemed to welcome the kindness shown to her and before long had begun to reveal her own situation.

She lived across town, she said, off Oxford Road. She had been in Reading only a few weeks, having previously lived for a while at 26 Piggotts Road, Caversham, a short walk over the river. She was a widow lady, she said; she had lost her husband and her own three children. Her husband William had been a labourer in Bristol. When he had died she had been forced into the workhouse and had been all alone without a friend in the world – but she had met a woman in the workhouse who took her out with her and said they could live together as sisters. That was who she lived with now – Mrs Thomas. This woman took in babies to nurse, little dears, which was why seeing the photographs in the window upset her so. Mrs Thomas had promised to pay her to help look after the little ones – a shilling a week she had said – but in reality all she received in return for cleaning the house, making the beds and other household chores were her meals. The babies were often taken away – she didn't know where to – but she missed them terribly; she always grew very fond of the blessed creatures. Mrs Thomas adopted the children, she said, "in consideration of a money payment". They were mostly illegitimate, and there was one at the house now who did not look well at all. Number 45 Kensington Road, that was where she lived, she said. Just off Oxford Road. The tram stop was just at the top.

Mrs Bennett informed her husband of the incident when he returned home from work. Charles Bennett listened carefully; as an NSPCC officer he was only too aware of the failure of the authorities to keep track of all persons involved in the often shady business of fostering and adopting children. He certainly had no knowledge of any such individual being registered to adopt children in Kensington Road and resolved to investigate without delay.

# 4 Kensington Road

The local Reading newspapers of 1896 reported a gloomy January; hard, grey days followed each other with steely clouds louring over rooftops. The winds were harsh and cold, but despite the weather, all over town would be found straggly mobs of children hanging around on street corners or pushing each other up and down the roads in makeshift carts fashioned from sugar crates, shivering in thin jackets or huddling in doorways to keep warm.

It was on just such a day that Charles Bennett chose to follow up the information given to his wife by the old woman in his parlour. Number 45 Kensington Road was a small, neat, two-up, two-down red-brick house, sandwiched tightly into a terrace of almost identical buildings which marched the entire length of the street. At one end was the junction with the main Oxford Road; the Reading Union Workhouse stood across the way, next to the Hospital for Infectious Diseases with its cholera-infected wards. At the other end was the cropped green of the county cricket ground with its genteel pavilion, the newly built Battle School and the brickworks, whose tall chimneys and kilns, coated in clay dust, sprawled in a disorderly heap.

45 Kensington Road, *Weekly Dispatch*, 19 April 1896

The middle-aged, slightly coarse-looking woman who answered the door eyed Charles suspiciously, her heavily built figure filling the doorway. Her dirty brown hair, streaked with grey, was dragged back severely from a centre parting into an untidy bun. She had a deeply lined, almost masculine face, a fleshy chin and loosely drooping eyelids. The straight, hard set of her mouth and a glimpse of blackened tooth stumps did nothing to warm her features. Had Charles looked more carefully, he would have noticed how easily she carried her bulk and how her large hands were at odds with the rest of her, being pale and smooth with long, tapering fingers.

Charles introduced himself as an officer of the NSPCC and asked if it was true that she had been adopting children. The woman, who identified herself as Mrs Thomas, invited Charles into the house and readily admitted to having one "dear" little nurse child of about six months old, the daughter of a Miss Neilson, and a young lad, Willie Thornton. She had already had a visit from the chief attendance officer of the school board regarding the boy. She hadn't thought to send him to school as his mother was meant to be coming for him in a few days' time. But she had been put under pressure, and the boy now regularly attended the Battle Board School, just up the road. She told Charles that she did indeed adopt unwanted children for sums of money, but that she had placed many of them in good homes. She was rather evasive when asked for details regarding the children, but did admit to being unregistered.

The old woman who had taken tea with Charles's wife a few days before was sitting quietly in a corner. When Mrs Thomas introduced her as "Granny", Charles was careful not to disclose her as the source of his information.

The interior of the house, although fairly spartan and frugally furnished, seemed clean enough. The table and chairs were decidedly plain and the floor beneath the oddly assorted mats looked well swept. There was a row of tin boxes in the kitchen containing infants' food, and Charles also noticed a cradle and a sewing machine which appeared to be new. In front of the fire was a clothes horse hung with various items of infant apparel. The condition of the six-month-old baby gave Charles some cause for concern and after requesting the mother's address he was reluctantly given the name of Mr G. Neilson, the child's uncle. Charles informed Mrs Thomas that henceforth she would be receiving periodical visits from him. She replied that she "would be pleased to see him at any time". As he left Kensington Road that day, the NSPCC officer was unaware that he had just had his first dealings with Amelia Dyer.

Charles Bennett reported back to the NSPCC Headquarters and informed the local Reading police that unregistered adoptions were being carried out at 45 Kensington Road. He also took it upon himself to write to Mr Neilson telling him of his suspicions regarding the care of his sister's child.

George Neilson, who lived in Manchester, had already become wary of the woman he knew as Mrs Thomas. He had agreed to pay her ten shillings a month to care for his sister's illegitimate daughter, but after paying the second monthly instalment he had received a letter from Mrs Thomas informing him that if he were to give her the sum of £2 she would be happy to relieve him of all further liability. Mr Neilson thought this "very queer" and travelled to Reading in order to satisfy himself as to the wellbeing of his niece. On finding Mrs Thomas absent from home, he decided to inform the local police of the situation, telling them that he "did not think things were altogether as they should be". He then left Reading, asking the police to let him know if "anything was wrong".

The suspicions of a number of concerned parties had at last been aroused.

Mrs Thomas was furious. Believing that the Neilsons alone had reported her to the NSPCC and the police, she scribbled a number of highly indignant letters – they survive today and are held in the Metropolitan Police Crime Museum at New Scotland Yard. The letters are chaotic, lacking in punctuation and full of spelling errors, as if she was literally shaking with anger at the time of writing. One such letter reads as follows:

> To Mr Neilson Sir I have daily been expecting a letter from you I am surprised you do not write I was more than surprised at the manner you behaved by reporting me to Inspector Bennett, he have seen Baby every week this last weeks She have been very ill Indeed she had the Dr last Tuesday Wensday he came twice and again now this morning but, She is alright again now and will not call again 2 bottles of medicine he have charges me 2/ for and 2/ each visit I shall have the Bill next week and will send it on of course after the way you have acted I cannot pay it you don't send any money and now it seems you don't trouble now I shall expect some sent on by return of post. I must give her up she is

got quite well again now but she never was a strong Child Miss Neilson have written to me but since acting in the way she did I shall not write anything she wants to know about Baby Mr Bennett will no doubt tell her. I have always done my duty and love that dear child dearly but now after the way I have been treated I should not think of writing to her. Not later than this day 2 weeks you must find another home for her dear little soul I would have kept her and done my duty by her but not now.

  I am Sir Yours
  A. Thomas

This letter was followed a week later by another, this time written to the mother, Miss Neilson. Mrs Thomas had been receiving regular visits from the police by this time and her anger had been fuelled; a number of phrases are underscored with a heavy black line to emphasize her outrage:

To Miss Neilson a week ago I sent and told Mr Neilson I should keep Baby no longer than Saturday next Feby 29. After behaving as you and Mr Neilson you pretend you know nothing what this is for when the same Saturday your Brother was here a month ago yesterday *you reported the circumstances to Inspector Bennett* you thought the child was not properly done by and the man came here he saw the child clean and comfortable. *I can tel you I was not a little put out by it would you like a policeman coming here every week to see the child no I am sure you would not neither do I.* I would have kept her and done my duty by her but I shall not now after this. I have done my duty by her you can write to Mr Bennett and he will tell you all you wish to know. More than that she has been ill I have paid 11/ for the Dr neither have your brother kept up the payments promised it is 8 weeks next Wensday since he sent any I have only had 50 shillings in different payments and he positively refuses to pay any more I will have Baby ready next Satturday and you must either come or send someone for her if not you will be put to a lot of expense and trouble I shall not keep her after that date under any pretence whatever. If you had any complaining to make why did you not speak to me in a strait forward manner when you was here not to behave in that manner if I had only known it when you came on the Monday you should have taken her with you *then but rest assured what ever you do with her Mr Bennett will follow you pretty sharp I will see to that* so please remember Saturday Feby 29

  Yours A. Thomas

The Neilson baby was not in the best of health. Its neglected condition had prompted Charles Bennett into taking action, and Granny had been sufficiently moved by the child's plight to report her employer. It is doubtful that a doctor was ever called to 45 Kensington Road.

Charles Bennett regularly visited the Neilson baby until 7 March, when, acting upon instructions from Mr Neilson, he arranged for the child to be handed over into the temporary care of a local couple, Mr and Mrs Pope.

Mrs Thomas continued to present herself as the aggrieved party and in her final letter to Miss Neilson it is clear her anger and indignation had not abated; she pointedly refrained from addressing Miss Neilson by name.

45 Kensington Road
Oxford Road Reading
Wensday 4th March 96
Mrs Thomas writes to say Baby is quite fit now to be removed and you will come for her on Satturday next March 7th without fail. Last Satturday the Dr said she could go but I have let her stop a few days the child will be ready Satturday morning and unless you come for her I shall take her to the house and the Warrant Officer will then fetch you. I have had advice on the matter also I have seen Mr & Mrs Pope about it be sure you are not later than middle day.
A. Thomas

Unperturbed by her close encounters with the authorities, Mrs Thomas continued, from January until the end of March 1896, to advertise for and take in several other children. She had practised a monstrous trade for almost thirty years, but it was about to be brought to an abrupt end.

# 5 The Sting

It was not until the beginning of April 1896 that the police obtained their first clue as to the identity of the person responsible for disposing of the brown paper parcel containing the body of a six-to-twelve-month-old baby girl in the River Thames. The mail clerk at Reading Station was able to identify the parcel as having come by the London and South Western Railway from Bristol and to confirm that it had been addressed and delivered in October of the previous year to a Mrs Thomas of 26 Piggotts Road, Caversham. The parcel had weighed about 15lb. He was also able to inform the police that Mrs Thomas had since moved away from Caversham and now resided at an address in Reading: 45 Kensington Road.

Police Sergeant Harry James, a personable looking man at the height of his career, was as meticulous in his appearance as he was in his work. A well-groomed, thick, walrus moustache complemented his pleasant features and lent him an air of proud authority. His winged collar was pristinely white and creased precisely over a thickly knotted tie; a heavy wool suit, with well-defined shoulders, hugged his neat figure. A photograph of him at the time shows a man who was not entirely strait-laced: the lower buttons of his jacket are left undone to reveal a glimpse of waistcoat and watch chain and his tidy bowler hat sits at a decidedly jaunty angle.

After making a number of discreet enquiries Sergeant James discovered that a Mrs Thomas had indeed resided at 26 Piggotts Road, Caversham, along with a grown-up daughter, a son-in-law, an old woman known as Granny, and a varying number of children whom she was in the habit of adopting. The daughter and son-in-law had by all accounts since left for London, and Mrs Thomas had moved across the river to Kensington Road, where she had become known to the local NSPCC officer, the school attendance officer, and had also been reported to the police for the unregistered adoption of children. A disturbing picture was beginning to emerge, and Sergeant James and his colleague, Detective Constable James Anderson, an earnest young Scotsman, began to make extensive enquiries. They discovered that a woman had been seen leaving Kensington Road on the morning following the discovery of the baby in the Thames. She had been carrying a scruffy looking carpet bag and was heading in the direction of the river. The two officers decided to proceed in their investigations with the utmost caution, wary of alerting Mrs Thomas to their suspicions.

To this end, a young woman (possibly a police matron – these were often the wives of serving officers) was persuaded to act as a decoy. She was instructed to call at the house in Kensington Road on the pretext that she had been recommended to Mrs Thomas by a friend in London (whose name was not to be mentioned) for the purpose of arranging the adoption of a baby. The woman who answered the door, however, was not Mrs Thomas, but a short, stout, bustling woman whose apparent energy belied her seventy-odd years. Her name was Jane Smith, but she was referred to by all who knew her as Granny, a sobriquet which sat comfortably with her soft, kindly features. She informed the young lady caller that Mrs Thomas was away from home for two days or so, but that if she wished she could make an appointment to come back and meet her when she returned. A time was agreed upon.

Two days later the young woman once again knocked upon the door of 45 Kensington Road. This time it was opened not by Granny but by a bulky, middle-aged woman who greeted her in a brusque and businesslike manner; she was at once most anxious to know who had recommended her. The reply she received was that the "friend" in London who wished to adopt out her unwanted illegitimate baby had made it clear that she did not wish her name or address to be given. Apparently satisfied by this answer, Mrs Thomas agreed to take the baby for the sum of £100. The young lady, however, baulked at this: the sum was far too high (it being the equivalent of the yearly salary of a butler), and, after further negotiation, the price of £50 was fixed upon. Mrs Thomas was careful to stipulate that the infant should be brought to her after dark.

The nature of the business being conducted at Kensington Road had become abundantly clear. So, on the evening of Good Friday, 3 April, DC Anderson and Sergeant James made their way to the by now familiar doorstep at precisely the time the fictitious baby was due to be delivered.

Mrs Thomas was in the backyard chatting to some neighbours and it was Granny who, with a gleam of satisfaction in her eyes, admitted the police into the house. She seemed almost to relish their presence and the words spilled from her lips as she willingly answered their searching questions. Her tired old eyes kept flitting toward the back door and when Mrs Thomas came in from the garden to see who the male voices belonged to, Granny quickly shrank back, cowering, into the background.

Producing the incriminating sheet of brown parcel paper bearing Mrs Thomas's name and former Caversham address, DC Anderson asked the now visibly shaken suspect to account for the fact that it had been found wrapped around the body of a young baby, discovered strangled and dumped in the Thames.

But her real name was not Thomas, mumbled the suspect, it was Dyer – although she sometimes adopted the names Thomas, Weymouth and Harding. Her explanation was that her mother's maiden name was Weymouth; Thomas was the name of her first husband; and that she had dropped the name Dyer (that of her second husband) because he had treated her very badly, and had broken up two homes, and she did not want him to find her. As for the parcel paper, well it was true that she had received just such a package while she was living in Caversham, but she had recently cleaned out a cupboard full of rubbish, and the paper must have been put out to the dustbins as usual.

Such a faltering response prompted the officers to make a thorough search of the house. In a small tin canister on the kitchen mantelpiece they found some printed forms relating to infant vaccinations. There were also dozens of pawn tickets for children's clothing, a number of letters and, in a cupboard in the kitchen, more piles of babywear. There was also a rare stench as if something were decomposing there. In a sewing basket the officers also found a quantity of macramé string and white tape similar to the materials found on the body of the murdered baby fished from the Thames. In the woman's bedroom they discovered a large tin box; it also gave off an almost unbearable odour, and bore the gruesome traces of having at one time been the receptacle for a body. The explanation given by the suspect was that the tin box had once held a quantity of old clothing which had become musty. It was a feeble response, and Sergeant James and

DC Anderson had seen and heard enough. They arrested Amelia Dyer and took her, and the suspicious tin box, to the police station.

⊨⊫

The familiar blue glass lamp was burning outside the door of the station as Dyer was led up the stone steps and into the outer police office. The walls were plastered with police notices, some of them illustrated with photographs of unsavoury characters wanted for burglary. A duty sergeant manned the desk, stiff-collared in a dark blue, brass-buttoned uniform with a black varnished belt buckled securely around his waist, there to hang his truncheon.

Mrs Thomas, now revealed as "Annie" or Amelia Dyer, was taken into the charge room to wait while the police matron was sent for. (As there were no women police officers at this time, it was necessary to have a matron to deal with and perform searches upon any women arrested and brought to the station.)

Reading Police Station, *Weekly Dispatch*, 26 April 1896

As she sat quietly waiting, Mrs Amelia Dyer produced from her pocket a small pair of scissors; but before she could do herself any harm – if that had indeed been her intention – they were wrested from her by an officer. The suspect then proceeded, very stealthily, to remove the lace from one of her boots; by the time the police were aware of this, she had tied the length of it around her neck, the knot resting just below her left ear.

# 6 Beginnings

There was little about Amelia's early years which might have led her to a feeble suicide attempt in a provincial police station. She was born in 1838, the youngest of five children. She spent her childhood in the hamlet of Pyle Marsh, a cluster of houses nestling in the mining district to the east of Bristol. Her father, Samuel Hobley, was a respectable, hard-working man, a cordwainer – a master shoemaker. Her parents valued education, and Amelia's brothers did well for themselves: by 1861, Thomas, her eldest brother, had stepped into his father's boots, as a shoemaker; James was a ship's carpenter and William, just two years her senior, a cabinetmaker and carver. These were solid, respectable trades. Amelia's education had also been funded by her father (at a rate of two shillings a week in a Church-run National School, for the children of the working classes), until she was fourteen.

In this respect, Amelia could consider herself especially lucky: only a quarter of the twenty thousand school-age children of Bristol received any schooling at all in the year of her birth; most were destined to remain illiterate. Amelia, however, reached adulthood with a sound, if basic, grounding in the "three Rs"; she wrote competently with a sweeping cursive hand, and she had acquired a reasonable grasp of grammar. Moreover, she had discovered a love of literature and poetry that she was to sustain throughout her life.

Things could have been worse. Far worse. Bristol was no place to be poor. By 1860, it was pock-marked with slums. Crumbling Georgian tenements, long since uninhabitable, were home to thousands of families. Lashed across the underbelly of these tenements were six hundred inter-connecting passageways, known as "courts", where entire families lived in single rooms. Here, in dark, damp spaces, crawling with vermin, dozens of families shared a single standpipe and privy. Misery and disease were the hallmarks of daily life and gang crime, theft and violence were rife.

Amelia had escaped the squalor on her doorstep. She had enjoyed a simple but comfortable childhood, in a close-knit, stable community, amid the honest values and Christian morals typical of her class. But for all that, she had not escaped hardship.

In 1848, when Amelia was just ten years old, her mother, Sarah, died. Amelia was to be forever haunted by the memory of her mother's final days. At the age of forty-five Sarah contracted typhus fever and Amelia witnessed her mother's spectacular mental decline: altered, dysfunctional speech and elaborate and horrifying delusions followed by wild hallucinations and periods of mania. Amelia's father entrusted his wife to the care of Dr Fox, who ran Bristol's first purpose-built private asylum just a few miles away, in Brislington. Fox attracted some of the most prominent lunatics of the day: he could even claim the (now somewhat dubious) honour of having been called to Windsor to help treat King George III. His name was synonymous with the treatment of the well-heeled unhinged. He accepted patients from whichever class could afford him; but he also reserved a few beds for pauper lunatics.

For a while, Sarah's fever appeared to abate, but once she was allowed back home there was no respite for her ravaged mind. Amelia had looked on in horror: although her mother was able to breathe and speak and chew and swallow, she was nevertheless left entirely vacant, unable to express even hunger or thirst. Then meningitis set in and death followed swiftly.

Eleven years after the death of her mother, Amelia's father died of bronchitis, by which time Amelia had already left home. She was later to recall that when she left school at the age of fourteen she was sent to live with an aunt in Bristol's marketplace. Thereafter, she served an apprenticeship with a corset maker. Then, in the late summer of 1861, at the age of twenty-three, Amelia took a room in a lodging house in Trinity Street.

❧

Trinity Street was a small row of damp and draughty Georgian terraced houses, running perpendicular to the harbour. To the east was a skyline of ships' masts and rigging and to the west the cathedral. College Green, with all its sophistication and opulence, was just a street away.

Number 2 Trinity Street was home to fourteen people. Three rooms were occupied by boarders, paying for their meals as well as their lodgings. The lodging-house keeper was Fanny Ross, thirty-eight-year-old mother of three, who cleaned the rooms, cooked the meals and, for an additional charge, took in laundry. The extra rooms were converted into income from her lodgers.

When George Thomas took rooms with Mrs Ross, he wasn't a typical boarder. A mature man with a good trade as a master carver and gilder, he had buried his wife just a few months earlier. At the age of fifty-seven, he was considerably older and more experienced than the men living around him. Later Amelia recalled that her acquaintance with George Thomas began while she was still living with her aunt. Intriguingly, George had left a good home with his married son in Clifton to move into these meagre lodgings, suggesting that he came to Trinity Street in order to live with Amelia. Certainly it didn't take long for the couple to formalize their relationship: five months after the death of his first wife, George Thomas and Amelia Hobley were married at the Bristol Register Office.

It was, by Victorian standards, an unceremonious occasion for a young woman's first wedding. There was no father at her arm; no mother dabbing an eye in the front pew. She had already become estranged from at least one of her brothers, James, for reasons now lost to time. Neither a Hobley nor a Thomas acted as witness. It seems that neither family knew of the union. Perhaps they even disapproved of it. The couple's marriage certificate gives a tantalizing indication of how the newlyweds felt about their substantial thirty-three-year age gap: George claimed that he was forty-eight, shaving nine years off his actual age. Amelia added an extra seven years to hers, insisting that she was thirty. Mr and Mrs George Thomas thereby effectively halved the difference between them.

Two years after her marriage, Amelia Thomas took up a position with the Bristol Royal Infirmary, as one of Bristol's very first team of nurse pupils to undertake regular nurse training. The BRI was a well-regarded and well-funded voluntary hospital. Behind its imposing edifice were four storeys of vast, wallpapered wards, the whole placed in the nightly care of a single nurse. Amelia gained experience on general, surgical and medical wards in three-month rotations.

Nursing was a thankless occupation in 1863, certainly no job for the genteel or those of a delicate disposition. It was demanding, gruelling work, from which Amelia emerged with all the characteristics of a mid-nineteenth-century nurse: an emotionally sturdy, dispassionate and self-reliant woman. Amelia worked sixteen-hour shifts, starting early in the morning and working late into the night. Medical expertise would not have formed part of her training: this was regarded as entirely the concern of doctors. But with anaesthetics, pain relief and surgery still unsophisticated, pain and infection would have been commonplace. A report on conditions in the outpatients department at the BRI in the mid-century paints a colourful image:

> The atmosphere of the room in which the patients waited was described as tainted and poisonous; a policeman was employed to keep order and when a fresh batch was wanted, the door of the common room was opened by one or two of the attendants and the crowd of maimed and diseased wretches shouldered and fought their way into the place where they were seeing the Physicians and Surgeons who had to arrange and sort them as they came in.

In 1864, when Amelia was twenty-six, she fell pregnant and was not permitted to continue working once her pregnancy became obvious. Later that year, she gave birth to a daughter, Ellen Thomas. At about the same time, a fortuitous meeting with a midwife named Ellen Dane was to introduce Amelia to a means of earning an income beyond anything she had thought possible, setting a course she would steer for the rest of her life.

# 7 From Angel to Angel Maker

Ellen Dane hailed from Southport, where George Thomas had family. She came to Bristol in the late 1860s and for a brief period she had stayed with George and Amelia. Dane earned a living taking women into her own home for the duration of their confinement, nursing them through the latter stages of their pregnancy and acting as midwife during their labour. Many of the women she nursed were driven by the need for secrecy; they would arrive when their pregnancy could no longer be disguised and would often remain as long as six months. In exchange, Dane could command a considerable monthly fee.

Dane offered one additional and highly sought-after service. Advertising in the small ads columns of newspapers under a pseudonym, she would take charge of unwanted newborn babies, either as "nurse children", fostered for a weekly fee, or else undertaking a permanent adoption for a one-off cash payment referred to as a "premium". Dane had identified a niche market and she was not alone in her trade. Since the Poor Law Amendment Act of 1834, a father could no longer be held financially accountable for the raising of his illegitimate offspring. This spectacular piece of Victorian wisdom was considered an effective deterrent against pre-marital relations: the intention was that the prospect of financial ruin would encourage more women to maintain their moral integrity. But deterrent it was not: by the 1860s, illegitimacy had reached pandemic proportions, and Dane and her like offered unmarried mothers what seemed to be an easy remedy.

In reality there were few others. Employers and families would turf a woman out as soon as her pregnancy began to show, driven either by a dread of scandal or by economic necessity. The workhouse was an option for some, but only at the discretion of the Guardians; many deemed "immoral" were turned down.

Once a baby was born, a woman's options were even bleaker. Few orphanages would agree to adopt any but "respectable orphans" – those whose fathers were dead rather than anonymous. The feeling was that immorality bred immorality: the "sins" of the mother would inevitably be revisited upon the infant, in the form of similarly loose morals. The Muller Orphanage in Bristol was typical: though priding itself on its ecumenical welcome to orphans of all religious denominations, it nevertheless stipulated that Muller orphans must be "lawfully begotten".

> On Saturday morning, the body of an infant was discovered, wrapped in an old newspaper, lying in the path from the Observatory to Clifton Down.
> *Clifton Chronicle*, 1856

Day after day, such newspaper reports stood testimony to the scale of the problem: many mothers, cornered and desperate, smothered their babies or abandoned them in public places. Mothers were rarely sentenced for "over-laying": smothering their babies to death during the night by apparently rolling over them in their sleep. Nonetheless, the term was often cited by coroners as a cause of death. Those abandoned babies who lived were raised in the workhouse.

The weekly fee offered by Dane would have given precious hope to those women genuinely looking to secure a future for their child. But it was a dangerous path to follow:

> There was held in the parish of St. Luke's, last summer, an inquest on the body of a neglected infant, aged seven months. The woman to whose care she was confided had got drunk, and left the poor little thing exposed to the cold, so that it died. The mother paid the drunken nurse four-and-sixpence a week for the child's keep, and it was proved in evidence that she (the mother) had been earning at her trade of paper-bag making never more than six-and-threepence per week during the previous five months. That was four-and-sixpence for baby and *one-and-ninepence* for herself.
> James Greenwood, *The Seven Curses of London*, 1869

The weekly fee was only profitable for Dane because she had found a means of keeping down the cost of fostering infants. Neglect was her method of choice, a gradual but persistent underfeeding coupled with regular doses of over-the-counter narcotics. Opiates and alcohol, sold as anticolic cordials, had the added benefit of keeping the infants docile and suppressing their appetite. Over a period of weeks, these methods would result in what Victorian death certificates labelled "marasmus": wasting away.

Where she thought she could, Dane would suggest that a woman offer her child up for permanent adoption, at a hefty but one-off premium, usually of around £5 or £10; more if she thought the mother could afford it. For many unskilled, working-class women, this amounted to something approaching an annual salary, and was beyond their means. But many adoptions were funded by the father of the child: a one-off payment could often be procured as a means of permanently easing a gentleman's embarrassment.

This system of fostering and adoption was known as baby farming, and in the 1860s it was still entirely unregulated. In the small ads of national and local newspapers there would occasionally appear an advertisement offering a baby for adoption which stipulated that *no premium* would be paid. In eliciting a response only from those prepared to adopt a baby without cash exchanging hands, these unhappy individuals were clearly hoping for a genuine and humane answer to their predicament. But such people were rare: many more saw this system for what it was, and understood they would have nothing further to do with their child after the transaction had taken place. Day after day the newspapers advertised infants adopted for a cash premium.

Adoption premiums wouldn't cover the cost of raising a child for very long, but Ellen Dane worked around this. Like many in her trade, she was not a sole practitioner. She acted as an intermediary, passing the babies she adopted on to baby farmers in other cities, paying a cut-price rate and pocketing a handsome profit. The lesser sum was accepted in return for anonymity; the intermediary would be well known to the infant's mother and therefore in a more precarious position.

Amelia watched Dane's occupation with fascination. Amelia was a nurse; she had received training in midwifery. She knew she could see women through their accouchement without difficulty. Whether George Thomas acquiesced in her plan to bring women into their home is not known, but it was not to be an issue for long. On 18 October 1869, George Thomas died. His death certificate gave his age as sixty-two and his cause of death as "Diarrhoea". His wife Amelia, present at his death, was left a young, widowed, single mother.

There seems little doubt that Amelia could have found a way through widowhood, that she could have chosen a respectable way of life to support herself and her daughter. She was later to claim that George had left her a considerable sum of money. But she also had extended family in the city – a sister, brothers, cousins. She had a trade and an education. She was a trained nurse and a competent midwife. She had options, but none that offered the instant money which Dane enjoyed.

Amelia was determined to earn her living as a baby farmer. Like thousands of other single mothers of her day, she now made the decision to pay for her child to be raised elsewhere. At the age of fifteen, Amelia's daughter, Ellen Thomas, would explain to a magistrate and jury that when her father died she had been "farmed out", sent away to live elsewhere. Ellen explained that she had not come to live with her mother until 1872. What became of Ellen during those three years is uncertain, but in 1871 the census return for a family living on the Sea Mills Road, in the village of Stoke Bishop, just outside Bristol, included one intriguing entry.

Stoke Bishop was just two and a half miles out of the city, to the north-west of Durdham Downs in Clifton. William Hemborough was a forty-year-old mason who lived with his wife, Esther, aged thirty-eight, and a house full of children. The Hemboroughs were not a conventional family. With an eight-year gap between their two elder children, a daughter and a stepson of the same age and two infants very close in age, the heavy copperplate script of the census return all but spells out *baby farm*. And last on the list of occupants in the household was a six-year-old "orphan" named Ellen Thomas.

─◁▷─

Dane's reputation for neglecting the infants which passed through her hands finally reached the ears of the police, and, fearing arrest, she set sail for the United States at the end of the 1860s. But by this time, Amelia had become intoxicated by the fast money Dane had made and had been exposed to a grim network of women embroiled in the buying and selling of infants for maximum profit and minimum risk.

In 1869, Amelia Thomas began advertising for children in Bristol. Operating under the pseudonyms "Mrs Harding" and "Mrs Smith", she took in women for the accouchement and began to establish a regular supply of unwanted infants to Dane's contacts in London and Liverpool.

# 8 *The Brixton Baby Farmer*

In the 1860s the editor of the *British Medical Journal*, a young doctor named Ernest Hart, together with a group of physicians known as the Harverian Society, launched an investigation into infanticide in Britain. Their findings were published and passed on to the Home Secretary, Sir Spencer Walpole, in January 1867. But Walpole's sights were firmly fixed on franchise reform and the report elicited no response. Undeterred, Hart kept up the pressure for legislation. In January 1868, he placed an advertisement in a national newspaper offering a child for adoption. He received more than three hundred replies, and the series of articles he subsequently published gained him the support of several leading members of the government.

The tide was beginning to turn. Infanticide in the metropolis had become such a problem that in the late 1860s Scotland Yard assigned a team of specialist officers to investigate the problem, led by Detective Sergeant Relph.

On 5 June 1870, Relph answered an advertisement in *Lloyd's Weekly Newspaper* and entered into a correspondence that was to result in the country's first high-profile baby farming trial, focusing on two sisters from Brixton named Margaret Waters and Sarah Ellis. Relph's investigation would also unwittingly uncover Amelia Thomas's connection with the Brixton Baby Farm.

> Adoption – A good home, with a mother's love and care, is offered to a respectable person wishing her child to be entirely adopted. Premium 5*l.*, which sum includes everything. Apply by letter only, to Mrs Oliver, post-office, Goar Place, Brixton.

The advertisement was typical of its kind. Ostensibly it offered a comfortable, maternal solution to an unwanted pregnancy; but some of its phraseology would nevertheless have been clearly understood by a young woman wishing to rid herself of a problem forever. Firstly, the stipulation that the child be "entirely adopted": no further visits from the mother would be entertained. The moment of exchange was to mark the end of all contact. Then, the "premium 5*l*": £5 cash payment for an infant's life. This was a woman interested in cash, not in filling her home with the sound of a child's laughter. "Which sum includes everything": an assurance of a one-off payment and a guaranteed end to any parental responsibility.

Sergeant Relph – still pretending to have a baby he wished to put up for adoption – met "Mrs Oliver" five days later. After their meeting he trailed her to an address in Brixton, where "Oliver" (Sarah Ellis) was discovered to be aiding her sister, Margaret Waters, in running a baby farm.

Number 4 Frederick Terrace in Brixton extended over four floors, from basement to attic. Relph's first impressions gave little reassurance of the "mother's love and care" Ellis had advertised: he found the house sparsely furnished and was assaulted by an overpowering smell. In a back kitchen, Relph discovered five three- and four-week-old infants lying in filth, three under a shawl on an old sofa and two stuffed into a small crib on a chair. The children were barely clothed; the few rags which clung to their bodies were saturated and stank of urine and faeces. The babies were huddled in so small a space that none of them would have been able to move even had they wanted to; though they appeared to have no such inclination. They were ashen-faced and emaciated, their bones visible through transparent skin. They lay open-mouthed, in such a state of torpor that movement seemed impossible to imagine. They lay with eyes fixed, pupils unnaturally contracted, scarcely human.

Relph later told a crowded courtroom that what most affected him was the noise: a cavernous silence, so abnormal for a room full of infants. The life was ebbing fast from these five: "...instead of the noises to be expected from children of tender age, they were lying without a moan from their wretched lips, and apparently dying in that condition" (*The Times*, 22 September 1870).

On a nearby table was an empty, uncorked phial which reeked of laudanum – an opiate strong enough to suppress the appetite and induce in a child a stupefied, docile state. These children were those ill-fated adoptees of Waters'. The one-off premium paid by their birth mothers had been reserved entirely for her own gain, not a penny of it having been spent on the children where she could avoid it. Their deaths were being hastened by a miserable and absolute neglect.

In another room lay five more infants. Older, cleaner and some-what better fed, these individuals were clearly favoured, their lives deemed worthy of being sustained a little longer. They were Waters' nurse children, lodging with her for a weekly fee. The longer she could keep them going, the more income she would receive. But these too were dying: one after another they would succumb to a death which was more drawn out but just as inevitable.

Relph returned to the house later that same day, having first sent for Dr George Puckle to examine a three-week-old baby named John Walter Cowen. Puckle immediately had the baby removed to a trust-worthy wet nurse to be suckled, but little John's skeletal body had been too much abused by neglect and laudanum, and two weeks later, on 24 June 1870, he died. Dr Puckle was convinced that starvation and opiates had caused the death of John Walter.

Waters and Ellis were arrested and taken into custody. The nurse children were taken to the workhouse where three of the older infants were reclaimed by their mothers. Two remaining older children rallied well. But, like little John Cowen, the four young babies who had been permanently adopted by Ellis and Waters were in an unnatural, torpid state. With a peculiar, glazed gaze which did not respond to light, these four were emaciated and inanimate and ravaged with thrush. None of the children weighed any more than 6 or 7lb, though the oldest of them was four months. All four died within a few weeks of being received into the workhouse.

On Thursday 22 September 1870, the two women were brought to trial at the Central Criminal Court. Margaret Waters, aged thirty-five, and her sister Sarah Ellis, twenty-eight, were charged with the wilful murder of the infant John Walter Cowen. Waters admitted to having adopted forty babies over four years. Ellis insisted the figure was higher.

Another Scotland Yard detective assigned to the case, Sergeant Ballantine, acted for the Crown in court, and he began by instructing the jury that the death of this infant was to be regarded as something more than a peculiarity of the constitution of the infant itself. This death was the result "of a system pursued by the prisoners".

Dr Puckle told the court:

The body [of John Walter Cowen] was extremely emaciated, the bones almost protruding through the skin. It was miserably wasted, and nothing but skin and bone. It had been a fine child. It was in a thoroughly insensible state. The eyes were closed, the limbs hung down, and the child appeared to be in a profound stupor. I raised the eyelids and found the pupils very much contracted, and not in a natural state. I tried very much to rouse it but to little purpose. It was under my observation for 20 minutes. Diarrhoea or thrush would not account for the state in which it was. My opinion is that the child was in a state of narcotism from some drug ... The children on the sofa were all very quiet, and that struck me afterward as a remarkable thing. I was in the house nearly half-an-hour and there was no crying or motion from any of them.

At the trial, Margaret Waters' fourteen-year-old servant also gave evidence. She told the court there were eleven infants in all; the five youngest infants would be left all day to lie on the sofa, and were only fed on the rare occasion they gave out a feeble cry. She said that she was used to keeping watch over the children at night, as Waters and Ellis would frequently leave the house under the cover of darkness, not returning until one in the morning. Often, she said, they would leave with one baby and come home with an entirely new one; or with none at all. Meanwhile, the bodies of five infants had been found wrapped in rags and tossed over garden walls or left lying under railway bridges all over Brixton.

Sarah Ellis was acquitted of the charge of murder, the judge instructing the jury to find that there was insufficient evidence to convict her. Instead, she was sentenced to eighteen months' imprisonment with hard labour for conspiring to obtain money (from adoption) under false pretences. But in the case of Margaret Waters, the jury were faced with contemplating a crucial point of law: did the evidence prove conclusively that Waters was conscious that her improper feeding of the infants, and the administering of narcotics, would hasten their deaths in order that she might profit financially? The judge told the jury that he was in no doubt that, "From the moment the child Cowen was received into the establishment, the hand of death was upon it", but he posed the question: "Did she intend by that course of treatment and line of conduct to shorten its life?"

The jury took just three-quarters of an hour to return a verdict of guilty of murder and, after a verbose objection by Waters herself, the judge donned the black cap.

Margaret Waters was hanged at Horsemonger Lane Gaol, Southwark, on 11 October 1870:

But that women could perpetuate the slow murder of infants, could watch them from day to day sinking with glazed eyes from stupor into death, and all in the pursuit of some precarious gain, is the most ghastly instance afforded in our time of the wickedness of which human nature is capable ... The depravity displayed by these two women is horrible and inhuman but it will not be forgotten that their infamous livelihood was rendered possible by a depravity scarcely less shocking in other persons. It is impossible to doubt that the majority of those who gave up their children to be adopted by Mrs Waters were cognizant of their probable fate, and were content to abandon them to it ...

*The Times*, 24 September 1870

It was the brief mention in the national press of one of the children in the Margaret Waters trial, a fourteen-month-old referred to by Waters' servant girl as "Little Emily", that would cause the heart of one particular Bristol nurse to miss a beat. Margaret Waters was paid a £5 premium for the permanent adoption of Emily three months before her trial. She had never had to meet the child's mother face-to-face: the adoption was arranged via an intermediary, Amelia Thomas, operating under the name of Mrs Harding.

Emily had been born to a twenty-nine-year-old widow named Elizabeth Gilbert, in April 1869. Mrs Gilbert was already struggling to raise two children on her own, scraping a living running a small general store in Holborn. She had been attended to during her pregnancy by a fifty-eight-year-old apothecary named Dr William Harding.

Dr Harding lived a life of modest privilege in a four-storey red-brick Georgian terrace in Fitzrovia – at 4 Percy Street, just off the Tottenham Court Road. In the late 1860s, Percy Street had an air of quiet, residential grandeur about it, which it is still possible to detect even today in the neat railings, the window boxes, the fanlights of polished glass above panelled front doors and the brightly tiled entrances. The Harding family's census returns for 1861 and 1871 encapsulate everything that Victorian English society found most estimable.

William Harding was a member of the Royal College of Surgeons and the Hall of Apothecaries. He remained married to Catherine all his life, and they had four children (by 1871 the eldest son, Percy, was a professor of mathematics and another, Alfred, a student of medicine).

They kept two domestic servants and one young male assistant to Dr Harding's private apothecary practice.

But Sergeant Relph knew of the murky truth behind Harding's respectable veneer, and his investigations had also uncovered the connection between this Fitzrovia apothecary and Amelia Thomas.

In August 1870, with Margaret Waters and Sarah Ellis already in custody, Dr William Harding had also appeared before the Central Criminal Court at the Old Bailey. Despite his professional association with the mother of Little Emily, and therefore his connection with the Waters' case, his was an unrelated charge: that he had procured an abortion upon a young actress named Isabella Tewson, which had resulted in her death.

Abortion, practised either with the use of drugs or surgical instruments, had been illegal in England, under the Offences Against the Person Act, since 1861. If the abortion could be proven to have resulted in the death of the pregnant woman, the individual could be tried for manslaughter, a capital offence. Only a dying actress's swansong stood between the apothecary and the gallows (on her deathbed Tewson had gripped Harding's hand in an effort to identify him as her abortionist). But there had been no corroborating evidence, and so Harding had been acquitted.

Four months later, Sergeant Relph revealed in an internal Scotland Yard report that he had kept up a close surveillance of Dr Harding since the acquittal. Relph reported that Dr Harding kept rooms in Windsor Terrace, just off the City Road in Islington, a couple of miles from his Fitzrovia home. Police surveillance of Windsor Terrace, and discreet questioning of the neighbours, confirmed that very few people were to be seen coming and going from the apartments. In fact, Relph ascertained that Harding had little need to practise at the time as he was able to live comfortably off an allowance from his elder brother, from the family's estate in Ludlow, Shropshire.

Nevertheless, Elizabeth Gilbert, the young widow from Holborn, had clearly sought the intervention of Dr Harding in her pregnancy in 1869. Dr Harding's attempt to give her an abortion had failed, and, upon the birth of Little Emily, Dr Harding told Relph that the baby had immediately been put out to a nurse. Intriguingly, Relph's report on Dr Harding and Little Emily states: "... shortly after its birth it was received as a nurse child by Mrs Harding at a weekly payment of five shillings. It remained in her care until the month of June following."

The surname Harding, shared by the nurse and the apothecary in the case of Little Emily, is difficult to ignore. He can hardly have been referring to his own wife, who was most probably unaware of her husband's covert and disreputable practice from the cover of a separate address. Furthermore, no gentlewoman would have taken in babies to nurse for a few shillings a week. Clearly, the Mrs Harding in question must have been someone other than his lawful wife. Whether Amelia Thomas's choice of pseudonym was simply a coincidence or the result of an illicit relationship with the Fitzrovia apothecary and abortionist in 1869 is now impossible to determine. But in June 1869, Little Emily was handed over by "Nurse Harding" to Margaret Waters for permanent adoption for the usual £5 premium.

Relph reluctantly concluded his report by saying that the police would be unlikely to gather any evidence sufficient to secure a prosecution against Dr Harding:

> I have no doubt this man occasionally lends his professional assistance in cases of abortion, but the operation would take place at the residence of the person undergoing it – no third person would be present and this being so the evidence of the woman being uncorroborated would not be admissible to support a prosecution, both persons being equally guilty. Thus rendering it extremely difficult to bring to justice persons guilty of this class of offence.

Harding was in fact careful to use Windsor Terrace for correspondence only, hence the absence of human traffic noted by the neighbours. Any women he attended to were treated at their own addresses, and he insisted upon no witness being present. Within the limitations of nineteenth-century law, he was untouchable.

❧❧

One other curious detail emerged during the trial of Waters and Ellis. A series of letters were found in Waters' house, suggesting that she had been involved with a nationwide trade in infants. Twenty of the letters were of particular interest. Since 1869, a midwife had regularly supplied Waters with unwanted newborns from a house of confinement she was operating in Totterdown, Bristol. The Tottterdown midwife went by two names in these letters: Mrs Smith and Mrs Harding.

It was a tangible thread linking Amelia Thomas to Margaret Waters. Amelia Thomas was farming babies under the alias "Harding". Neither Scotland Yard nor the Somerset Constabulary (which policed Totterdown) picked up the thread: no visit was made to the Totterdown address. No enquiries were made to establish Mrs Harding's true identity. But throughout 1869 and 1870, Amelia Thomas was evidently running a substantial baby farm of her own, earning a handsome income supplying Margaret Waters with babies to kill.

⚖

If polite London society hoped Waters' execution would bring an end to the abhorrent trade in infant lives in the metropolis, their hopes were soon dashed. The press continued to report clear evidence that her legacy lived on. Scotland Yard offered rewards for information leading to the arrest of anyone guilty of infanticide, and even offered pardons to any accomplices who came forward. But the scale of the problem was vast.

### DISCOVERY OF ANOTHER BABY

> On Wednesday Mr Carter held an inquest at the "Malborough Arms" tavern, South Street, Camberwell, on the body of a male child which was found on Monday last ... John James Boulton, a gentleman's gardener, stated that on Monday last he was passing the garden of a lady's residence at Dulwich when his attention was directed to a parcel which was lying on the ground therein. He immediately went in and opened it and found it contained the body of a deceased child ... This makes the third body which has been found since the execution of Margaret Waters, the baby-farmer.
>
> *Morning Advertiser*, 28 October 1870

In fact, it soon became apparent to the whole country that Waters was not the only one plying such a trade. In the years following the execution of Margaret Waters, further arrests were made for baby farming. Mary Ann Hall and her accomplice Mrs Cumming were arrested at the end of 1870. In 1880 Elizabeth Thompson was charged with baby farming in Liverpool. In the late 1880s, Millie and Joseph Roadhouse were apprehended in London for baby farming. Finally, in 1889 another Camberwell woman, a Mrs Bogle, who had been adopting infants on a prolific scale for twenty years, was given a fifteen-year sentence with hard labour. In every case, their baby farms had been regularly supplied with infants from a house of confinement run by a midwife in Totterdown, Bristol, known variously as Mrs Smith or Mrs Harding. The midwife was never pursued.

⊰⊱

The horrors perpetrated by the Margaret Waters case caused such public outcry that Ernest Hart of the *British Medical Journal* was able to establish the Infant Life Protection Society, which proved to be the final push needed to goad the government into action. In 1871, Sergeant Relph was called upon to discuss his experiences of illegitimacy and baby farming in the capital in front of a Parliamentary Committee. The Infant Life Protection Act was subsequently passed in 1872, calling for the registration of all nurses caring for more than one infant under the age of twelve months.

# 9 The Lunatic Pauper Palace

As another year spluttered into life on New Year's Day 1871, Amelia Thomas ought to have been counting her blessings. Within a few short years, most of her contacts had paid a heavy price for the trade they shared. Ellen Dane had fled the country to escape arrest; Margaret Waters had been hanged; and Ellis, Cummings and Hall were all serving time with hard labour. Dr Harding, with whom she had had, at the very least, a working relationship in 1869, had only narrowly escaped the ultimate sanction.

Amelia would have followed these cases avidly in the press; after all, they had been high-profile trials, which had, according to *The Times*, "excited much interest". And those punished had been her colleagues. Several of the children she had sent to them were named in court; letters she had written were cited; her pseudonyms were printed in the national press.

If she took urgent action, she could still escape arrest: after all, her name was not Harding. Nor was it Smith. Her Totterdown address could easily be vacated. She closed her house of confinement, and instead searched the small ads of local papers for something very different. More by necessity than choice, Amelia Thomas sought once more to earn an honest living.

—⧗⧗—

Early in 1871, Amelia became a nurse attendant at the Bristol Lunatic Asylum.

It was an odious prospect: for a salary of £1 a month, in addition to a uniform, meals and a beer allowance, Amelia would once again be working long and hard for her money. But it was a relatively easy job to come by for it was arduous and sometimes dangerous work, with no holiday allowance; few women remained in the post for a full year.

But it offered Amelia accommodation and, for the moment, that was attraction enough.

The Bristol Lunatic Asylum in Fishponds stood on a commanding site, a long avenue of year-old limes extending across its grand, turreted frontage. The ten-year-old building was largely bright and airy; the wards were comfortably furnished with beds, heavy wooden tables and long wooden benches, and a smattering of comfortable chairs. The asylum Visitors saw to it that "objects of interest" – plaster busts, prints and vases – were scattered throughout the wallpapered wards, in order to "enliven". It stood in stark contrast to the much-despised St Peter's Asylum in the city, and quickly earned a reputation as Bristol's "Lunatic Pauper Palace".

Amelia was to report to the head female attendant, Miss Louisa Yeames. Yeames was devoted to her post and had the respect of her employers. She was a thirty-year-old spinster from Yorkshire, and had been in charge of the nursing staff at the asylum since the previous year. It was an unenviable job. The attendants were not always the most professional. The sobriety of some was often in question (hardly surprising in an institution which budgeted more for the purchase of wine, spirits and beer than it did for medication), and the behaviour of others left much to be desired.

Nevertheless, the emphasis at the Fishponds Asylum was a liberal one, by the standards of the day at least. Dr Henry Oxley Stephens, the asylum's first medical superintendent, had retired at the end of the previous year, but from the start had insisted his staff adopt that most current of maxims "Treatment Not Punishment". He hotly disagreed with any thinking which suggested that a lunatic brought his condition upon himself by indulging in vices. He instead believed that lunacy was consequent to "a variety of troubles and misfortunes, mental, moral and physical, to which we are all liable". Miss Yeames was keen that Amelia remain mindful of this sobering thought in all her dealings with the patients. Kindness, she insisted, was to be an attendant's chief motivation. This wouldn't always be easy, she realized; some patients had violent or self-destructive tendencies and these could be most testing to manage. Yeames assured her staff and Board of Guardians (the directors) that, despite the prevalence of mechanical restraint elsewhere, at Fishponds it was to be strictly a last resort, limited to those instances of the direst necessity. Indeed, its use had been entirely forbidden under Dr Oxley Stephens. Still, it had to be conceded that patient safety occasionally required a reliable method of restraint.

Amelia was made aware of the various means of restraint: preventive gloves, for example, which crossed the stomach and were tied behind the patient's back, restricting arm movement entirely; metal cuffs, locking together the wrists; and straitjackets, for the restraint of excessively violent patients, such as the criminally insane. Miss Yeames was insistent that each and every instance of restraint was thereafter meticulously detailed in the asylum's Medical Record, priding herself that this journal would bear witness to the sparing use of such measures on the female wards. But Amelia was soon to discover that if individual patient attention and a general enlightened tolerance were the much aspired to ideals of the medical superintendent and his esteemed head female attendant, they amounted to little more than an unworkable nonsense for the ward attendants.

In 1871, the wards were full to capacity and beyond. A few patients were being accommodated in the day rooms, or else in corridors. The workhouse would routinely transfer all incurable and unmanageable patients into the asylum, while the asylum superintendent tried in vain to secure the transfer of the criminally insane out. Added to this, the water supply was barely adequate and of dubious quality: gastro-intestinal disorders, enteric and typhus fever tested the medical capabilities of the institution still further.

It was undeniably a laborious way for Amelia to choose to earn a living. The care of the psychotic, the epileptic or the syphilitic was the grimmest part of her job. These conditions were little understood and hopelessly incurable: medical intervention amounted to a meagre attempt to manage symptoms, not treat causes. Sedation was prioritized for the epileptic and the psychotic, and the emetic was the most favoured sedative: even the most unruly patient could be forced into compliance by extended periods of vomiting. The emetic of choice at the latter end of the century was apomorphine, a narcotic so highly toxic that it brought on hours of vomiting. Some asylums still made use of the rotating chair, a mechanical means of achieving that same quietening nausea.

A military-style regime restricted the staff as much as the patients. Every door was to be kept securely locked. Every excursion, even down a corridor, was to be punctuated with head counts. Even patients' footwear was subject to restriction: for those deemed liable to damage their shoes, lockable boots were issued, cumbersome things which could only be removed by an attendant with a key.

Each day was filled by a strict regimen of housekeeping, feeding,

47

cleaning and exercising the patients in the "airing yards". On bath days, patients were stripped in batches and taken to communal bathrooms. Amelia would help her fourteen patients, one by one, into a tub of water (the asylum aimed to provide fresh water for each patient but rarely managed this until it was connected to the mains supply in the 1880s). She would scrub each woman down from head to toe with a soapy, long-handled brush, until the skin was marked and red, afterward leaving each bather to stand naked until she had fine-combed her hair through with turpentine to kill off any infestations.

Before she could get her patients dressed again, Miss Yeames would inspect them individually, wanting her to account for every bruise, mark or scratch on their bodies. Then Amelia would hand out fresh clothes, in which the patients would remain, day and night, for the coming week. Finally she would dress their hair. Loose hair for the female patients was forbidden, but then so too were grips and pins, since they might be used as weapons. So Amelia and the other attendants fixed every woman's hair in place with a needle and thread.

Mental health nursing was never a great calling for Amelia. In fact, she soon learned it was an occupation she did not much care for at all. She was one of only eleven female attendants set to nurse 136 female patients. Her patient care, in common with the work of all attendants, amounted to little more than crowd control. A wholesale restrictive routine was the easiest way she could manage fourteen women in her care.

If mechanical restraint appeared in Fishponds' Medical Record to have been little used, on the wards it was very much part of the furniture; an indispensable means of managing dangerous or self-harming patients, used frequently, though rarely entered into the books. And any patient deemed too violent to be at large could expect to spend long stretches of their days cuffed into chairs or strapped into a straitjacket, being let out at brief intervals and only then once in seclusion. Whatever ideals the hospital boasted, then, the strain placed on the nursing staff created a stealthy culture of low-level aggression toward refractory patients. The annual Commissioners' reports of the early years of the 1870s make it clear that the hospital Visitors recognized this. One Commissioner noted having seen a patient with a black eye and facial contusions, and was informed by him that he had been "set upon" by two attendants for arguing with another patient after leaving the dining hall.

If she was lucky, Amelia would escape the worst of her lot by supervising mostly melancholics, suicidal maniacs or those with "depressive agitation". These women were generally calmer and more compliant, as they could be managed effectively with narcotics. Opiates were standard issue and they were indulged just as eagerly by the attendants as by the patients. They elevated melancholic spirits, rendered the agitated docile and induced sleep. One of the asylum's suicidal maniacs in the 1870s, recorded simply as "E.W.", made frequent and inventive attempts to end her life. She tried swallowing an entire box of dominoes, and, on another occasion, 14oz of pebbles. Most spectacular were the 24¼oz of iron screws, which she had dislodged from the window shutters over the course of one night and swallowed before breakfast the following morning. (Despite periodic painful stomach spasms, she was left largely unharmed. The thirteenth screw was finally passed six months later, at which point the annual Commissioner's report noted that E.W. was transferred out of the asylum.)

All fit and able patients were expected to spend part of their day working around the asylum. Those with trades were put to good use: shoemakers and binders, carpenters, smiths, painters, mat makers, bakers, laundresses, cooks, dressmakers and seamstresses – all were expected to offer their specialized services, in exchange for an extra allowance of bread and cheese and a half-pint of beer at tea time. Such useful occupation was considered therapeutic; but every year, the annual report boasted an estimate of how much expenditure this policy saved the asylum.

For recreation, the asylum chaplain kept a ready supply of books which he distributed every week to literate patients. A programme of entertainments was introduced: cricket, piano and harmonica recitals, theatrical performances, picnics, outings to Bristol's zoological gardens.

Amelia began to see that for the well-behaved lunatic a short spell at the asylum wasn't so bad. It was certainly a more attractive proposition than the workhouse, where the harsher regime and extreme depersonalization made absolute economic sense, but created a living hell for the inmates.

In fact, it was possible for a female lunatic to work the system to her advantage. If she remained largely even-tempered, and was deemed to be suffering from a manageable, transient and therefore "curable" condition, the asylum might even represent a refuge, a respite. It offered a troubled woman a constant supply of dull but nevertheless edible food, free beer and tobacco, as well as time to read, to sew, to walk in the gardens, attend chapel and even enjoy in-house entertainments once in a while. Moreover, she had daily access to mood-enhancing narcotics. For Amelia Thomas, this may have come as something of a revelation.

The year 1871 turned out to be a bad one for the Bristol Lunatic Asylum. The annual report published at the start of 1872 contained a catalogue of complaints. It had been a year of increased overcrowding; the death rate had risen, and they had been forced to open their doors to a greater number of the incurably insane. To add to their unease, the asylum Commissioners complained of a worrying element of poor record-keeping throughout 1871. In particular, they listed instances of restraint which had gone unreported, and drew attention to the unrecorded deaths of two patients. Finally, they highlighted the failure of the medical superintendent to bring to their notice the case of a female attendant who had been dismissed following an unseemly inci-dent with a patient. The attendant had been deemed overly aggressive: she had argued with the patient, wrestling with her and shoving her to the ground. That she had been rightly dismissed was not in question; that the incident had gone unrecorded was very much so.

The attendant went unnamed in all reports, but by the start of 1872, of the eleven female attendants at the Bristol Lunatic Asylum, Amelia Thomas was no longer on the payroll.

# 10 Totterdown

In the autumn of 1872, Amelia married again. Her second husband, William Dyer, had just turned twenty-seven, and (according to subsequent census entries) he believed his new wife to be just twenty-nine (curiously, a year younger than she had claimed to be upon the occasion of her first marriage, eleven years earlier, when she was actually only twenty-three). In fact, in 1872, Amelia Thomas was already thirty-four years old. But her deception did not extend beyond this one detail: Dyer knew Amelia to be a widow and a mother, and he became an instant stepfather to her seven-year-old daughter, Ellen Thomas, who now returned to live with her mother.

Before he married, William Dyer had lived in Bristol with his parents and his younger brother, just outside the Bedminster parish boundary, in Philip Street, which ran between the Redcliffe Hill Bridge at its eastern end and Bedminster railway station at its west. His father, Francis Dyer, was a stays cutter in a firm of corset makers, an intricate and highly specialized craft. His youngest son, Henry, was twenty-one years old in 1871, and the census records that he worked as a cab driver. William was unskilled and illiterate: he marked his marriage certificate with a cross. In common with many of his neighbours in St Mary Redcliffe, William was employed as a labourer at the Conrad Finzel's sugar refinery, renowned as the city's best employer, and an easy walk from his home in Philip Street.

In the autumn of 1873, William and Amelia had their first child, Mary Ann, known to the family as Polly. She was followed three years later by a brother, William Samuel. The Dyers fell victim to the high infant mortality rate, burying at least two other children between 1872 and 1879 (and possibly more: Amelia would later claim to have given birth to thirteen children during her lifetime). The Dyers gave up a room so as to take in a lodger, Jane Williams, to help pay the rent. For the first five years or so of their marriage, their lives were unremarkable.

But in 1877 Bristol's best employer was hit by the combined forces of rapid expansion, trade slump and the increasing predominance of the port of Liverpool. The Finzel refinery was forced to make extensive cuts to its workforce and Dyer was among the five hundred workers who lost their jobs. Two years later, however, William was working again, this time as a labourer at the Purnell and Webb vinegar brewery. Though he most probably earned a lower wage than he had at Finzel's, the family's financial crisis was essentially over. But by then, a crisis on an altogether bigger scale had been unleashed.

⊰⊱

By the time Polly Dyer was old enough to form her earliest memories of her mother, the family was living in Poole's Crescent, on the steep slopes of Totterdown, a suburb of Bristol which sat just over the river inside the Somerset county boundary. Poole's Crescent was one of a tangle of streets built in the 1860s and 1870s to accommodate the railway workers for the newly built Temple Meads Station.

If Ellen's early childhood had been unsettling, Polly's was about to become far more so. Ellen had at least spent her early years largely removed from her mother's influence. Polly had no way of escaping.

When Father lost his job, it was Mother who took decisive steps to see the family through their financial difficulties, returning once more to the baby business. Polly later recalled that from 1877, when she was just four years old, her home in Poole's Crescent had been filled with ladies. Some would stay weeks, others months. Some came from far away – from London, Dublin even. But eventually every one of the ladies would succumb to the same end: the "accouchement". The sound of women in labour was a constant in Polly's childhood. Mother would disappear behind a locked door and eventually emerge exhausted. Sometimes, a day or two later, Polly would see the new mother, nursing an infant at her breast. But often there was no infant: just a death certificate, pronouncing on another "stillborn"; and an undertaker.

Contemporary Scotland Yard files reveal that many midwives knew how to engineer the appearance of a stillbirth where it was called for: the baby would be smothered at the very moment of delivery when the head emerged, its mouth stuffed with a wet cloth, its nose covered with another. That way, the compression of the chest still inside the birth canal would prevent it from taking breath. It would die silently, and, if the woman was lucky, its skin might not entirely discolour, a telltale sign of asphyxiation, thus throwing any doctor off the scent. Scotland Yard even detailed cases where the madam of a brothel smothered infants during delivery without the consent of the woman giving birth.

There was a grim skill in this. Hesitate, and in a moment the newborn infant would be lying on the bed gasping for air. Even then, so long as its cries went unheard, all was not lost: many infants who died naturally in the birth canal would also die blue. Even modern pathologists cannot easily tell the difference between a natural suffocation during labour and a suspicious one immediately thereafter without an internal post-mortem. A nineteenth-century doctor would be able to pronounce upon this type of infant death as nothing but a natural occurrence.

Polly may have known differently from the doctors who certified the babies "born dead" in Poole's Crescent. She may sometimes have caught the first spluttering cries of a newborn. With the blind acceptance of a four-year-old, she may not have pursued any further the troublesome question of how a dead baby cries. Instead, it may have sat, stored in a dark recess, to be revisited in her maturity.

Not every birth in the house elicited a doctor and a death certificate. Some babies lived, and remained a while after their mothers had left. Sometimes a different woman would come to collect a baby, handing Mother money. Polly well recalled the glint of sovereigns before Mother secreted them away.

RESPECTABLE Person to Adopt a little Girl three months old. Premium. References exchanged. – "Secrecy". Daily Press Office.
*Western Daily Press*, 14 February 1877

Some of Mother's nurse children were not born in the house at all, but were brought there. Daily the post brought more letters to the door; every week, Polly was sent to post letters from Mother. Letters addressed to ladies in other cities. Letters addressed to newspapers: to the *Western Daily Press*; the *Bristol Times & Mirror*; *Christian World*.

-⊟⊨-

MARRIED LADY wishes to have CARE OF A CHILD. Would adopt one – Address Mrs Dyer, 14 Poole's Crescent, Bath Road, Bristol.
*Christian World*, 27 June 1879

It was a perfunctory advertisement, in comparison to the others among which it sat.

J. R. Pearce of Somerton, whose ad appeared just above Mrs Dyer's, proclaimed herself "A RESPECTABLE WIDOW", residing "in a healthy village". More sinisterly, Pearce had added the assurance "A delicate child would have the greatest attention". She might well welcome the sickly infant: such a child could be neglected to the point of death without too much difficulty, its death later explained as an unavoidable tragedy and put down to its natural frailty. But at least other advertisements offered some assurance of the suitability of those offering their services, such as Mrs Chappell from Lower Edmonton, London, who offered the "Highest references" to those who cared to take them up. Mrs Dyer offered no such guarantee.

⋇

Polly watched Mother and Ellen tend to the nurse children, preparing feeds with boiled bread, and bottles of water, cornflour and a little condensed milk. It was busy work. The babies kept coming: sometimes they were tending to as many as six at a time, as well as Polly's brother William Samuel, barely walking in 1877.

The babies wouldn't have seemed like Polly's own little brother. He was plump and rosy-cheeked; he laughed when he was happy and bawled when he wasn't and fed heartily. Mother's nurse children had yelled loud enough in the beginning, and for so long at night that Mother couldn't get any rest. But she had seen to that: she sent Ellen twice a week to fetch "twopenny-worth of Godfrey's Cordial" from the druggist on the Wells Road. Sometimes she sent her more often, depending on how many babies were in the house, and how fractious they were at night. It was a wonder, that cordial.

The druggist's wooden counter was so highly polished that Polly could have seen her reflection in it. Behind the counter was the "drug run": row upon row of tiny square drawers, each with a neat, round, ivory handle and each filled with powdered or caked medicine. Above the drawers was a glass and mahogany cabinet, groaning under rows of bottles, jars and packages, filled with an array of coloured liquids, powders and pills; as enticing as a sweet shop.

Godfrey's Cordial was usually kept by apothecaries in a great jug on the counter. Ellen would have had to hand the druggist her empty bottle and ask for "twopenny-worth". The apothecary would pour it through a funnel into her little glass bottle. Get the dregs of the jug at the end of the day and you'd have more of the laudanum and less of the syrup and molasses; that way, you'd get more for your money in terms of the effect it had on the recipient. *The Quietness*, Ellen and Polly would have heard it called. *Five drops of that on the end of a spoon at bedtime, and they'd go off as quiet as anything, sleeping all night without a sound; all day too, often enough.*

Soon after Mother had taken to quietening the babies with Godfrey's Cordial at night, they had stopped needing so much food, too. They took to sleeping, mostly. They were wrapped in muslins and left to sleep all day in wooden crates which served as bassinets. Soon they'd got to be so thin and drawn that they hadn't the strength to take a bottle at all. Polly wouldn't have cared to look at them much after that: the skin drawn tight; blue and grey and sunken, like miniature crones. The sound of their breathing was different, too: heavy and laboured, as if they'd just run up the Wells Road.

Mother could at least rest at night now that the little ones had been quietened. Life could carry on around them pretty much as if they weren't there at all. The weekly fee kept rolling in; the babies were kept dosed up by Mother. Mother began to suffer terribly with her teeth: pregnancy put neglected teeth at risk and her later medical reports chart her declining dentition. She needed something to ease the toothache: Mother knew well enough how to deal with pain; she was fond of saying, "I'm part doctor myself".

Had Polly seen the little clear glass bottle, its distinctive grooved sides warning the poor-sighted and the illiterate of its deadly contents? It was filled with a sticky brown liquid and clearly labelled "Laudanum – POISON". Mother had no need of pretence; no need to soak off the labels, to disguise the contents. It was purely medicinal; she could right enough have had it prescribed to her by a medical man for the relief of her toothache, had she not been so adept at self-diagnosis. Laudanum; "Elixir of Opium": sherry, opium, saffron and cinnamon. Foul-tasting, bitter liquor, but worth swallowing for the sweet relief it brought. The druggists sold it commonly to those troubled with neuralgia, toothache or persistent rheumatic pain.

Mother knew poison: she had worked in hospitals; she had experienced enough to keep her from its dangers. She had seen its pull often enough, on the lunatics in the asylum. Those who had begun with a few drops to ease pain, and had soon found they needed its comfort daily. Before too long, a few drops would become a spoonful. After a while, a tablespoon a day was swallowed. How easily the feeble-minded were ensnared: she would never fall victim. Just a drop or two on the end of a spoon every few hours was enough; she could cope with her days then.

# 11  The Totterdown Baby Farm

WANTED, to place a baby with a respectable person. – address with terms – "Mother" Daily Press Office.

*Western Daily Press*, 26 January 1879

The ladies kept coming and so did the babies. Mother would routinely set off to the railway station with a newborn baby, returning later alone. The next morning she always had a story: the baby's mother came for it; some poor couple fell head over heels with it on the platform, and adopted it on the spot.

Ellen recalled there were generally four little ones in the house, besides Polly and Willie. Then in March 1878, when Polly was four and a half, there was trouble. One of the babies died. Polly remembered the commotion. More strangers in the house: a doctor first, then an undertaker. Unwelcome intruders; she would have been glad to see the infant go.

After that, the babies kept dying; two more over the next twelve months. It didn't much matter: Mother could always find new ones. The letters kept coming. By the summer of 1879, there were six nurse children in the house. Even with Ellen's help, Mother was struggling to cope. Mother's teeth must have been hurting pretty badly, too: she relied more often on her sticky brown poison to ease the pain.

A medical man and his wife wish to recommend a home for 2 or 3 young children from birth and upwards. Healthy and pleasant neighbourhood of Bristol. Motherly and home comforts guaranteed. Terms from 7s a week according to requirements. Address "Mother" Daily Press Office.

*Western Daily Press*, 3 July 1879

Over the last year or so, Polly had watched the three babies deteriorating, as they succumbed to their slow deaths. One of the babies in the house that July seemed to Polly as if she might be the next to go. She was a three-month-old child called May (though everyone called her "Little May" as there was already an older nurse child called May at 14 Poole's Crescent). Little May slept pretty well all the time, though Ellen remembered that Mother still quietened her every night with five drops of Godfrey's Cordial. The infant took less and less from her feeding bottle. Mother said there was no need to wake the babies for feeding unless they mithered for it. Little May was too weak to express hunger, and so went mostly unfed. And Little May wasn't the only child who was fading. There was Bessie, too; only a month in the world and already thin and grey and beginning to take on the sunken features of one far beyond her age.

> Respectable married couple want a child to nurse or adopt one. Small
> premium. 14, Poole's Crescent Bath Road.
>
> *Western Daily Press*, 31 January 1879

Mother said she hadn't liked the look of Little May; the life was half gone from her eyes and her breath had become unnervingly laboured. Mother said it was time she went, and sent Ellen off to post a letter marked "Mrs J Williams, 14 Moor Street, St Philip's Marsh, Bristol".

Mrs Williams was an old friend of Mother's; she had lodged with them when William was first born. She arrived at Poole's Crescent later that same day. Mother told her she had received a letter from a lady in Dublin, who had asked if she could come to the house until she'd had her baby. Mother still had six babies to nurse, and she told Mrs Williams she was worried that she'd never cope with all of them and the lady in the house as well. There wasn't the room, for one thing.

"I'd be doing myself more good," Mother said, "with the lady, than with two or three babies." Mrs Williams agreed to ask her husband's permission. Two days later she sent word that she would come and collect the babies the following Wednesday.

On Tuesday 29 July, the day before Little May and Bessie were due to go to Mrs Williams, Mother was fretful about Little May, saying she had taken a turn for the worse. She had what Mother called "the Red Gum", her mouth and face and frail body covered in sores. (Lots of babies born to syphilitic mothers soon became severely ulcerated;

"the Red Gum" may describe this condition). The sores over the infant's skeletal trunk and inert limbs were enough to make a six-year-old shudder if she looked too long. Before the end of the afternoon, Mother had sent Ellen off with another letter for Mrs Williams, asking her to come to the house later that evening instead.

Mrs Williams came to the door at around half past seven. Mother said that as the lady from Dublin was arriving early on Thursday, she could do with Wednesday clear to get the house ready. Would she take the babies now? She gave Mrs Williams instructions to feed them bottles of condensed milk and cornflour along with a little boiled bread. Mother made no mention of her worries about Little May, and wrapped her well so that Mrs Williams didn't notice the child's red gum.

Mrs Williams didn't want the Godfrey's Cordial Mother offered. Mother asked what she intended to do when they became restless without it. But Mrs Williams said that was no matter; she said she'd never felt moved to resort to it before and wouldn't do so now, thanks all the same, and she left, taking Bessie and Little May with her.

14, Poole's Crescent – Respectable person wants a child to nurse.
*Western Daily Press*, 3 July 1879

Polly couldn't recall a lady from Dublin appearing that week, but babies continued to arrive. Before long, Mother soon sent two more infants to be nursed by Mrs Williams. But two weeks after she first took Little May away, Mrs Williams brought her back. The child was not doing well; she wouldn't take her boiled bread and showed little interest in her milk either. Bessie wasn't much better. She said she couldn't manage all four babies, especially since one of the boys Mother had sent her was also poorly and needed a lot of nursing. She asked that Mother come back with her to St Philip's Marsh to take a look at him.

Mrs Williams was right about Little May: she was worse than ever. It was so much trouble just trying to keep her clean: she had diarrhoea. And there were still four other infants at Poole's Crescent for Ellen to tend to whenever Mother was out.

While Mother was tending to the sick boy at Mrs Williams's house, her friend Mrs Hacker arrived at Poole's Crescent. She said Mother had sent word from Mrs Williams's house that she was to come and collect Little May and another nurse child, named Evalina, to be nursed at her house in Victoria Terrace, St Philip's Marsh, for a few days. (Mrs Hacker had already taken two babies from Mother, but she could manage two more as she had now passed them on to another friend to nurse.) Mrs Hacker had screwed up her face when she pulled back some of the clothing and caught a glimpse of how dirty they were underneath. Ellen did her best but Mother hadn't let her wash them very often.

Mother brought two babies home with her from Mrs Williams's late that Tuesday night. Mrs Williams was left nursing only Bessie, making sure that Mother was informed by letter of the child's progress and telling her she had had to call out Dr Paull, who prescribed medicine for Bessie's diarrhoea.

The sickly boy died in Poole's Crescent the following day.

Three days later, Mother sent word that Mrs Williams should return Bessie to Poole's Crescent as the child's father was shortly expected. Polly remembers seeing no sign of the father, but Mother gave Bessie a dose of Godfrey's Cordial and sent it back to Mrs Williams the next day.

Mother also had a letter to be posted to Mrs Hacker, asking her to bring back Little May for a night, as her mother was due to visit on the Saturday. She asked that Mrs Hacker be sure to travel after dark: she didn't want the neighbours suspecting anything, what with so many babies coming and going. Mother was always very keen that they should keep their business away from the neighbours: they were not the sort to understand. Mother was making angels: Jesus wanted the nurse children far more than their own mothers did. She was adamant her trade in infants was not for the neighbours to worry about; she would rather they didn't know.

Mother was on the doorstep when Mrs Hacker arrived, and took Little May directly into her arms, making a point of remarking that the little one wasn't looking too well. Mrs Hacker disagreed. She said she thought May a good deal stronger: she had even cried on the way over to Poole's Crescent that evening.

But Mother must have been right, for Little May had been the next to die.

Mother and Mrs Hacker left the house together late that same Friday night, taking Little May with them. Mother had persuaded her to take the baby to Dr Milne's surgery, in Harford Place, Bedminster. Against her better judgement, as she later recorded, Mrs Hacker had eventually agreed. It was approaching midnight as they set off, and Mother was still urging her to agree to them acting as sisters. Mrs Hacker conceded that Mother should tell Dr Milne the child was her own.

Little May came back to Poole's Crescent with Mother, with some medicine Dr Milne had prescribed to treat what he had said was a disorder of the gut. She lay as still as a stone, her mouth open, her eyes fixed and glassy, like the fish at the market. The next day Mrs Hacker appeared at the door several times and asked Mother to let her have Little May, promising she would hand her back the instant her mother arrived. She grew increasingly agitated when Mother declined each time. Mother absolutely refused to concede, which was typical: all who knew her agreed there was really little point in challenging her; she would never be moved. But finally, after a strong exchange of words, Mother at last allowed Mrs Hacker in to see the child.

Little May was "all wrapped up in her bed, the empty tube of a feeding bottle still in her mouth". She was awake, her eyes fixed and staring. Mrs Hacker tried to talk to her, to get her attention, but the child didn't stir; she rarely did. In fact, none of them had ever seen Little May smile. Mrs Hacker was worried: she said the child didn't look right; there was something wrong. Mother grunted in reply, and Mrs Hacker recalled her having put the blame upon Mrs Williams for not doing right by the child.

That next day was Sunday, and despite Mother dosing up the child with Dr Milne's medicine and a few more drops of Godfrey's Cordial, Little May grew weaker and weaker. Eventually, in the middle of the evening, Mother took her back to Dr Milne. But it was no use; Little May died at nine o'clock in Dr Milne's surgery.

Dr Milne wrote Mother out a death certificate, Mother informing him that the child's name was "Ann May Walters Dyer". He wrote that "intestinal disorder and convulsions" were the cause of death. He'd not seen her convulse, but Mother was part doctor herself, and he believed her when she told him the child had fitted.

The next day, Mother wanted to keep word of Little May's death quiet. She told Ellen and Polly to say nothing and went out. While she was gone, Mrs Williams called at the house to see Mother. Ellen kept quiet, as instructed. Mrs Williams said Mother had written to her explaining that Sergeant Dewey of the Totterdown Constabulary had called, asking for the address of Little May's mother in London, after which the woman had come to take May back home. She wondered, had the child already gone from the house? (Polly would have wondered at this, knowing Little May couldn't be in London with her mother. She was lying dead on the sofa in their front room.)

Mrs Hacker was next, arriving just after Mother and demanding to see the child; she would not let up. Mother did her best to send her off, but eventually admitted that the child was dead. She led Mrs Hacker into the parlour, where Little May's body was lying on the sofa, wrapped in blankets. Afterward, she warned Mrs Hacker to say nothing of the child's death and sent her on her way.

Mrs Williams arrived later with bad news. Bessie had also died the previous day. She wanted to know what Mother proposed to do about funeral arrangements. She said Dr Smart had come from Redcliffe Crescent to see Bessie, and had given a death certificate, stating "atrophy and convulsions" as the cause of death. Mother urged Mrs Williams to register Bessie's death herself, insisting it would go better for them all if she were to say the child had been born in her house. Mrs Williams agreed to do so.

Mother was twitchy after Mrs Williams left: three deaths in five days. From that day on, she kept the little bottle of laudanum in her apron pocket.

---

Mrs Hacker hurried home to St Philip's Marsh after her conversation with Dyer that Monday morning. She was fretful about the death of Little May, busying herself tending to Evalina, the fast-fading nurse child who remained in her care. The child's blueish appearance and listless demeanour were worrying; she had already taken her to be examined at the Children's Hospital. And there was something else about Dyer's behaviour that was concerning her: why had she insisted on pretending that they were sisters? Why had she lied to Dr Milne, claiming that Little May had suffered a fit? At the time, Mrs Hacker had not dared to contradict her. Now her part in the demise of this little one was weighing on her conscience.

Elizabeth Hacker spilled out the day's events to her husband Charles as soon as he arrived home that evening. He hadn't hesitated: she was to go and recount every detail to the first policeman she saw. She did exactly that.

She had never been able to make up entirely for the pitiful state in which Evalina had first arrived. The dirt on the child's body was deep-grained: she had not been properly clean since. The unnatural sleep, the lack of appetite and the unresponsive, glazed wakefulness had eased somewhat. But she knew from Ellen that Dyer had administered Godfrey's Cordial on a daily basis: the woman had offered her some to quieten the child's restlessness. The Hackers had children of their own and she had never once resorted to the drug. She knew enough about raising infants to recognize that boiled bread and cornflour could never sustain a human life. She had done her best by Evalina, giving her prompt medical attention and new milk. But on the Saturday following the deaths of Bessie and Little May, Evalina too passed away. On her certificate Dr Stephens of the Children's Hospital stated atrophy as the cause of death: like the others, she had simply wasted away.

❧

When Jane Williams went to 14 Poole's Crescent on the morning of Monday 18 August, Dyer seemed less interested in discussing funeral arrangements for poor Bessie than in getting the child's death registered. Again, Dyer insisted it would "go better for them all" if she wasn't the one to register it. At Dyer's insistence, Jane went to the Bristol Register Office and waited in line to see Mr Hunt, the city registrar. She was prepared to claim that Bessie had been born at her home in St Philip's Marsh, but was not happy to act as the child's mother, as Dyer had asked her. She clutched the death certificate signed by Dr Smart and hoped all would go well.

Mr Hunt was not happy. He listened to the woman's story that this infant had been born and raised in her home and had simply failed to thrive. He studied the death certificate uneasily. He asked her if she was the infant's mother. She admitted she wasn't. Finally, he refused to register the death, informing Mrs Williams that the matter was now out of his hands and would be passed over to the City Coroner, Mr Wadborough.

# 12 Polly and the Post-mortem

Sergeant Dewey already knew that Mrs Dyer was not altogether trustworthy. She had first come to his attention following the death of the boy on 13 August. A pitiful sight, his body had been, haggard and wretched. Dewey had recognized instantly that this was a case of neglect. The boy's body had been lying wrapped in blankets in the parlour, and two other infants at the house were barely clinging to life. When the woman Hacker informed him that another of Dyer's nurse children had expired, this time a girl named May, he had written to the Somerset County Coroner, Mr Biggs, without delay.

*Totterdown,* Bristol
19th August 1879

Sir,
I have to inform you that a female child died at Dr J Milne's surgery, Harford place, Bristol, on Sunday evening, the 17th inst., where it was taken by a married woman, named Dyer, living at 14 Poole's crescent, Bath Road, Totterdown, who had been taking children to nurse for years; and last Wednesday, the 13th inst., another child died at her house. This numbers five within about twelve or eighteen months, one of them being her own child. For this child that died on Sunday last she obtained a certificate, and gave the name of Ann May Walters Dyer, which is not correct. Dr Milne saw this child first on Saturday, the 16th inst., at 12.30 and prescribed for it. The mother, as he thought she was (Mrs Dyer) reported next day that the child was dead and he gave a certificate. The age was stated as nine weeks – the cause of death convulsions and intestinal disorder.

Dewey was eventually able to determine that the child Dyer had claimed was hers was in fact May Walters, born to Dorcas Walters, a domestic servant from London.

On Thursday 21 August, Dewey learned that the City Coroner was opening an inquest into the death of another of Dyer's nurse children, Elizabeth Thomas – "Bessie". Days later, Mrs Hacker informed him that Evalina was now dead.

Four of Dyer's nurse children dead in two weeks.

He wrote informing the Somerset County Coroner of the Bristol inquests, pointing out that they pertained to the same nurse as in the case of May Walters. The County Coroner ordered that a post-mortem should be carried out without delay on May Walters, at the Dyer's home in Poole's Crescent, Totterdown.

❧

The body of Little May lay on the parlour table for seven days. Polly, still not quite six years old, knew it was there. The parlour curtains were kept drawn and Mother remained largely out of sight, relying heavily on the little bottle in her apron pocket and sending Ellen out to fetch more.

On Thursday afternoon, four days after Little May's death, Polly's home was suddenly overrun by men. There were two police officers and two doctors: Dr Milne, whom she knew, and another who introduced himself as Dr Gardiner. Both doctors carried weighty black bags and one clutched a set of scales under his arm.

The men spent much of the afternoon in the parlour, muttering terms of which Polly could have had no understanding: "emaciated"; "empty intestines"; "want of nourishment". She heard the sound of weights against the cold steel of the scales; Dr Milne announcing a body weight of just 6½lb, an estimated age of nine weeks. (In fact, Little May was at least three months old.) The conversation took on the tone of a dispute, the nature of which must also have been lost to Polly: Dr Gardiner repeating the words "narcotics" and "laudanum" with great emphasis, Dr Milne responding with "convulsions".

After they left the house, they had not taken Little May's body with them as Polly had hoped. Instead, it remained on the parlour table. Then Mother had decided she should be taken in to see the body. Polly had been terrified: the parlour was plunged into shadow; curtains drawn, lights dim. Little May's body had been "all cut about" by the doctors – wounds opened up in her little stomach and sliced into her chest and then roughly sewn together again. Polly had wanted to close her eyes and block out the sight of it; but she hadn't been able to, and had never forgotten it.

~❈~

Two days later, the house was filled with men again. Mother had been wailing and crying half the night. Polly understood little, but surely sensed the fear. Suddenly, late in the morning, Ellen had run to fetch help: she said she was afraid for Mother's life and believed her to have taken too much laudanum.

The police, when they came, were inexplicably stern with Mother, despite her obvious indisposition. Mr Carr, the surgeon, had given her an emetic, which made her vomit violently. An empty laudanum bottle sat on the bedside table. Polly and Ellen knew there was more.

Sergeant Dewey had been in the house before, and took the stairs two at a time straight to Mother's bedroom. Their exchange was reported verbatim for the benefit of the Coroner's Court later that afternoon:

"You foolish woman; you are making things ten times worse!"

Mother answering: "I've not taken much."

A second, younger policeman, who had followed Sergeant Dewey up the stairs, was ordered inside the bedroom while Sergeant Dewey spoke to Ellen quietly for a minute or two.

It was hard for anyone to make out Mother's words now: she was groggy and her voice sounded sleepy.

"You have another bottle about here," Sergeant Dewey barked. "I must have it!"

Downstairs, Polly cowered at the anger in the policeman's voice. She knew the bottle would be in the right-hand pocket of Mother's apron, just as it always was. Minutes later Dewey came downstairs, two empty bottles in his hand, their labels cautioning "Laudanum – POISON", should anyone be left in any doubt.

~❈~

It was no small dose, as Amelia had claimed. In fact, it was a wonder she was alive. Two bottles of laudanum were easily a fatal dose for anyone who had never been exposed to opiates before. Only a habitual laudanum drinker could have tolerated such a large dose.

In the nineteenth century, stories of opium dependency were well chronicled: men and women who for years consumed a daily dose sufficient to take out a shipful of unexposed crewmen. Men and women who would consume a half-pint of laudanum every day and yet continue to function and go about their business. As the writer Thomas De Quincey opined in his *Confessions of an English Opium-Eater*, only a fool would time his doses so as to sleep during the day: unconsciousness would come sure enough, but space out the doses carefully and first would come eight or ten daylight hours of clear-headed lucidity.

Yet for those who had never indulged, a medicinal dose of opiates sufficient to induce unconsciousness for surgery, for example, could easily prove fatal. Opium is a fickle narcotic; it was one in which this woman had clearly indulged before.

※

Mother continued to vomit. She vomited throughout the arrival of a houseful of well-dressed gentlemen, who let themselves in and examined every square inch of the house and its occupants, before finally crowding into the parlour where they scrutinized the body of Little May.

One of the gentlemen came out of the parlour and, after a brief word with Sergeant Dewey, followed him upstairs and into Mother's bedroom. He stood over her for several minutes, and questioned her in harsh tones. As he descended the staircase, he announced to the other gentlemen, now filing out of the parlour, "The woman has all the symptoms of poisoning by opium. She'll not be fit to attend today."

※

As the sickness wore off Mother grew more excitable. Sergeant Dewey returned that evening, by which time she was raging, shouting, "I am determined to do it!" and, "I can't live!" Her breathing was strange: fast and light. She was light-headed, as if she would swoon if she tried to stand. With a sunken-eyed, ghostly countenance, she stared through those who faced her, as if looking at some spectre beyond. Sleep mostly escaped her but when it came, it brought with it no rest, and she cried out and thrashed about in her bed, troubled by the most fearsome nightmares. Eventually, she descended into a heavy and unnatural sleep, from which she could not be stirred. Awake or not, a police officer remained at her side morning and night for the duration of the week.

The doctor had said he feared Mother might never wake. But by the following afternoon, she was able to sit up and have brief conversations again. When Sergeant Dewey returned in the early evening, she was downcast, muttering miserably that she didn't understand why she was still alive: "I took about the right quantity. I am half doctor myself."

The wind began picking up that Sunday night. By Monday morning, the South-West was plunged into the bleak half-light of a late summer storm, the wind wild enough to warrant a special mention in the local press. The rain started that night and continued into the next day, falling in torrents and wreaking havoc on garden fetes and village flower shows. Inside 14 Poole's Crescent, Mother was maudlin and taciturn, not helped by the lingering effects of the laudanum overdose. Polly was confused and frightened. And in torrential rainfall on the morning of Tuesday 26 August 1879, a black prison van pulled up outside Poole's Crescent and took Mother away.

Polly recalled that it would seem like years before she would see her again.

# 13 *Criminal Intent*

The City Coroner would normally have taken the lead in a case where multiple victims of one perpetrator had come to the attention of two neighbouring authorities. But both coroners had agreed with Dewey that, in this instance, it would be beneficial to have two courts on the case, creating a greater possibility of sustaining a conviction.

At the Victoria tavern in St Philip's Marsh, Mr Wadborough conducted the inquest into the deaths of Elizabeth Thomas (Bessie), and Evalina Townsend, on behalf of the city. He drew attention to the fact that both infants had been nursed primarily by the woman Dyer, and that two others had died in her care. While carefully instructing the court to consider only the cases brought before them, he added, "The fact of all the children appearing to suffer in the same way, and being instructed into the care of other people when they appeared to be dying, is very remarkable."

Mr Biggs, the County Coroner, held his inquest at the Turnpike Inn, a small coaching inn on the Bath Road in Totterdown. Biggs shared Wadborough's gravity:

> It is idle to disguise that this enquiry into one child opens up a very wide question as to the deaths of many children placed under the charge of this woman Dyer.
>
> *Bristol Times & Mirror*, 25 August 1879

To the consternation of the court, Sergeant Dewey took the stand at the commencement of the proceedings, announcing that Mrs Dyer had just now taken an overdose of laudanum and was lying, near death, at the house in Poole's Crescent.

Suicide was a criminal offence under nineteenth-century British law. Those found guilty of a genuine attempt to bring about their own death were frequently imprisoned. The coroner was highly disgruntled to learn that the woman already accused of criminal misdemeanour had been permitted by the local constabulary to carry out this latest offence.

"Did she do it with criminal intent?" Mr Biggs asked Dewey.

"Oh, yes. I took the bottles out of her pocket not long ago."

Mr Biggs was noticeably irritated by this inconvenient turn of events. "We shall not be able to conclude this inquiry without her evidence."

The coroner was at pains to make sure the sergeant realized his duty to the court: it was his responsibility to see to it that the woman be kept in his charge, and kept alive, until able to take the stand. "What course do you propose to take? If the enquiry adjourned I should hold you answerable for producing her."

Sergeant Dewey shamefacedly accepted his charge, assuring Mr Biggs he would take the woman into police custody on the charge of attempted suicide.

The foreman of the jury, a Mr Parfitt, was moved to speak out in Sergeant Dewey's defence: he was a Totterdown man, familiar with and supportive of his local sergeant. He wasn't happy with the coroner's implied accusations of ineptitude. After all, Dewey had not yet had time to take decisive action. "It is only within the last hour and a half that she has done this."

Mr Biggs took a moment to consider the matter, before turning again to face the police sergeant before him. "Supposing no fatal consequences ensue, you will produce her at the adjourned inquiry, I assume?"

"Most decidedly."

Satisfied, Mr Biggs then called for the jury to proceed to 14 Poole's Crescent to view the body of the deceased child. He accompanied them, determined to see for himself the woman Dyer in order to ascertain her chances of survival.

※

When the inquest was reconvened later that same day, Mr Biggs was struck by the cunning shown by Dyer in her attempts to disguise her part in these deaths. By ensuring that the fast-failing infants were put out to nurse within the city boundaries, and thereafter insisting these women register the deaths with the city registrar, Dyer had moved beyond the reach of the Somerset administration in which she lived; she had "apparently thrown dust into the eyes of the authorities". This, combined with the secrecy with which she had conducted herself, left him in "no moral doubt that these children were hurried to their grave by improper food and drugging".

The problem was proving it. It could not be stated with certainty that Dyer had drugged the child May after Mrs Williams had taken her into her care: a verdict of manslaughter required that they show some direct act on the part of the woman. He told the court,

> It is true that general neglect, incompetence and carelessness might constitute a criminal charge, but that has not been shown to such an extent as to justify the hope that if sent for trial there would be a conviction ... so far as this case is concerned we are powerless to deal with one of the worst matters that has ever come under my notice. It is perfectly clear this woman's establishment has simply been an infant's hell, and if ever the inscription the Italians spoke of in connection with another region should be inscribed anywhere, it should be placed here. "All hope abandon ye who enter here." This is baby-farming in its worst and most vile aspect.

With obvious regret, Mr Biggs told the jury that he was obliged to tell them the same as his esteemed colleague Mr Wadborough had done the previous day. They would have to return an open verdict. However, proceedings could be taken out against her for acting in breach of the 1872 Infant Life Protection Act, by whose terms a nurse was not permitted to care for more than one infant under the age of one year for longer than twenty-four hours, without first having registered the house with the police. Also following the death of an infant residing in such a baby farm, a keeper of such a house was obliged to bring the attention of the coroner to the death.

He addressed Mrs Williams in the strongest terms: "You have been residing on the edge of a precipice for some time without knowing it."

After twenty minutes the jury returned their verdict, reluctantly affirming "that the deceased died from natural causes", but appending the following rider: "The jury are of the opinion that Mrs Dyer, who had charge of the deceased, is deserving of severe censure for the manner in which the children under her care are treated."

Sergeant Dewey, conscious of the coroner's admonition of his account-
ability, had Dyer on twenty-four-hour watch until the moment came
when the constabulary's prison van, the Black Maria, could be sent to
escort her to the Police Court at Long Ashton for trial on the morning
of Tuesday 26 August 1879. Dewey must have breathed a quiet sigh
of relief as the woman stepped into the van in driving rain, watched
by a crowd of onlookers who had gathered, despite the storm. He had
kept the woman alive and delivered her to the magistrate. His duty
done, justice could now be served.

⊣⊢

Dyer was remanded in police custody for three days, following an
initial hearing. Then, on Friday 29 August, the magistrate Sir A. H.
Elton heard her case at the Long Ashton Police Court petty sessions.
Like the coroners before him, he took a grim view of Dyer's crime.
He was prepared to treat the attempted suicide with little more than
a few stern words and an instruction for the prison chaplain to take a
special interest in her soul. But in sentencing her on the graver matter
of the infant deaths he said:

> You have pleaded guilty to the commission of gross negligence, and
> the bench find it necessary to impose on you the highest penalty in
> their power, namely six months' imprisonment with hard labour ...
> that it may act as a warning to others. You have narrowly escaped
> standing there upon a much more serious charge, but we have no
> evidence before us as to how those infants came by their deaths, but
> there is very little doubt that you treated them with great negligence.
> I mention this that you may think it over in the hours now before you.
> You will be imprisoned in Shepton Mallet gaol.

# 14 Silent Servitude

That Friday storms continued to rage across Somerset. The two dray horses pulling the Black Maria hung their heads after a twenty-four-mile journey in driving rain, their necks sleek and shimmering, stretched by the last long pull uphill from Wells to the gaol at Shepton Mallet.

Inside the Black Maria, Dyer was locked into a windowless cell; a small ventilation grille in the door offered no more than a glimpse of the passing countryside. A police officer sat within the van but outside of the cells, and the driver was perched up top, a gabardine cloak his only protection against the inclement weather. It had been a long and uncomfortable journey: even going flat out, two drays pulling a heavy load could have covered eight miles an hour at most. But Amelia's discomfort was nothing compared with what lay ahead.

Her sentence may have been the toughest that the magistrates could afford her, but she had in fact escaped lightly. The Victorian passion for harsh punishment of any crime against property meant that theft carried with it far tougher sentences than those for many other misdemeanours. (Just a few years earlier, for example, a local man, George Tipney, had served twelve months' penal servitude for the theft of a piece of bacon valued at just ninepence.) But as she climbed down from the van on that last Friday in August, and was led up the four stone steps and through the vast studded and arched wooden doors of the main gate of the Shepton Mallet House of Correction, February, and the end of her sentence, must have seemed an eternity away.

Beyond the walls of the House of Correction, locals spoke in hushed tones of the brutal regimen within:

> ... its very walls look forbidding, and within its courts and corridors reigns a dismal silence, broken only by the forbidding chink of keys,

the creaking of a lock, the grumbling of a heavy bolt, the measured footsteps of a warder, or more rarely, by the penitential moan of some poor conscience stricken sinner.

Alas that there is need of such a place on Christian soil.

John E. Farbrother, Headmaster of the
Shepton Mallet Grammar School, 1860

The same "dismal silence" assaulted Dyer's ears as she stepped inside. The gaol had a rigorously maintained "Silent Order", imposed upon all prisoners throughout the day. The order extended beyond mere verbal communication: any gesture exchanged by prisoners was severely punished.

Amelia was stripped, inspected by the prison medical officer and given a dress and petticoat, a pair of stockings, a loose cotton shift, neckerchief, pocket handkerchief, cap and a pair of shoes. Her clothing was not the standard pale grey issue, but yellow, to denote hard labour. A badge was pinned to her chest bearing a number which corresponded to that above her cell door. She would have to grow accustomed to responding to this number: it was to be used instead of her name for the remainder of her sentence.

She was led into D-wing, where the female prisoners were housed, through endless corridors and locked wooden doors. It was already late in the day when she arrived at her cell. Very little natural light could seep in through the tiny barred windows set high into the cell walls. Beyond the barred window she could hear the constant distant rumble of the treadwheel, and above that an irregular repetition: the clean echo of iron against stone.

These were the sounds of the male prisoners sentenced to penal servitude. A rectangular building, three storeys high, nestled alongside the boundary wall of the gaol. At ground level were six heavy, arched wooden doors. This was the treadwheel shed: four great wheels, each with twenty-four treads. Male prisoners served out an agonizing eight hours, every day of their sentence, behind these doors. Lined ten abreast at each wheel, they climbed an interminable staircase (amounting to something just short of a Himalayan peak every three days). Men ruptured chest and stomach muscles working the tread-wheel. Builders and domestic servants fared better: they were used to the action of climbing ladders or mounting staircases for much of their working day. Skilled artisans, or any others accustomed to a more sedentary life, found it almost intolerable. For the remaining two hours of the prisoners' working day, men and boys were led into a series of enclosed yards and set to stone breaking, using heavy, hand-held mallets.

Amelia would not share the same occupation as her male counter-parts, but in common with them she endured the deprivation of basic comforts. Other prisoners were afforded the luxury of a thin mattress, two sheets, a pillow and a coverlet. Amelia, and those like her, slept on a hard wooden bench.

That first morning, after a comfortless night, she was to discover that the days began early. Housed in a little tower built into the apex of the chapel roof was a large bronze bell which tolled every morning at a quarter to six. This was the signal for the prisoners to stir; to wash, dress and then clean their cell. (The washing of hands and face was permitted once a day. Once a week, they were to clean their feet also. Once a month they were indulged with a tepid bath.)

For the first hour and a half, the female prisoners were occupied carrying out domestic duties around the gaol: cooking, laundry, cleaning, all carried out in absolute silence. At eight fifteen, the silence was again shattered by the bell, summoning all prisoners to chapel. Line by line, the female prisoners were paraded, two steps from those in front, from the first floor of D-wing across a high covered wooden walkway into the chapel. The prisoners sat in stony silence; each seat was enclosed on three sides by high wooden screens, which precluded any communication between prisoners and offered only a view of the chaplain, as he threatened the unrepentant with eternal hellfire from the pulpit.

After chapel, Amelia's days were to be occupied with hard labour: hour upon hour of "oakum picking".

Inside the oakum sheds the air was clouded with dust; it caught in the throat and settled on shoulders and laps like ash from a bonfire. The women sat in serried ranks in absolute silence, bent over the work in their laps. Mounds of old rope, sodden and tar-soaked, were to be unravelled, each piece pulled apart little by little, until the hemp was teased out like cotton wool, and every last one of its fibres picked out. The fibres were used in the ship-building industry, mixed with tar to waterproof ships' hulls.

Oakum picking was a painful occupation. The ropes were tough and the sinews cut deep gashes in the women's hands. In many work-houses a sharp tool was provided in order to tear the threads apart. But in prisons tools were prohibited and the task thus made all the more unendurable. After just one morning, Amelia's hands would have been blistered and blood-soaked, nails torn from the skin of the fingers. After six months, her hands were scarred and calloused, their skin as thick as a pig's. Like the treadmill, this was a task designed to be hard work without any of the satisfaction gained from an end product: although the treadwheel at Shepton was used to power a working mill, the prisoners were never permitted the satisfaction of seeing the flour they milled. Toil was regarded as an end in itself.

There were precious few moments of relief in the day. Two half-hour breaks were permitted, and brief evening reading sessions – of the Bible or the Prayer Book – by dim gaslight. Night-time communication between prisoners went unregulated. Prisoners could send and receive one letter in every quarter, and in exchange for sustained good behaviour they could also earn a twenty-minute visit every quarter.

Mealtimes were no cause for excitement: the menu was always the same and never entirely sustaining. It consisted of a pint and a half of gruel, a pound of bread and a pound of potatoes, with a meagre 6oz of beef, boiled on the bone, so that much of its weight was made up by the bone itself. No tobacco, no beer, and certainly no opiates.

But unstinting hard work didn't go entirely unremunerated: a reward system, known as "stages", was in place at the gaol. A full day's toil was worth one point. Carelessness or insufficient industry: zero. Indolence or insubordination took a point off a prisoner's total. Earn fifty-six points and Amelia would be rewarded with a slate and chalk and secular reading matter, along with one day's remission for every seven days left of her sentence. She could strive to move up through the stages, converting more of her punishment into rehabilitation, and reducing her sentence in the process, a day at a time.

If she chose to kick against the regime, however, her experience of gaol would have been insufferable. Solitary confinement was routinely imposed and for extended periods. The room reserved for the purpose instilled dread into all who had experienced it. Known as the "Dark and Silent Cell" it was a damp basement room, its walls bricked up solid with just one small ventilation hole in the ceiling. The thick wooden door blocked out any additional light and sound: but there was little in any case. The corridors outside were poorly lit and the cell was deliberately positioned far away from the other prisoners: once incarcerated, a prisoner could neither see nor hear any sign of life. Whippings were commonplace, the prisoner strapped at the ankles and wrists to an x-shaped frame, and lashed with a cat-o'-nine tails.

Restraint, too (leather cuffs for women, irons and straitjackets for men), was standard practice. Lie in late, fail to sweep out your cell satisfactorily, or be caught talking, and an inmate would be whipped.

Whether Amelia Dyer passed her sentence in silent servitude, or else raged against the regime at every opportunity, the Shepton Mallet House of Correction left her scarred. When she was finally released in February 1880, she resolved that nothing would lead her back. From now on, she determined to stay one step ahead of the law.

# 15 Polly and the Ballad-Monger

Polly hadn't understood why Mother had climbed into the black van, nor was she sure where it had taken her. Father had spared her the truth, saying Mother had gone to the country until she felt better. In the meantime they weren't to mither about her. But one day, not long after Mother had gone, Polly discovered the truth from a most unexpected source.

Father had sent her on an errand into Bristol. She set off down the Wells Road, heading toward the Bristol Bridge and the busy High Street on the other side. The Wells Road was one of the main thoroughfares into the city. On a typical day, it was teeming with traffic. Contemporary photographs show tradesmen's carts taking produce into the city centre; furniture removers; cabs and private carriages; maybe even a hearse, the black ribbons on the horse's head bobbing sedately as it made its sombre progress. An omnibus heading down into town would cross paths with another on its way back up the hill; two dray horses drew each tram, often augmented by another pair, harnessed before the long pull up the slopes of Totterdown.

Women went about their business of buying the family's food for the day, from the butchers, bakers and grocers of the Wells Road. Barrow boys sang out a small chorus, of pies, muffins, sweets, ices and fruit. Children looked longingly at glistening pyramids of red apples, stacked into broad baskets by the apple hawker.

On this particular morning, Polly saw that a crowd had gathered around a man singing a ballad on the dusty wooden pavement. Adults and children were cheering him on. Ballad-mongers and organ-grinders peppered the city streets, making the walk into the centre more exciting. They sang all sorts of songs – of fairy tales and love stories; of murder and intrigue; of tax laws and boxing matches – their tunes simple, rhythmic and melodious, like hymns. Their love stories rarely ended well and their tales of murder made women and children shudder in a macabre delight.

At first, Polly couldn't catch the words of the ballad above the noise of the street. She had to get quite close before she heard anything at all. People were pushing through the crowd and dropping a halfpenny into the hat which lay at his feet, in exchange for a copy of the large broadsheet upon which the words and tune were printed. Polly tried in vain to catch a glimpse of the song's title.

Babies, she realized. He was singing about babies. She picked out a phrase: "… taken in to die".

Fearfully, she tried to move away but found herself hemmed in by the gathering crowd. She tried to bustle her way through, squeezing between felt trousers and full skirts. She remembered several children she knew had been standing at the back of the group. Just as she caught the eye of a boy she recognized, she heard the ballad-monger sing out two words she hadn't ever expected to hear: "Amelia Dyer".

The boy was still staring at her. A look of recognition flashed across his face. He opened his mouth and drew breath as Polly pushed through the crowd and broke free, but too late. She heard the boy cry out, "There's one of her kids!"

She froze. All eyes were on her. For a second there was silence. Then the ballad-monger spoke. "Poor girl; she can't help it."

Polly began to move away, drawing the youths with her like a reluctant piper. The ballad-monger cautioned the crowd – leave her be; don't be following her. No one paid him any heed. Polly walked the rest of the street to the sound of hoots and boos from an entourage that would not be shaken off.

The ballad-monger's sensationalism was the tabloid journalism of its day: he capitalized on his audience's emotional response to local and national news stories. The lyrics of this ballad, recalled in snatches by Polly in adulthood, encapsulated the anger felt by the people of Totterdown. Their gut feeling about this crime was intensified by his simple rhyme and melody so that some of the crowd took out their anger on the woman's six-year-old daughter.

Polly later remembered no violence, nor even the spoken threat of it. But it had been none the less scarring: she had been pursued and set apart, her anonymity ripped from her. And, in the cruellest possible way, she had been made to realize that Mother was not recuperating in the countryside as Father had said; rather, she was incarcerated in that very hell which was so often fodder for the ballad-monger.

# 16 Mother Returns

It was a different Mother who finally came home one cold day in February 1880. She was filthy, her hair sticking to her head, an insufferable odour about her. The clothes she had left home in now hung loosely from her shoulders. She was forty-three, but looked older now – more lined, her eyes sunk deeper into their sockets with deep, dark shadows.

Polly and her family noticed other changes, too. Her teeth were fewer and blacker. She couldn't rest all night on her bed, although she looked more in need of sleep than ever she had done when the babies had given her no respite. Her hands, too, were different, the palms thick and coarse, her nails torn, flaked and brittle. She kept them out of sight, under her apron whenever they were idle, and rubbed them with goose fat every night.

Father had done his best to keep everyone going in Mother's absence. Polly's troubles had undoubtedly not been limited to the ballad-monger, but, as with any scandal, gradually the story had become old news. It seemed, however, that the cascading implications of Mother's crime affected the whole family: soon after Mother's imprisonment, Father lost his job at the vinegar brewery. Now, he attended an invalid gentleman in his own home, for a pitiful wage. Ellen fled the Dyer household after Mother's trial and was only briefly referred to sixteen years later by Polly, who reported that Ellen had married well and was living in London.

The Dyers had a family network upon which they could rely for support. Henry, Father's brother, had left Bristol with his wife Laura, to settle in Westminster, where he worked for the Metropolitan Police. But Polly's grandfather, Francis, was still working as a stays cutter in Bristol. In times of difficulty, working-class families often pooled what few resources they had: William Dyer may well have had financial and practical assistance from his family to help him through his wife's absence.

But for all their difficulties, Polly had passed six months of relative normality. She and her brother went to school. Father went to work. No ladies came to stay at their house; no babies were born there; none died there. There were no clandestine visitors after dark. No reason to hide from the neighbours. No little bottles marked "Poison". No police officers, undertakers, coroners or jurors.

And then Mother was back and for now at least she was in search of an honest living. She turned to the trade she had first learned as a young woman, before she became a mother. Perhaps at the instigation of her father-in-law, she took a position as a forewoman for a firm of corset makers.

※

There were several firms producing corsetry in the city: it was a boom time for the trade. The latest fashion for the bustle pulled the front of a lady's skirts narrow and flat, throwing more emphasis upon the waist: a cinched-in waist was more of a necessity than ever.

This surge in demand was well timed: the sewing machine, first introduced in the 1850s, meant that mass-produced corsets, made to suit various combinations of bust, waist and hip sizes, could be made more economically and purchased off the peg. Bristol's new department stores were the perfect outlet, their lingerie departments specializing in meticulous fittings. No longer must a delicate lady wear only white against the skin: manufacturers added allure by making corsets in a variety of fabric and colours and finishes, enticing browsers with artful packaging, such as "La Fiancée", offering the perfect silhouette and guaranteeing romantic success.

It was a world of gloss and frippery which stood in stark contrast to the dark place from which Amelia had just emerged.

Corset-making had always been a male preserve, a specialized trade requiring considerable strength to manoeuvre the heavy machinery through layers of chemically stiffened fabric and around sections of whalebone. But mechanization and mass production made for rooms full of machinists – a production line, rows of young girls each with a specific instruction to sew up the same section of every garment. It was monotonous work, and, despite mechanization, it required a robust, sturdy young girl to carry it out.

Amelia may have gained some knowledge of the work of the corset maker from observing her father-in-law, but the forewoman's job demanded knowledge of every stage of stays-making; she must have been able to demonstrate prior competence in the trade.

A forewoman was also required to maintain discipline: this was a pitifully low-paid, repetitive occupation which demanded absolute accuracy. Mistakes could not be tolerated. Moreover, factory girls, many of whom were only fifteen or sixteen years old and away from home for the first time, living in lodgings, were notoriously a handful:

> The chief characteristic of the factory-girl is her want of reverence.
> She has a rough appearance, a hard manner, a saucy tongue, and an
> impudent laugh ...
>
> Anon., *Toilers in London; or Inquiries concerning*
> *Female Labour in the Metropolis,* 1889

A forewoman worked long hours, in a stressful and demanding role, for very little pay; Mother didn't remain long at the stays makers.

⋈

Totterdown was a close-knit community, and Mother had felt the need to hide from the neighbours even before her trial and incarceration. Many locals would have made it known that they were none too happy that the "Totterdown Baby Farmer" had returned. Mother felt it was time to leave.

Therefore, with nothing to lose except the last shreds of his dignity, Father borrowed some money and took his family away from the scene of their shame.

⋈

In 1881 William Dyer found employment as a labourer in a brewery on Stokes Croft, a vibrant and bustling street to the north of the heart of Bristol. He moved his family into lodgings close by, at 2 St James' Square Avenue; number 1 on the avenue was the slaughter house. Amelia tried to work her way back to respectability. At first she took in laundry, and then she set up a small general store, an ill-advised venture in an area with a prohibitive £100 annual ground rent and a glut of competitors. By 1884, the shop had failed and Mother had grown entirely disillusioned with scratching out a meagre living.

# 17 The Fishponds House of Confinement

WANTED, respectable Person to take a Baby. Must charge moderate.
– Address E.R. Letter Exchange, Bristol.

*Western Daily Press*, Wednesday 2 January 1884

In 1884, when Polly was eleven years old, the family moved into Fishponds, to the north-east of Bristol, and Mother began the baby business again. The next few years were an unsettled time – no one place was to be home for longer than a year. Polly grew increasingly disorientated by the relocations: she recalled that sometimes they moved into a house on a Saturday and were clean out of it again by the following Tuesday.

Father wasn't at all happy for Mother to be taking in babies again. Why would she risk trouble a second time? He became increasingly withdrawn and taciturn: Polly remembered him as "a most sulky man" and said that "scarcely a week went by when he and Mother did not have words". For Polly and Willie, it was anything but a happy home.

Mother paid her husband little heed. Soon, there were lots of babies in the house, just as before. But this time there was a significant difference in Mother's method of operation: this time, she made sure the infants didn't stay for long. Polly reflected upon how the babies would come and go "in the strangest fashion ... here today; gone tomorrow".

Sometimes, the women who came to the house were very grand, arriving in fine carriages and dressed in the most exquisite fabrics and the very latest designs. They seemed to have hundreds of pounds at their disposal and sent Mother or Polly out for whatever they desired. Polly would marvel at the quantity of gold coins Mother would be left with.

RESPECTABLE Couple would like to Adopt a child of gentle birth. Premium required. – Mater. Hayward's Letter Exchange, High Street.

*Western Daily Press*, Friday 18 April 1884

Mother was impressed by the women of wealth and high birth who were increasingly calling upon her services. One day in 1884 a grand carriage pulled up at the house, an incongruous sight in such a modest row of terraces. A fine-looking woman stepped out, clutching a baby girl named Annie. She brought a breathtaking pile of gold sovereigns, which she left on the parlour table: £80 in all. It was more money than Polly had ever seen; more than Father earned in two or three years. Mother was seduced by the baby's breeding as much as the handsome fee, and so Annie stayed.

Always there were ladies. They would come to stay and in due course would deliver their babies; sometimes the baby remained in the house after the mother had gone, but, Polly recalled, frequently there were funerals.

One lady paid handsomely for the funeral of her baby. She told the family she was a relation of a general in the army (but they could never rely upon much of what the ladies said as being the truth). When her baby died in the house, she paid the undertaker £5.5s. for the funeral: the equivalent of half a year's salary for many of the unskilled women who came to Mother for help. The funeral was a most elaborate affair for an infant so unwanted as to be delivered in such disreputable circumstances.

£10 offered to any Respectable Person who will ADOPT a fine healthy boy. – Immediate, Letter Exchange, High Street.

*Western Daily Press*, Friday 23 May 1884

RESPECTABLE Person offers comfortable HOME for Child. Terms moderate. – Mother, Intelligence Office, 33 Lower Ashley Road.

*Western Daily Press*, Thursday 12 June 1884

Whenever a young woman came to the house, Polly would hear Mother promise time and time again that she would treat the baby as if it were her own. But as soon as the money exchanged hands, the door would close on a mother's love for ever: Mother never did as she promised by these children.

In 1885 the Dyer family took up lodgings in a house in the Causeway, a main Fishponds thoroughfare. Father managed to get a position as a labourer in a nearby factory, and the family settled for another year or so.

In 1886, when Polly was thirteen, the family had moved again, this time to Pound Lane in Fishponds, a short walk from the Bristol Lunatic Asylum. Toward the end of the year, a beautiful woman came for the confinement with Mother. She was very young, the daughter of a well-to-do gentleman farmer. Mother was scathing about the baby's father, saying that he was more than likely the household's coachman. Certainly the lady demanded the same anonymity as most of the others, keeping all her details private. In early 1887, she gave birth to a little boy named Alfred, whom she left with Mother to raise as her own. Some two or three days later, the lady's father came to the house, accompanied by two solicitors. They sat in the parlour and spoke to Mother in grave tones, and when they left Polly watched her count out another mountain of gold coins – another £80 – that had been left for her on the table. Alfred, with his privileged background, also stayed.

--- ⊣⊢ ---

In September 1888 the country became gripped by reports of a brutal murderer who was mutilating the bodies of his female victims in the East End of London, and taunting the press with letters, which he signed "Jack the Ripper". Polly and Mother could not have avoided the press frenzy: on every street corner in every city, newspaper vendors sang out the latest headlines:

SAVAGE BUTCHERY AND MUTILATION PUBLIC TERROR
TWO MORE WOMEN MURDERED IN WHITECHAPEL AND
ALDGATE.

*Daily Telegraph*, Monday 1 October 1888

Sensationalist journalism described "the butchered women ... found weltering in their blood", and observed that the murders "cast a shadow of gloom and horror".

--- ⊣⊢ ---

Later that autumn, the Dyer family moved again; this time to Ridgeway Road, just a few streets away from the Causeway, where Mother continued to farm babies.

Mother became increasingly furtive. Polly noticed that she was once again resorting to the little bottle of laudanum she kept in her apron pocket. At the same time she became increasingly brutal in her treatment of the children, and Polly felt the worst of this, growing wary of her mother. What Polly hated the most was being asked to lie to Father. It was a frequent request: he was increasingly intolerant of Mother's adoptions.

One morning Mother left the house early to catch a train in order to collect a baby. She would not return until after Father was home from work that evening but asked that Polly tell Father she had not long left the house and would soon be back. Polly hesitated: she knew she could not lie convincingly.

"I can't do that, Mother," she had answered, daring to say no.

Mother raged against the rebuttal; how dare Polly refuse to do her bidding? "What? You won't?" Mother reached for the nearest object she could find and raised it high above her head. She sent a glass beaker hurling through the air, hitting Polly on the side of the head and drawing blood. It left a scar she would carry to her grave.

If Mother was weighed down by the constant need for secrecy, Father was far more so. Their arguments worsened, Mother later claiming he had been brutal to her. But, in truth, it can hardly have been a happy environment for a man and his children. There was a constant stream of ladies in various stages of pregnancy and labour in the house. Newborns were "delivered dead" as often as they survived; the undertaker was a regular visitor. Babies appeared and disappeared. Polly commented on the frequency of fatalities; her father cannot have failed to. And constant house moves were unavoidable if his wife was to keep out of trouble.

Mrs Dyer is a skilled midwife and whilst she was at Fishponds, Bristol, she had many lady patients. There is little doubt from the information in the hands of the police that Mrs Dyer was in the habit of advertising for "ladies in trouble" who could "get over it" and "no one would know it". In one case the police are certain that a lady placed herself in communication with Mrs Dyer who promised her that for £50 "the baby could come into the world and go out of it, so that no one would know". This letter and many others are in the possession of [the police].

Weekly Dispatch, 1896

Meanwhile, business was booming and the family was living in increasing comfort. Shared lodgings became individual rented homes. Polly admitted that the "baby business" kept the family in decent accommodation and paid off their credit accounts with local butchers and grocers.

If Dyer didn't approve of his wife's occupation, he appeared either unable or unwilling to eradicate it.

⊲⊳

In March 1889, Bristol was devastated by one of its worst floods on record. Early in the month, a heavy snowfall was followed by forty-eight hours of rain. Nearly three inches of rain was recorded to have fallen over Fishponds, most of it over an eight-hour period. The River Frome burst its banks and an area of Bristol covering 150 acres was submerged. Police delivered bread and other provisions to stranded households from small rowing boats. A relief fund was set up, and in a matter of a few weeks it had raised a staggering £11,700. In all, it took 15 tons of disinfectant to purge the 2,700 homes across the city, which had been left with sewage deposits once the water subsided.

If Amelia Dyer was a superstitious woman, she might have taken warning from these apocalyptic conditions: trouble was just around the corner. Not every young mother wanted to sever all ties with her baby after handing it over to Dyer. Not every woman understood that the one-off premium would effectively end all contact she was ever to have with her child. Some cherished a naive belief that Dyer would deliver her promise of providing their baby with a "mother's care".

In truth, with the exception of Annie and Alfred, none of the babies had remained longer than a few days in the Dyer household throughout the 1880s, their fates a mystery which would never be entirely solved. It was only a matter of time before one of these mothers demanded her baby back.

# 18 The Governess's Baby

In 1890 an attractive and well-educated young governess from Exeter found herself "in trouble" and entered into a correspondence with Amelia Dyer. Dyer's letters in response were persuasive, with their sweeping script and homespun promises of care and discretion, and she decided to trust that Dyer would help her out, albeit for a fee.

Her faith in Dyer was to prove entirely misplaced.

The governess was never named. Her age, place of birth and address were never given out. But the story of her four-year fight for the child she entrusted to Dyer was taken up by the Bristol police force at the time, and was to be recounted by Polly from the witness stand of the Central Criminal Court six years later, and transcribed by the national press. It was a true-life Victorian melodrama. The governess's determination to do the right thing might not have ended well for her, and hers is a story that was no doubt played out time and time again in the lives of many young mothers, long since forgotten. But it was to herald the start of a dramatic new chapter in Amelia Dyer's criminal career.

The governess wrote to Dyer early in 1890, in response to a newspaper advertisement. She was desperate. She had fallen in love with the elder son of the family by whom she was employed. The two had carried on an illicit affair, and she had become pregnant. The son offered to marry the governess, but his father would have none of it: a governess was not a suitable match, not least because she was clearly a woman of loose morals. The son was packed off abroad in an attempt to distract him from the affair.

The young governess found herself out of work and alone.

The governess exchanged several letters with Dyer and agreed the financial terms upon which she would nurse her through the pregnancy and labour. Should the baby live, she had no choice but to arrange that it would thereafter be adopted by Dyer. A final sum of £15 would then be payable two months after the birth.

In the early spring of 1890 the young woman moved in with Dyer, before the pregnancy became too advanced to be disguised. She remained at Dyer's house in Horfield, near Fishponds, for a considerable time – probably for as long as six months and certainly until after she had delivered her child. In all this time, she clearly came to trust that the nurse was the right woman to raise her baby. Dyer proved adept at sustaining a role day and night for the lengthy duration of the governess's stay in the house. In due course and with a heavy heart, the governess gave Dyer her baby for permanent adoption.

Two months later, in the late summer of 1890, Dyer and the governess met for what was supposed to have been the final time. It was to be an opportunity for the governess to see that her baby was being well cared for, and for her to hand over the final payment, and thereby relinquish all further responsibility. She was to learn for the first time that her nurse was not as she had at first seemed.

At that meeting the governess realized instantly that something was wrong. Dyer was nursing a child, but she was convinced it was not her child. Dyer was dismissive: infants change considerably in the first six or eight weeks of their life; this was her child as surely as night followed day. But the governess pulled back the child's clothing to examine the hips for signs of the birthmark with which the child had been born. There was nothing there.

Dyer was apparently entirely "nonplussed". How could this have happened? She assured the governess that they would meet again, in a few weeks' time, and that this time she would have the "dear little baby" in her arms. In the meantime, she wondered would she consider parting with a little of the balance of payment; just something for her "to go on with"? The governess refused to hand over another halfpenny until Dyer produced her child, alive and well.

According to later accounts in the press, the governess's young beau re-entered the story at this point. He had finally persuaded his family to grant them permission to marry and now that the ring on her finger gave respectability to her child, the young woman determined to remove the baby from Dyer's care and bring it home. With her husband at her side, she went to meet with Dyer for the second time.

The nurse failed to keep the appointment. The young mother was distraught. Her friends and relations had already remarked upon the noticeable physical strain etched on her young face. This was too much to bear. Unable to rest until she found Dyer, and with her, she prayed, her child, she returned to Horfield later that same night.

It was the early hours by the time she reached the house. Rage at the enormous betrayal of trust, and fear of what might have become of her child, had driven her far beyond the point of paying heed to courtesy and decorum. She pounded on the door until Dyer appeared. The governess stood trembling on the doorstep, battling against her distress in order to speak her mind. She demanded that Dyer hand back her baby.

By contrast, Dyer was cold and perfectly poised. That side of her which was so rarely given a public face was unleashed on the governess: a devastating menace. Dyer must have been aware of the threat posed to her by a desperate mother, and yet reportedly nothing about her demeanour that night suggested to the governess that Dyer felt either fear or remorse. With steely control, Dyer demanded further payment before producing the child.

The next forty-eight hours can only be imagined: Dyer, fighting to keep her nerve, plotting her next step; the young mother, unable to find solace even in sleep. Finally, the couple knocked on the door of Dyer's rented Horfield home for a third time.

Dyer greeted them in the same dispassionate manner. There was no baby in the house and she offered the young couple no reassurance that they would be reunited in the foreseeable future. In fact, Dyer was not prepared to give them any indication of the child's where-abouts. Even when the couple showed her the £15 they were prepared to hand over in exchange for their baby, Dyer remained resolute and the meeting ended abruptly.

The governess was frantic, but could not leave matters there. She was convinced that Dyer was hiding the child somewhere in the city, and so embarked upon a clandestine three-week surveillance oper-ation. Day and night she watched Dyer's every movement. She would have got to know what the contemporary newspapers described as Dyer's "peregrinations" around Bristol very well, had it not been for the fact the Dyer was shrewd enough to realize that she was being shadowed and altered her habits accordingly. In the end, the governess learned nothing.

The husband could sit back no longer and permit his new wife to hasten her own decline. He returned to Dyer's house and confronted her once more. Finally, Dyer appeared to capitulate: the baby, she revealed, had been so greatly admired by a couple on the platform of Temple Meads Station that she had been persuaded to hand it to them for adoption and it had been taken to live in their farmhouse.

It was not a convincing story, coming as it did after weeks of Dyer's menace and procrastination. But it represented the couple's only hope, and however unlikely the story, they were compelled to follow the trail. Dyer sent them firstly to several addresses in Bristol; when these addresses produced nothing, she came up with another. Then, after several weeks, she claimed to have received news that the couple who had adopted their baby were currently residing in Cheltenham. With mounting desperation, the pair scoured Cheltenham for word of the elusive couple from the railway platform who had allegedly disappeared and taken their baby with them.

December 1890 was the coldest in Bristol in more than a century. Snow lay on the ground for four weeks, nine inches in all by Christmas Day. Temperatures fell to five degrees below, and rarely climbed above zero day or night. When the rain came, it froze as it fell, covering the city in a sheet of ice.

For the governess and her husband in their joyless search, the chill weather could not have seemed more appropriate. They found no trace of the couple or their baby in Cheltenham. By January the non-tidal "Floating Harbour" in the city centre was still covered with several inches of ice, so that the people of Bristol had been able to enjoy weeks of skating. But there was no New Year cheer for the governess. For many months she danced Dyer's pitiless *pas de deux*, cherishing faint hope of recovering her child in Bath, Gloucester, Exeter and London in turn. Each journey fruitless; each preceded by yet another confrontation with Dyer, who offered her further leads which she had no alternative but to follow up before discounting. Dyer's sustained deception was an act of heartless cowardice, but for now, at least, the governess could do nothing but listen to her.

Finally, the governess and her husband accepted that they could not continue to fight this woman alone. No longer mindful of the risk to their reputations, in January 1891 they took their story to the Bristol police.

# 19 Mother and the Boarding House

By the time the census was taken in March 1891, Amelia Dyer had ostensibly disappeared. The governess and her husband could find no trace of her. William Dyer, now resident at 7 Ridgeway Road, Stapleton, informed the census official that he was a widower. Their children, Polly, now almost eighteen, Willie, fifteen and a general labourer, and the adopted children, Annie, seven, and Alfred, four, were apparently motherless. Polly kept house and her father went out to work as a labourer.

But the family knew that Amelia was alive and well; Polly was later to admit as much. Furthermore, Amelia's continued existence was also known to another census official, this time gathering information in the nearby coastal town of Portishead.

Amelia Dyer is listed on the 1891 census as a servant – a nurse. The house in which she was employed was in Woodhill, a row of large, genteel, semi-detached residences on high ground overlooking gentle grassy slopes running down to the sea at Portishead. The boarding-house keeper was a forty-one-year-old widow named Annie Anderson. Annie's twenty-one-year-old son was a law student; neighbouring houses were occupied by people of independent means, or else solicitors, bankers and the master of the docks. This was a leafy, picturesque neighbourhood for the quiet middle classes. In fact, it was the perfect environment in which ladies of a delicate constitution might choose to take up temporary residence in order to "take the air".

Mrs Anderson's seven lodgers and boarders were women of various ages – from their mid-twenties to late sixties. Most were single; a few were widowed. None was married. One, twenty-five-year-old Agnes Lucy, was deaf and blind. All but two were of independent means. Amelia Dyer was the only nurse employed in the house, along with a cook and a housemaid.

The boarding house in Woodhill offered her a brief respite, a temporary anonymity. It was a discreet and genteel world into which she had stepped. She was essentially a domestic servant: seeing to the personal needs of the ladies in the house, in their airy, scented bedrooms; assisting those who were not entirely firm-footed in their daily perambulations; perhaps pushing one or two in wheeled chairs along the promenade. Certainly it was a far cry from the murky activities of her recent past. What is more, her anomalous presence in this place of sober propriety is another indication of her expertise at carrying off the semblance of respectability: she had easily gained the confidence of the women who paid her to adopt their children, in particular the "inconvenienced" daughters of the genteel. Here in Portishead she was now the consummate private nurse.

Yet somewhere a former governess was spending her days in misery, mourning the loss of the child snatched from her by this very same "affectionate woman".

⇥⇤

Polly and Willie were made to swear not to let on to Father that they knew of Mother's whereabouts; Mother had threatened to kill them if he found out. Polly cited her father's disapproval as a source of much dispute between her parents; now he was defiantly pronouncing his widowhood while Mother was in hiding from him. Was Mother fearful of his aggression? Or was she afraid he would hand her over to the Bristol police, perhaps acting on the advice of his brother, who was still working for the Metropolitan Police?

In any case, for as long as William Dyer remained ignorant of his wife's whereabouts, the governess and her husband could entertain no hope of tracing their baby.

# 20 Polly and the Piano

Mother's absence continued for several months. Meanwhile, the rest of the family were left in a house which was comparatively grand. Polly proudly boasted "we had a piano and everything". The piano was a vital piece of furniture for the social aspirant, creating instantly the illusion of a middle-class household. By the 1890s, it was also widely accessible, available for lease or hire purchase, in most cities:

> FOR HIRE, a PIANOFORTE Terms 1s per week – Address BBM Daily Press Office.
>
> *Western Daily Press*, Saturday 21 June 1884

But the house and its furnishings had been affordable only for as long as Mother had filled it with pregnant, fee-paying young women. Now Mother was in hiding and all the ladies had gone. So when Father lost his job again, in the early summer of 1891, the family had no hope of paying the quarterly rent.

Polly claimed she was left to deal with their landlord, who began to threaten eviction. The Dyers' was clearly a matriarchal household: despite Mother's absence, it was not Father whom Polly consulted about the financial shortfall. Mother's instructions were that she was to raise the rent money by selling the piano. Obediently, Polly approached a gentleman who inspected the piano and thereafter agreed to pay £10 for its purchase – good news for Polly, whom Mother had told to settle for nothing less. Polly handed over the piano and used the proceeds to pay the rent.

Polly insisted she had been unaware that the piano was never theirs to sell. It had been secured by a hire-purchase agreement, and, once its owner discovered it had been sold by Polly to a third party, he raised a summons for her arrest. Days after the sale, Polly was met at the gate of the house by a gentleman caller, who she claimed said to her, "Miss Polly, I am astonished to have for you what I have in my pocket," at which point he served her with the summons. The solicitor's overly familiar tone, as recalled in adulthood by Polly, seems unlikely. She claimed that he addressed her by her pet name, rather than her surname. Polly also claimed that the solicitor expressed a degree of shock at having to serve her with a court summons, as if he had met her before and knew her to be of good moral standing. It is an unconvincing account. Nevertheless, wary of Mother's threats not to reveal her whereabouts to Father, Polly duly faced the magistrate alone.

The magistrate condemned Polly's wickedness and she was held in remand, the magistrate refusing to release her until £10 bail was met – the very sum they had needed in the first instance for the quarterly rent. The demand for bail drew Father into the crisis. Having known nothing about the intended sale of the piano, he borrowed the £10 bail money in order to secure Polly's release.

The affair forced Mother out of hiding. She calmly assured Polly all would be well. Curiously, she approached the "good and steady young fellow" with whom Polly was at that time "walking out". Mother had learned of the young railway guard's £9 in savings, and persuaded him to part with it for Polly's sake. This sum, along with an IOU for the balance, she handed to the purchaser of the piano; the instrument was thereafter returned to its rightful owner, effectively settling the matter out of court. All charges against Mary Ann Dyer were subsequently dropped.

The legal crisis over, the Dyers were nevertheless left without an income and in debt to the tune of £19: £10 which Father borrowed for Mary Ann's bail money and £9 which Mother had negotiated from the young railway guard. It seemed inevitable that Mother should set up in the baby business again.

Another house move: this time to Fillwood Road, just a few streets away. Here, Polly said, Mother took in "an awful lot of ladies and a great many babies. I recollect there being seven ladies in the house at one time." The Dyers were soon solvent again. Mother adopted another child, a little girl named Lily, for a very handsome £30.

The Dyers did not remain long in Fillwood Road. In the early autumn of 1891 they moved again, this time to Glenworth House in nearby Eastville. The address may have changed but, as Polly recalled, "It was the same thing over again. The ladies came and had babies, and there was hardly a month passed without the doctor and the undertaker being in the place, for there were several funerals. I can remember two in one week."

Countless, nameless infants. Coming into the world and slipping out of it again, so that no one would know.

The governess and her husband had not given up. Buoyed by the intervention of the police, they had continued to pursue Dyer. Finally, in late October 1891, more than twelve months since the birth of their child, they knocked on the door of Glenworth House. At their side was a police officer.

# 21 Mother and the Sharp-Pointed Knife

If Mother was disturbed by the sight of a police officer at her door, she did not immediately seem so. With her usual imperturbability, she insisted she had been telling the truth: that a couple on the railway platform had fallen for the child and had taken it from her for adoption. Naturally, she was not able to provide them with any further details as to the family's current address.

Amelia Dyer, *Weekly Dispatch*, 3 May 1896

Dyer's sangfroid was not long-lived: it soon became apparent that the psychological impact of the incident was considerable. Dyer had been through the dark, grim regime of prison and hard labour once before: she was capable of doing anything to avoid arrest again.

When young Willie returned home from work on the afternoon following the policeman's visit, he found Mother in the back garden, "half-fainting". She had slashed at her throat five or six times with a sharp-pointed knife Polly used to peel potatoes. By the time Father came home, Mother was raging and incoherent. She talked of hearing voices; destructive voices. They urged her to kill herself, she said. Worse, they warned her that Polly was trying to murder her.

Whether Mother's suicidal and delusional paranoia was feigned or laudanum-induced is now impossible to tell, but for two weeks her terrifying frenzy continued. With her father and brother out of the house all day, Polly became the focus of Mother's fury. She claimed she had long been accustomed to hearing Mother's threats against her life should she dare to cross her – "she threatened my life on several occasions" – and she already had a scar on the side of her head from the glass Mother had thrown at her in 1888. But Mother's vehemence now became far more sinister. Polly later described to a journalist how one fracas resulted in Mother throwing a knife at her head. Polly ducked behind the open door to the room, but the knife embedded itself in the hand with which she gripped the door, leaving another scar.

Finally, on 13 November 1891, William Dyer called for the local relieving officer to send in a physician, a Dr Bernard, whose assessment would determine whether or not his wife's mental state warranted confinement in the asylum.

General practitioner and surgeon David Bernard lived only a fifteen-minute walk from the Dyers, in a sizeable household made up of his wife, their two adult sons and a staff of four. But however privileged he appeared to be, forty-nine-year-old Bernard was no stranger to the lives of the less fortunate of the city: he was the medical officer for the Barton Regis Workhouse.

The fifty-three-year-old woman Dr Bernard found in Glenworth House appeared to be at the point of mental collapse. She was, as he later wrote on the medical certificate, "... highly excitable and very voluble". He found her to be "a stout, fat and flabby woman". Her skin was coarse and thick and she was "of florid complexion", broken-veined and weathered; like a drunk. She was unkempt: her skin filthy; her hair feral; her teeth decaying, blackened or entirely missing; her tongue dirty and thickly coated. She ranted incessantly, spitting in fury, fuelled by terror; and repeating over and over that the voices in her head wouldn't rest until she had brought about her own annihilation. She must die! She must do it!

The woman's husband and daughter reported that she had made three attempts on her own life in the past two weeks. The nature of one such attempt at least was evident: the marks from a knife which her daughter described as having made a "nasty wound" in her neck. Dr Bernard interpreted this a little less dramatically, describing simply "five or six slight scratches or cuts, of a recent date" below her left ear. Nevertheless, he was in no doubt that the daughter was telling the truth about her mother's violent episodes and concluded that Amelia Dyer was a danger to herself and to others. He referred her to the County Asylum in Gloucester.

# 22 Lunacy

Gloucester was a thirty-mile carriage ride from Eastville in Bristol; it would have been late in the day by the time Amelia arrived.

The County Asylum in Gloucester was spread over two sites. It was not to the newly built, expertly designed site that Dyer was delivered on the evening of 13 November 1891 but to the crescent-shaped façade of the ageing First County Asylum at Wotton. This sprawling tangle of original buildings and extensions, described by its own Commissioners as the "Rabbit Warren", housed on average eight hundred patients. Its manicured lawns, ivy-clad railings and the neatly planted borders would have at least offered that same semblance of respectability which Amelia had first encountered as an attendant at the Bristol Asylum in Fishponds.

Upon arrival, Amelia was given a thorough medical examination, and the details of Dr Bernard's medical certificate entered in the patient case file book. The nature and duration of her attack were recorded, along with her personal circumstances and the patient's perception as to the cause of her indisposition (in this case, "domestic trouble"). Her heartbeat and breathing were monitored and recorded; her pulse and the condition of her abdomen determined; the acidity of her urine was noted. Finally, the asylum doctor, Dr Harold T. Johnson, made an assessment of her mental state: "Dull, lazy manner, quiet and orderly, answers questions. Does not know why she cut her throat, will not talk much. Clean, appetite good."

Evidently, several things about Amelia had changed since her first encounter with Dr Bernard earlier that day. Firstly, the raging aggression had stopped; so too had the voices. She was now left "dull", "quiet and orderly". Secondly, at some point she had taken the opportunity to clean herself up. If Amelia's "fits of madness" were feigned, staged in order to avoid, if only temporarily, the clutches of the law (such as was to be argued five years later by a weighty school of thought, with catastrophic consequences), then Dyer would at this point have put into practice those lessons she had learned as an attendant at the Bristol Asylum. She would have been keenly aware that some small effort with one's personal appearance and a degree of quiet cooperation were essential if a female lunatic was to enjoy the best an asylum had to offer.

But there was another explanation. Sustained and significant laudanum abuse can account for the volatility, the aggression and the paranoid delusions Amelia exhibited for the two weeks prior to her hospitalization. And as the laudanum wore off, so too would the excitability, the crazed "volubility" described by Dr Bernard, giving way to the "dull, lazy manner" she displayed at Wotton.

Certainly, three days later Amelia's case file reads very differently:

November 20th

Is quiet and orderly. Industrious and doing sewing now. Clean and tidy in habits.

App good. Health good.

Was she recovering from a laudanum binge? Or was she playing a shrewd game? Whatever the answer, her surroundings were pleasant enough. Light flooded in through the large windows of the day rooms, which were tiled up to dado level and hung with a selection of framed prints. Easy chairs, draped with crocheted rugs and throws (crafted by the female patients as part of their therapy), pot plants, reading matter and even a resident cat all helped soften the hard edges of incarceration. And outside were broad, tree-lined gardens, known as airing courts, where primly uniformed attendants would take the female patients along gravelled pathways, past the ornately covered pagoda, for their daily "airing".

Weekly entries in Amelia's case file suggest the perfect patient. The Commissioners of any late nineteenth-century asylum would have wished for nothing better than to have in their wards lunatics such as Amelia Dyer, with her cooperative, malleable and easily rectifiable "madness". Whatever "suicidal" tendencies patient number 9806 had exhibited upon her admission to the asylum on the night of 13 November 1891 had quickly been eased by a few weeks of daily opiates, used routinely to treat "suicidal mania", along with an ordered routine and purposeful activity.

Nov 27

Much improved. Orderly industrious sewing and caring for others all the time.

Dec 4

Same state practically well

Dec 11

Quite well

On 12 January 1892, Amelia Dyer was "discharged, recovered". She left Gloucester and travelled back to her home at Glenworth House in Bristol by train.

# 23 "Once more there were funerals"

Mother began looking for other accommodation almost as soon as she returned. She couldn't begin to bring in an income for the household until she could hide behind a new address. She set her mind to raising the necessary capital for the down payment in advance of a new rental, obtaining an infant for adoption – and with it a premium – by the end of her first week home. What became of this child was never established, but it did not leave Glenworth House with the Dyer family.

So it was that the Dyers moved back to the district of Polly's childhood, settling into a house in Totterdown for almost the entire duration of 1892. Mother very quickly began advertising to take ladies for the accouchement, and Polly recalled "as many as three and four in the house at one time. Once more there were funerals – there were always a lot of these when the ladies came. Some ladies left with their babies and some did not ..."

Those infants who remained with Mother would never do so for long: there appeared to be that same disregard for infant life to which Polly had always been witness. Mother made all the usual assurances: Polly recalled, "although I have heard Mother make all sorts of promises that she would treat them as her own, she did not do so, once they were out of the house and had paid down the money". The infant death toll at Dyer's hands during 1892 alone is incalculable: the same presence of the undertaker, with a ferociously high rate of infants "born dead"; an ever swelling number of "adopted" infants who were never to be heard of again.

This grim trade paid its dividends. Even Polly noticed that "Mother always seemed to have a lot of money". William's period of unemployment had ended and he had once again become a labourer at a Bristol vinegar brewery. His wages were as meagre as they had ever been and he would have been all too aware that their home could not be maintained by his income alone. If he disapproved of his wife's occupation, as the press later insisted, he appeared nonetheless to give it his tacit permission to continue.

Before the end of the year, Mother moved the family to more impressive accommodation. Number 144 Wells Road was a substantial grey stone house, with generous sized rooms spread over three floors. It was a curiously indiscreet location for a woman with an apparent disregard for the law and a consequent need for secrecy to choose to set up home, not least because it was the same close-knit community from which she had fled twelve years earlier. Nevertheless, it was to be home to Polly, Willie, Alfred, Annie and Lily, for nearly two years.

Polly said of their stay in the house, "during the whole of that time we had lots of ladies in and out, and as usual, plenty of doctors and many funerals". As before, Mother agreed to adopt the majority of the babies she delivered "for life"; and yet the number of permanent residents in the household did not alter. None of the babies remained in the house for long after the final exchange of cash.

Where she could, Mother was quick to snatch at an opportunity to make an adoption more lucrative. In one instance in 1892, a woman came for the accouchement from her home in Abergavenny, South Wales. Mother discovered that the infant was tongue-tied and refused to adopt it until she had sought the advice of a doctor on the subject, to ascertain whether the infant would be strong enough to withstand an operation to correct the defect. Acting under the misguided belief that Dyer's concern for the child's speech at least indicated her genuine intentions, the parents of the child scraped together a lump sum that would cover not only the adoption fee, but also the cost of the procedure and post-operative care. Thereafter the adoption went ahead and the couple parted with their child.

A week later, the child's body was carried away by the undertaker. The operation had never taken place.

## 24 Arthur

The lifestyle Mother had chosen to pursue may have been a lucrative one, but it brought with it the strain of living with permanent deceit. For now, at least, the governess's trail had gone cold, but with every adoption came the possibility of another mother chasing her child.

The raging anxiety that had first sent Amelia into the asylum had not entirely abated: Polly said of Mother's mental health during these years in Totterdown that she "seemed very down-hearted and very peculiar in her manner at times". In times of stress, the chemically dependent inevitably turn to their drug of choice for relief. The highs and lows of Mother's long-term laudanum addiction had now begun to produce unpredictable mood swings that were to be increasingly commented upon by those who saw Dyer frequently. These were made all the worse by a second addiction: Polly admitted that Mother now "drank brandy to excess", a bottle of which she had taken to carrying around in her apron pocket, along with the laudanum.

Father had generally been a quiet, reserved, brooding man, or so Polly recalls him. Increasingly, however, her parents' marriage had become troubled. Their arguments, along with Mother's periodic "peculiar" episodes, made 144 Wells Road an unsettling place to live. Polly decided it was time she found herself a husband.

There was one individual whom she had the occasion to encounter frequently. He was a foppish young man, with a well-trimmed, sandy moustache and fashionably long hair, who was habitually seen in a slouch hat and an immaculate frock coat. This was not a look favoured by landed or titled young men, but nor was it that of young working-class tradesmen; Polly's brother, for instance, would certainly not have dressed in this manner. This young man cut quite a dash.

Arthur Palmer, *Famous Crimes*, 1905

He kept what was known as a "fancy" store on the Wells Road, filled with covetable decorations to finish a lady's outfit: lace trims, fabric flowers, birds, feathers, ribbons and bows and buttons and pins of every description. It was just the occupation for a flirtatious young man.

The man's name was Arthur Palmer and he was twenty-three years old. He had been born in Parkstone, Dorset, to a printer from Warminster named Robert, and his wife, Clara, and had an older brother, Alfred Ray. When Arthur was born, the family had lived in modest comfort in Dorset, employing one domestic servant. But soon after Arthur's birth, Robert died, leaving Clara to raise her sons alone. She never remarried, and soon lost her domestic help, taking up dress-making in order to be able to raise her sons.

When Arthur and Polly began walking out, he had easily won Mother's affections. After all, he had an asset upon which Mother placed great emphasis: capital.

When Arthur was barely sixteen, he had been seduced by the prospect of crossing the Atlantic to earn his fortune in New York. With or without the consent of his mother, Arthur travelled to Liverpool, where he boarded the *City of Rome* on 1 May 1885, announcing himself a labourer and travelling steerage.

Such a journey was quite an undertaking for one so young, but Arthur's early drive and ambition did well for him. He worked hard in a fast-expanding New York City labour market and returned home with an accumulated wealth which gave him an air of superiority and funded his ostentatious dress sense. Polly claimed he had "put by" a staggering £800. Such a sum, even if exaggerated by half, would have been what an unskilled working man, such as Polly's father, could expect to earn in twenty years.

After a nine-month courtship, Polly told Mother that Arthur had proposed, and that he was planning on seeking an opportunity of speaking to Father. Mother's expression was far from the teary-eyed delight every young girl imagines her mother will assume on hearing such news. Polly recalled how Mother's face darkened. She answered: "Very well, let him speak to me first."

Arthur's meeting with Mother was memorable: he later recounted the conversation verbatim. He began by asking her why he should not follow tradition and seek the permission of Polly's father.

"It's nothing to do with him," she had replied curtly. "I can do just as well as him, and if you take my advice you will say nothing at all to him. Even if you did, he would have nothing to say about it."

Polly and Arthur were engaged in the spring of 1893. Father was not consulted, just as Mother had insisted. The engagement was simply presented as a *fait accompli*, further removing Dyer's active participation in the life of his family. Relations between William and Amelia were already strained and they were about to be put to the test once more.

# 25 Liquor and Laudanum

Over the course of 1893, Mother's house of confinement continued to thrive. Throughout the courtship and engagement of Arthur and Polly the ladies had come and gone; so had their infants, as nameless as they had always been. As many as seven women at a time took up temporary residence at 144 Wells Road, each paying a substantial fee for the privilege. Most of the women stayed at least two or three months before their confinement and some for as long as five or six. Polly said, "as far as I could make out ... at that time she had plenty of money".

While babies quietly disappeared in the background, Father continued to labour at the vinegar brewery. Mother swung from relative good health, when in "calm moments she was very kind and affectionate", to dark and "peculiar", drug- and alcohol-induced delusional melancholia.

At the beginning of December 1893, Mother's mood plummeted. Her anxiety levels raged out of control (a common symptom of long-term, habitual opium abuse); she could not be consoled. Polly sent for the young doctor who had been attending Mother since she had returned to Totterdown in 1891. Dr Henry McQuade was a thirty-year-old Irishman who lived just minutes from the Dyers. In what condition McQuade found Amelia Dyer has not been recorded, but whatever had triggered her troubles would soon become apparent.

On the afternoon of Friday 23 December 1893, a well-dressed couple approached the house on the Wells Road. There was no Yuletide cheer apparent on their careworn faces, but their tireless investigations had at last led them to the door of number 144.

It had been almost two years since the governess and her husband had last seen the nurse, three since the birth of their child. In all that time they had not given up their search. Whatever characteristic steely coolness Dyer presented them with on that December afternoon was short lived. As with their exchange of 1891, the details of the meeting have been lost, but its consequences were to prove considerable.

❧

Mother set off from the house almost immediately the couple left; Polly recalled her returning with threepence-worth of laudanum from one apothecary and the same amount from another. This amounted to a substantial overdose, comparable to that which had almost carried her off fourteen years before. Over the ensuing years, sustained use would have boosted her tolerance, as, little by little, she had raised her dose to stave off the agony of withdrawal.

By 1893 recreational opium eating or laudanum drinking was widely regarded as socially unacceptable, but in reality many doctors – as well as their patients – functioned well with an opium habit of their own. The feeling was that within the limits of your "level of individual tolerance" an opium habit was largely harmless, and certainly less offensive than alcoholism. As a household painkiller it therefore remained easily accessible and largely unregulated.

Perhaps less acknowledged by its late nineteenth-century advocates, in the long term a laudanum habit brought on mood swings and periods of considerable melancholy. It could certainly account for Mother's periodic "peculiar look". And when a substantial habit was combined with excessive alcohol consumption (as many who knew her acknowledged), erratic, anti-social and psychotic behaviour were predictable consequences. Moreover, a sudden withdrawal from the drug could produce the kind of delusional episodes she periodically displayed.

Now that the governess and her husband had tracked her down to her Totterdown address, Mother realized she was once again faced with a very real threat of arrest and imprisonment. Laudanum now represented a painless way out. Mother consumed both bottles on Christmas Eve, leaving Polly to cope with the consequences.

Dr McQuade instantly recognized the severity of Mother's condition and notified the relieving officer. Later that day Dr Frederick Thomas Bishop Logan came to examine Mother. Polly let him in without a word, and introduced him, saying simply, "There's somebody come to see you," before retreating to a seat in the corner.

Unlike McQuade, Dr Logan was not acquainted with the family

and could have had no idea what he would find as he entered the parlour. The woman was sitting in an easy chair by a roaring fire. Dr Logan took a seat away from her at a table and began to take out a notebook and pencil.

Suddenly Dyer made a move. In a moment, she was out of her chair. She grabbed the poker from the fireplace, and, raising it high above her head, rushed at the doctor, screaming, "I'll break your skull!"

The doctor wrestled with her for a minute or so, until he could gain control. He was left in no doubt as to her state of mind: "she was very excitable and wild in her manner ... she would have struck me a blow had I allowed her". Once she had been overpowered, Dyer became highly distressed, crying and muttering in despair. Logan sat her down and waited for her to calm sufficiently so that he could begin to question her.

Polly explained that Mother was periodically very violent and that she had sent for the local doctor earlier that day as a result of her suicide attempt.

"I've no peace in this world, only in heaven. I'll soon get there." Dyer wanted to leave the doctor in no doubt of her intentions, repeating several times that she wanted only death and that she would kill herself. "The voices tell me to do it," she said. "And the birds. They tell me 'go and do it'."

It was more than enough to convince Logan, who issued a certificate recommending that Amelia Dyer be taken to an asylum for treatment.

⟨⟩

The next day, Christmas Day, passed sombrely. Early on Boxing Day morning, the local magistrate made the necessary order for Amelia Dyer to be transferred to the Somerset County Asylum in Wells. She had once again escaped the retribution of the young governess, and therefore also the law. Exhausted from the laudanum overdose and the events of the previous forty-eight hours, for Amelia Dyer the ride to Wells offered a welcome reprieve from her worries.

# 26 "Frenzied Objects"

The asylum at Wells is a grand red-brick building, perched on a plateau in the Mendips, with breathtaking views of the city and its cathedral and a broad panorama beyond. The perfect symmetry of its towers and chimneys and pointed apexes is a testament to the balance the institution strove to establish, even as early as the mid-decades of the nineteenth century, in the troubled minds of the "frenzied objects" it called its patients.

If the Bristol Asylum aimed for well-ordered stability, Wells triumphed in it. Attendants were provided with no method of restraint from the 1860s and the use of seclusion was highly regulated. Firm emphasis was placed upon good nutrition, recreational and occupational activity, fresh air and regular sleep. Attendants were warned that patients deserved to be treated not just kindly, but "indulgently"; that they were "never to strike or speak harshly to them", and that they would be disciplined for failing to show respect. In return, the attendants' need for recreation and relaxation was acknowledged and respected.

Amelia was led directly through to the physician's reception, where she was given a thorough medical examination by Dr William.

**On admission** – a stout and robust looking woman, hair grey, conjunctival suffused, pupils equal and normal, very few teeth, tongue coated, pulse weak, 63, heart sounds weak and distant, lung sounds normal.
**Urine** – acid … slightly albuminous.
**Mentally** – very depressed and melancholy, converses coherently, taking a very gloomy view of her condition, and says she has been brought low by trouble. Had little sleep, talks of suicide saying that in the morning the birds told her "to go and do it", and she felt she was better off out of the world. Takes her food.

In common with all patients at Wells, she also had her photograph taken. Today, the images in the asylum case files offer grisly evidence. Often undernourished, all with an air of desperation, and in many cases in a state of complete personal neglect, the women are, by the rigorous standards of the day, half-dressed, their hair a tangled, hopeless mess, as if reflecting their mental turmoil. In some cases, the medical staff indulged themselves with a second photograph, revealing an astounding transformation: hair perfectly pinned, fully corseted, neatly dressed and a hat perched primly on the head. The patient clearly transformed into the self-possessed individual Victorian society required her to be.

Amelia Dyer's case file has the yellowed outline where her photograph had once been pasted; presumably it was removed and taken home as a macabre keepsake, or else sold to the press during her later notoriety. The dark-eyed image she displays in which she glares at the photographer is the most sinister ever taken of her (see plate 3) and has been widely circulated, but its provenance cannot be ascertained. It seems likely that this was the photograph taken upon her entry into Wells Asylum that December.

The easy regime at Wells soon worked its magic. After just two days of hot baths, plentiful food and some gentle sewing tasks, her case file recorded a marked improvement:

Dec. 28th  Expresses herself as feeling better.
Converses freely and seems brighter.

With a sizeable working farm on site, the asylum was all but self-sufficient, providing optimum nutrition at meal times. Fresh vegetables, home-farmed milk, and protein in the form of daily rations of cheese and meat, were seen as an integral part of every patient's cure. Meal times were made all the more pleasant by an in-house band of attendant musicians, who would frequently play light-hearted tunes through dinner.

Dec. 30th  Is going on very well.

The attendants' charge, to "promote cheerfulness and happiness", was evidently well adhered to. Amelia passed contented days strolling in the manicured gardens of the airing courts, sewing, reading "light-hearted literature" beside roaring fires, eating and sleeping at regular intervals, and, of course, accepting her daily dose of opium. Her progress was pleasing to her carers.

> Jan 5th – expresses herself as feeling much better and as having got rid of all her morbid ideas. Sleeps very well and takes her food.
> Jan 10th – continues to improve
> Jan 16th – bright and cheerful and takes an interest in her surroundings

It seems Wells Asylum was quite the holiday.

On 20 January 1894, Amelia Dyer left the asylum, the Committee fully satisfied that she had made a complete recovery. She weighed 17 stone 1lb: 3lb heavier than she had weighed upon admission.

⊰⊱

Mother had no intention of remaining long in the Wells Road after coming out of the asylum. She left William Dyer and moved with all five children to several different addresses across Bristol: to Montpellier, just north of St Paul's; to Stokes Croft, to where she had fled following her release from prison in 1880; and to Horfield, close to the Bristol Asylum. For several months, she could settle nowhere for long. Anticipating discovery and arrest at every turn as she must have been, she nevertheless continued to adopt infants: it was, as Polly admitted, her mother's only source of income. Without the premiums from permanent adoptions, she would have had no means of making the advance rent payments needed to secure lodgings for herself and her children.

It is hard to understand why Polly, now twenty-two and engaged, continued to live with her mother. She had long been

Polly Dyer, *Famous Crimes*, 1905

the victim of her raging brutality and cowered from her unpredictable mood swings. She is not recorded as having expressed a moment's affection for her mother; indeed, she was to prove quick to damn her given the opportunity. But for another few months at least, Mother exerted sufficient influence to keep her daughter at her side.

By early spring, Arthur approached Mother once more, this time to request that she provide the family details required for the marriage banns to be put up.

Polly's brother, Willie, was eighteen years old and a working man. He had been raised in mayhem just like his sister and for him, too, it was clearly time to leave Mother behind. That same spring he announced that he had enlisted in the Royal Navy; he would become a marine. Mother was left reeling. Her marriage had ended, though it had never been an especially happy one; her daughter was about to be married, and now she was to be parted from her son. Five months spent essentially on the run from the pursuing governess and her husband and the Bristol police had already taken their toll on her nerves; separation from Polly and Willie now pushed her beyond the brink of what she could withstand.

This time her incapacity continued far longer than the usual few days. She later described to a physician that she was rendered "unconscious for three weeks", finally awakening with the delusional sensation that her body was swarming with vermin: "I fancied that the rats were crawling all over me." Her memory loss and unsettling psychotic delusions almost certainly describe the consequences of a sustained period of heavy alcohol and laudanum consumption.

But events were about to become far worse: just three months after Dyer's release from Wells Asylum, at the end of April, the governess and her husband appeared at the door to Mother's lodgings in Horfield, a police officer at their side once more.

# 27 Melancholy Days

It is not clear why the police did not arrest Dyer that April. After all, the governess could identify her as the woman who had "adopted" her child; and the child was clearly missing. At the very least, Dyer had entered into a fraudulent contract to raise the baby as her own for life and had therefore obtained the fee under false pretences. She could have been arrested and charged on those grounds – as Sarah Ellis had been before her in the Brixton Baby Farmer case of 1870. Whatever the reason, the police failed to make the arrest, and Dyer was left alone once more.

This time she made the journey to Wells directly, hoping to be re-admitted without the suicide attempt, the medical certificate and the magistrate's order which had conspired to send her there on Boxing Day. The meticulous case notes kept at the Wells Asylum record the following encounter which took place toward the end of April 1894:

> One evening in the spring of 1894 [Amelia Dyer] arrived here late in a very excited state ... She had only a few coins in her pocket and had come all the way from Bristol having had nothing to eat all day. I took her in for the night and telegrammed to her friends next day as they did not come to remove her, I sent her back with an attendant.

Officials during the period often used the word "friends" to describe relations: it was clear that none of Dyer's were altogether too keen for her to return home.

Pasted beneath the entry in the asylum case notes was the following article from the *Wells Journal*, with a note to say that it had appeared in the paper a few days after Dyer's visit:

**Alleged suicide attempt** – Amelia Dyer was taken to the General Hospital last night by the police suffering from the effects of immersion, caused it was alleged by her attempting to commit suicide in the rivulet at Ashton Park.

It was not difficult to try to drown oneself in the city of Bristol. With the awesome height of the Clifton Suspension Bridge spanning the River Avon, the River Frome running through the city as well as the muddy waters of the Cumberland Basin, there were several opportunities. Indeed, Brunel's iconic bridge has over the years earned itself a reputation as Bristol's "suicide bridge" (although fate has intervened on more than one occasion in that regard. In 1885, for example, a factory girl named Sarah Ann Henley, jilted by her lover, jumped from the bridge and was saved by the billowing of her skirts, which acted as a parachute, carrying her gently down to the muddy banks of the river. She became quite a local celebrity and lived to the age of eighty.)

Dyer's "attempted suicide" in Ashton Park (in what was elsewhere described more accurately as a "brook") did little more than dampen the layers of her skirts. Nevertheless, on 26 April 1894, Amelia Dyer was discovered in an excited state, partially submerged in a foot or two of water in the rivulet. She was taken to the Bristol General Hospital, where, an hour or two after admission, she was seen by house surgeon, Dr Lacey Firth. He recorded seeing no evidence of the woman's "excited" state, although she was shivering with cold and in very low spirits. She was admitted to a ward, where she remained for thirteen days.

For the duration of her stay, Dyer remained downcast, but Dr Lacey Firth was satisfied that while she was certainly melancholy, and initially refused all food, she was not insane. She repeatedly told the doctor that she was troubled, that there was something on her mind.

Dr Lacey Firth reported that she received one visitor at the hospital. A well-dressed man, whose name the doctor did not record, conversed both with the doctor and the patient. He was searching for a woman, in whose care had been placed a child. To the man Dyer remained unresponsive, but later the visit had such a negative effect on her mood that it prompted the doctor to question her about her visitor. Dyer admitted to having known the woman the man had been searching for, who she said lived on a certain street in Bath, and she also gave some indication that she had been involved in the disappearance of the child. But she would not admit the exact nature of her actions or the whereabouts of the child.

※

Polly and Arthur were married days after Mother's release from hospital, at the parish church in Horfield. Arthur spent almost his entire savings making a home for Polly.

Willie had already set off for his new life in the navy, and Father was still resident on the Wells Road. Mother briefly returned to her husband after her discharge from hospital, but the marriage was clearly over, and she soon moved to York Road in Totterdown, a riverside address.

Marriage had added a certain haughty allure to Polly's tall, neat physique. A wedding ring was still a young woman's surest way into society, and her husband's savings had funded a well-furnished and comfortable home. Briefly, Polly must have felt removed from her mother's influence for the first time in her life. But it hadn't lasted long: within a few weeks Mother appeared at Grove House, Polly's Fishponds address, begging to be allowed to live with them.

Polly recalled that it "seemed quite a surprise to mother that Arthur had so much money to spend" on making a home for his new wife. Polly seems to have grown in confidence, buoyed by the material trappings of respectability which now surrounded her. Arthur had for a while now been employed as a commissions agent – a travelling salesman – selling corn and flour to Bristol tradesmen for a major London miller. But soon after Mother moved in with them at Fishponds he lost his job, "due to slackness of trade", leaving the couple without an income.

Polly was later to claim that when Arthur sold "almost every stick" of furniture they possessed, it was not because of his change of circumstances, but rather as a result of Mother's desperate plea for cash. He told Polly that Mother had approached him in a most distressed state, and had insisted that "if she did not have £150 at once she would very likely get into most serious trouble". Mother had promised to repay him the loan shortly; she expected to come into £500. Arthur had believed her and had raised the money against the sale of the household contents.

Polly recounts, "Here again the same business was repeated, I mean as regards the ladies coming and the babies being born." Infant life became the household's sole source of income. Arthur passed indolent days, happy to allow his mother-in-law to work to support him and apparently indifferent to the ebb and flow of women and infants. Polly was induced to enter into what she grimly referred to as "the baby business". She was soon to prove herself as prolific as her mother.

By the end of 1894, they had also opened their doors as a house of confinement. Alongside the ladies who came for the accouchement, Mother and the Palmers, Alfred, Annie and Lily and four adopted infants were all crammed into Grove House. One of the babies was born in the house; Mother had received £80 for its permanent adoption. Two others were the result of newspaper advertisements and had been born elsewhere, arriving with £30 and £40 premiums respectively. As the money rolled in, so the number of people in the house increased and tensions began to run high.

In December 1894 Mother suffered another fit of melancholia, and Polly awoke one morning to the familiar sound of Mother's distress. She had tired of this world, she said. It was time she sought peace in heaven; she must do it! She must do it! She threatened to drown herself in the river, and finally Arthur applied to the relieving officer for an order to have her certified.

Dr William Eden arrived at Grove House on 14 December. He reported that he had found her "very excited; when I went in she threatened to pitch me out ... I had very little conversation with her, she was in such a bellicose spirit; I heard what she had to say, and let her talk on, and in the end I came to the conclusion she was of unsound mind, and ought to be placed under control." His words give a sanitized vision of Dyer's condition: Polly had been under siege. The incessant and semi-coherent talk of suicide (Dr Eden also noted how Dyer "rambled on") would turn in a moment to raging aggression. Polly told Dr Eden that Mother had "run after her with a knife".

With Mother exclaiming, "God has forsaken me!", "The world is against me!" and "I must do it! I will do it", Dr Eden signed a certificate to the effect that she was "Excited and depressed by times. Says she is lost to God and the world is against her ... She is dazed and incoherent." Under the magistrate's order she was then transported to Gloucester County Asylum at Wotton.

# 28 *"They broke my spirit"*

In December 1894, the Wotton Asylum in Gloucester was as crowded and dilapidated as Dyer must have remembered it. Its labyrinthine corridors echoed with the torment of cross-grained humanity just as it had always done. The routine was familiar. Her particulars were recorded: marital status ("married"); occupation ("nurse"); religion ("C of E"); age ("54"). The family of five children she had cited on previous case files was now reduced to a brutal and intriguing "nil". Amelia Dyer was listed as a danger to others and to herself, and an assessment was made of her physical condition:

> Very stout woman, sallow complexion
> Grey hair teeth almost all gone
> Tongue thickly coated
> Eyes dark blue
> Margins of pupils slightly irregular
> React naturally
> Respiratory system: nat
> Circulatory system: heart sounds feeble & distant
> Pulse 84 reg, small.

This was to be Dyer's final stay in a lunatic asylum; it was also to be her most harsh. The asylum medical superintendent, Dr F. Craddock, was a slight man with a heavy moustache dominating his face; he wore his coat fully buttoned, the man inside it hidden behind a concentrated English reserve.

In the early 1890s Dr Craddock was troubled by his work. He compiled a statistical analysis of lunacy which he used in support of his most fervent belief: he argued that there was a worrying escalation of lunacy in Britain, the solution to which lay in the study of eugenics.

He argued in favour of the enforced sterilization of lunatics, believing that those of unsound mind would inevitably taint any offspring with the same affliction.

Craddock's intrinsic distaste for the lunatics in his care influenced a harsh regime. Amelia's final incarceration as a lunatic was to last three months, and that despite a note in her case file as early as 22 December to the effect that "there is very little wrong with her", and again a week later: "Is now apparently quite recovered." Little is known of her precise treatment during this time. She claimed to have been often placed in isolation, and to having spent long hours in a padded cell. Dyer's last spell as a lunatic seems to have had a lingering impact, all but crushing her. She later wrote in a letter to Polly, "I have no soul; my soul was hammered out of me at Gloucester Asylum."

# 29 *Money Troubles*

The governess was never to see her baby again, nor even to have the small comfort of laying flowers at its grave. She sank into quiet oblivion, just as her child had done. But in her relentless pursuit of the nurse who had almost certainly made an untimely angel of her child, she had instigated months of unremitting torture. As a result of her struggle, Dyer was to feel hunted for the rest of her life. Moreover, the governess's intervention sparked a chain of events that was to continue to force Dyer into the darkest recesses of Victorian society.

Dyer's story was marked now by an inexplicable poverty. She had taken in at least four infants for adoption over a short period of time, three of whom had brought with them £150 in premiums, enough to keep a modest household comfortable for several years. And that was in addition to the weekly fees paid by the ladies staying for the accouchement, and the additional high fees paid by those who wished their babies "born dead".

On paper, it seems it was a lucrative time and yet Dyer was apparently in dire financial straits. Mother had been so desperate for cash that she had induced Arthur to sell "every stick" of furniture. When Dr Eden committed Dyer to the Wotton Asylum for the second time, her particulars cited "money" as one of the factors contributing to her mental malaise (along with personal circumstances and domestic trouble). Evidently the Palmers, too, were suffering from financial hardship. In December 1894, they abandoned Grove House immediately upon Mother's removal. Polly ("Mary-Ann Palmer") is given as her next of kin; her address listed is Sambourne, Warminster, the home of Clara Palmer, Arthur's mother. Before they left, Arthur took Alfred, Annie and Lily, the children raised as Polly's "siblings" for ten years, as well as the four infants who had been adopted by Mother, and dumped them at the door of the Barton Regis Workhouse in Bristol. One of the infants was to die soon after admission, weakened by Dyer's characteristic neglect; two others were successfully reunited with their mothers, both living locally and "in a good position in life".

The family trade in infants didn't end now that Mother was incarcerated. Arthur and Polly needed cash and they raised it the only way Polly knew. Returning to Bristol for three months early in 1895, the Palmers set themselves up in the baby business independently from Mother for the first time, affecting the air of a young couple desperate for children.

It was a role Arthur appeared to relish. After a few months, his advertisements had become grandly verbose:

A Gentleman with a comfortable home wishes to ADOPT two CHILDREN without parents (boy and girl preferred). They must be healthy and of undeniably respectable parentage. Highest references given and required. Address. – Comfort, c/o Messers Atchleys, Solicitors, Bristol

*Western Daily Press*, 5–10; 19–23 April 1895

The wording was a master stroke, designed to elicit only the most refined, and therefore moneyed, responses. Casting himself in the role of a "Gentleman", and insisting arrangements be made via a solicitor (just as Polly had recalled the well-connected relations of Alfred had managed his adoption), Arthur had played to his target audience. These subtleties lent absolute credibility to his presentation. Having solicitors validate the adoption was an arrogant device the couple were to resort to again. Finally, his insistence upon "undeniable" respectability – only the strictly legitimate infant – was the final deterrent to the poor, working-class single mother, with her meagre premiums.

Arthur signed his name to one receipt after another, each one acknowledging the high premiums settled upon the dozens of luckless children to whom he had promised a loving home. Countless babies condemned: police later collated handfuls of these receipts, all signed by Arthur. And, with just one exception, none of the children he adopted in the spring of 1895 was ever heard of again.

Queenie Baker was a four-year-old girl adopted by Polly and

Arthur at the end of April. With a significant sum of money now at their disposal, the Palmers packed up their belongings and left Bristol in early May, heading deeper into the West Country on a steam train from Temple Meads, taking Queenie with them.

# 30 The Family Divided

By 13 January, Amelia Dyer had convinced medical staff at the Wotton Asylum that she was sufficiently recovered to warrant a trial return into the community. Where she headed for that cold, bleak January fortnight following her release is not known, but, significantly, her trial coincided with the start of the Palmers' new venture as independent baby farmers. By the start of February she was back at the asylum, her case file recording five days later that she was "again to all intents and purposes recovered, though not so much as previously". She was clearly not entirely buoyed up by a visit to her daughter and son-in-law, if indeed that is where she had been.

However, she was now a compliant lunatic, and one whose recovery, if not yet complete, was considered entirely imminent. She was duly removed from the County Asylum, where costly patient care weighed so heavily upon the local ratepayers, and transferred to the more economical wards of the Barton Regis Workhouse infirmary in Bristol.

⁜

If her weeks at the Wotton Asylum had been grim, the workhouse was grimmer still. Though a shift toward the employment of more female and working-class Guardians had effected a gradual softening of some of the worst excesses of the regime, it was still widely regarded as a place of dread. The days were monotonous, the routine harsh and the infirmary staffed by unqualified "pauper attendants", who could be notoriously brutal. The infirmary struggled to accommodate the sick, the mentally ill and the incapacitated side by side. Added to that was the pressure of housing the violently insane. Written into the workhouse regulations at Barton Regis was a stipulation that no one deemed dangerous, of an unsound mind, or who "may require habitual or frequent restraint" should be admitted into the workhouse for longer than fourteen days. But even two weeks is a long time for those living in an open ward alongside a dangerous and restrained individual. In such an environment, those with depression or psychosis would quickly deteriorate, and were often sent back to the County Asylum.

-=¤=-

The day the Palmers took Queenie by train out of Bristol, Queenie recalled being "waved off" at the platform by a "very big tall lady" who she had been told was her grandmother. Alongside her "parents", she climbed aboard a train bound for Plymouth. The city then, as now, was a major naval base, which must have rekindled Arthur's boyhood love of the sea. He was frequently reported to have passed himself off as a ship's steward home on leave, and had even been offered a position as such, on New Year's Day that year, working alongside his wife as steward and stewardess on board a private yacht. It would have taken them away to sea for three years and Mother couldn't tolerate that thought: she had forbidden them to accept the post, despite what she described as "a good wage" of eight shillings a month. Her word, it seems, had been enough to stop Arthur taking the job he had dreamed of since boyhood. But the pull of the sea was clearly strong, and so Arthur, Polly and little Queenie Baker sat in their compartment and waited for the whistle.

-=¤=-

After a brief consultation between the medical superintendent of the Wotton Asylum and the medical officer of the Barton Regis Workhouse Infirmary, Dyer was officially discharged from Wotton on 11 March, considered by both parties to be fully recovered. But still she was not ready or able to risk life on the outside: she pleaded poverty, saying her home had been broken up since her incarceration, and became an able-bodied pauper at the Barton Regis Workhouse.

It was a grim choice for her to have to make. There can have been little that distinguished her life as a pauper from her memories of prison. In both institutions she was labelled an "inmate". In both, her days were regimented by a series of bells. In both, her diet, her personal hygiene, her clothing and the manner in which she passed each day were entirely removed from her control. It was a system that, though reformed in 1880, bore the traces of its original conception as a punishing system for the eradication of the "idle poor"; a regime designed to reprimand and to castigate those who failed to support themselves.

Dyer was bound by daily roll calls, enforced periods of silence and rigid controls against smoking, drinking, use of "obscene or profane language" or card games. Permission had to be sought for the most basic human rights: the right to sleep when exhausted (forbidden outside set bedtimes, "except by permission of the master or matron"); the right of a parent to be with her child (restricted to one set period in each day, and only then in a room specially set aside for the purpose); the right to leave (without giving "reasonable notice"). Even her choice of reading matter was scrutinized: an enduring mistrust of the educated working classes meant that it was left to the discretion of the master or matron to decide upon anything deemed "improper ... which may be likely to produce insubordination".

What gave the house its *raison d'être*, as well as its name, was work. Picking oakum was a standard and soul-destroying occupation, but there were other tasks, too. Able-bodied women could be asked to nurse the sick and lunatic on the wards of the infirmary; or to tend to the infants in the nursery. Amelia Dyer had four of her own adopted children at the workhouse in May 1895: Annie, Alfred and Lily and a baby girl who had been one of the infants Dyer had adopted at Grove House. Ironically, Dyer may have been set to tend her own abandoned children. (The baby girl remained in the workhouse for another four months, until September 1895, when she was selected by the Guardians "to be emigrated" to Canada. She was later said to be doing "thoroughly well".)

Life for the elderly inmates in particular was nothing but a bleak and hopeless monotony. Elderly paupers were typically proud, dignified souls. They had worked hard all their lives, and would only enter the workhouse when their bodies were worn out so that they could no longer earn their own keep; although such was their dread of life in the workhouse that many chose begging and vagrancy as preferable alternatives. Those inside spent comfortless, regimented days on hard wooden benches, with nothing but a bland and inadequate diet to break up their day. Most elderly paupers went into the workhouse knowing they would almost certainly die there.

On the morning of Wednesday 24 April 1895, Mother obtained a temporary pass out of the workhouse to visit her daughter.

❧❧

It was a day fraught with emotion. Mother didn't bear isolation well; she had not waited long before returning to live with Polly after the wedding. She had even gone so far as to forbid the newlyweds to take up the position on board a yacht because she could not accept the ensuing three-year separation. Polly herself was later to reflect, "For as long as I was there, [Mother] was well." In spite of all that had gone between them, it seemed Amelia Dyer craved the company of her daughter. That April, after three years on the run from the Bristol police, considerable financial pressures, three torturous months as a certified lunatic and several weeks toiling under merciless hardship of the workhouse, Amelia was reeling. And now she found herself standing on a crowded railway platform, waving her daughter off to a life in a new city.

When she headed back into the workhouse two days later, she had resolved that her stay there was almost at an end.

❧❧

Dyer could have avoided the monotony and crushing loss of liberty of the workhouse. It was a dehumanizing system: an assault upon an individual's humanity and one which none would opt for, except those in desperate need. It is difficult to regard Dyer's need as desperate. For as long as she was prepared to continue to accept cash for infant life, as she had done for twenty-five years, there was no need for her to tolerate poverty.

Had she at last had a change of heart? It seems unlikely: she would return soon enough to her "nefarious practice". Her stay at the asylum may well have reflected her genuinely fragile mental health, but upon her discharge she made a choice to remain a pauper. Perhaps the hardship of the workhouse represented a lesser evil; a welcome refuge; a protection from a greater foe? Certainly she feared capture and arrest by the Bristol Constabulary, who had already proved unrelenting in their pursuit; but that had never stopped her from living at large in and around the city before. She had taken refuge in the asylum and the workhouse for the first six months of 1895, as if she

Caversham Weir and the Clappers footbridge, where seven of Amelia Dyer's victims were recovered.

# MURDER.

## £50 REWARD.

**WHEREAS** the dead body of a newly born female Child, with a piece of tape tied tightly round the neck, wrapped in pieces of towelling and brown winsey and a lilac apron, was found in Holford Mews, Clerkenwell, at 4.30 a.m. on the 8th instant; and a Coroner's Jury having returned a verdict of "Wilful Murder against some Person or Persons unknown,"

## FIFTY POUNDS REWARD

will be paid by Her Majesty's Government to any person who shall give such information and evidence as shall lead to the apprehension and conviction of the Murderer or Murderers; and the Secretary of State for the Home Department will advise the grant of Her Majesty's Gracious

## PARDON

to any accomplice (not being the person who actually murdered the said Child) who shall give such evidence as will lead to a like result.

Information to be given at any of the Metropolitan Police Stations.

METROPOLITAN POLICE OFFICE,
4, Whitehall Place,
20th June 1871.

**E. Y. W. HENDERSON,**
*The Commissioner of Police
of the Metropolis.*

[14915]  E. & S.—450—071.

"Wanted" poster issued in 1871 as part of a Scotland Yard offensive against infanticide in the capital.

Amelia Dyer, angel maker. This photograph was probably taken on Amelia Dyer's admission to Wells Asylum in 1893.

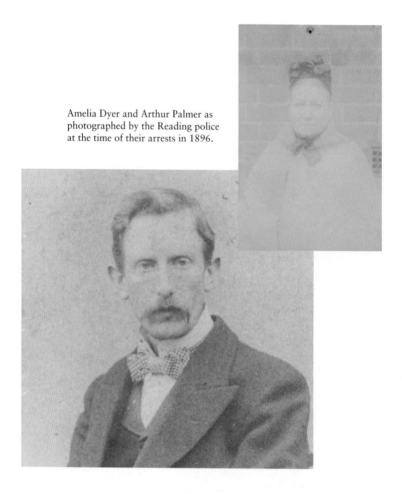

Amelia Dyer and Arthur Palmer as photographed by the Reading police at the time of their arrests in 1896.

MARRIED couple with no family would adopt healthy child, nice country home. Terms, £10.—Harding, care of Ship's Letter Exchange, Stokes Croft, Bristol. b

The advertisement that led to the adoption of Doris Marmon and Harry Simmons.

15 Kensington road
Oxford road Reading Berks
Sunday Jany 12. 96

Dear Madam   Seing an advertisement in the London W.. Dispatch,
Lady wanted to take a New Born Baby I beg to say we are wel to
do Farmers we have no Child I should be delighted to take your
little one we have a nice home and every comfort but no Child &
Child with me wil be well brought up under Church of England
Influence would have a Mother & Fathers love and I must tel you
my Husband as wel as myself are dearly fond of Children I should
never take a Child for the sake of Money I do realy want a nice
Baby I dont mind Boy or Girl I could love either I dont mind how
small a sum you wil pay if you wil kindly reply and tel me all
Particulars I feel we may come to an Arrangment and if at any
future time you would like to come and see me I would make you
Welcome to stay a few days for it is a lovely in the Country in
the Summer time Now my dear Madam will you kindly send a line by
return and tel me all Particulars and oblige Yours
                                                    Respectfully
                                                    A Stanfield

              address
                        Mrs Stanfield
                        45 Kensington road
              Oxford road Reading Berks.

A letter written by Amelia Dyer using the alias Mrs Stansfield, seeking arrangement
of an adoption, which was found in Kensington Road at the time of her arrest.
The typed text is the police transcript.

The front cover of the Olympia Sporting and Military Show programme that Amelia Dyer brought back from London and gave to Granny Smith.

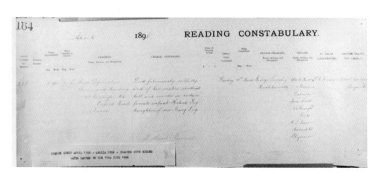

Police charge sheet issued against Amelia Dyer on the evening of 3 April 1896.

The officers leading the Amelia Dyer investigation posing with the carpet bag, white tape, string and bricks. Left to right: DC Anderson, Superintendent Tewsley, Sergeant James.

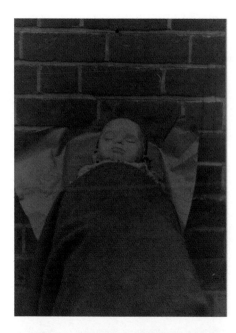

The bodies of Harry Simmons
(left) and Doris Marmon
(below), photographed
in the mortuary in April 1896.

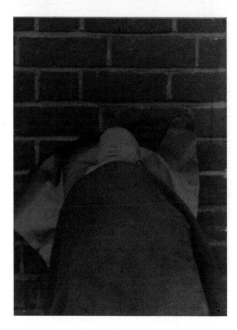

were in hiding. Furthermore, she had pleaded for a considerable sum of money from Arthur and then suffered apparent destitution, despite a staggering income. Dyer was clearly fleeing some greater menace, its identification now sadly beyond our reach.

᚛᚜

Jane Smith was a lonely soul, suffering the workhouse as her only option, the spark all but gone from her eyes. Fast approaching seventy, she had once had a home, a husband, a family. She had been born in Swansea and had moved to Bristol when she had married her husband, William, since which time she had never left the city. She took pride in her long service to a Bristol law firm as a cleaner. But now all that had gone: her three children buried many years since; her husband dead for over two years; her home lost with him.

Most of the old girls in with Jane passed their days in quiet introspection, and she had struggled to find solace in their company. There was one exception: a Bristol nurse, fallen on hard times; she had entered the house in the spring of 1895 and began to spend time with Jane. The nurse listened to her story, and confided in Jane her dearest wish: to live on the outside once more, making a quiet life tending to the unwanted babies cast aside by their unmarried mothers. Jane was encouraged to feel some small hope for her own future.

Jane Smith, *Weekly Dispatch*, 19 April 1896

# 31 Queenie Baker

Little Queenie, the Palmers' four-year-old adopted daughter, was taken to Gloucester Cottages, a smart street in a good part of the town of Devonport, near Plymouth, known as Morice Town, where the landlady, Mrs Barber, let them into one of the dwellings. The neighbourhood was dominated by the sea: the naval base at Devonport had been there for centuries and many households were headed by naval seamen, both active and retired.

But this was to be no home for Queenie, more a prison, for she was literally held captive. Day after day, she spent lonely hours locked in a small downstairs room, with little water and no food, while her new "parents" went out and left her alone. On 17 May, Queenie was told she was moving again. The man said that they were taking a trip, and that she was to come with him. Leaving the cottage, he had walked her through the streets of Devonport, finally reaching an area with which she was not familiar. He told her she was to stay put until he returned. And then he was gone.

It is not known how long the child wandered the streets. Eventually, a kind stranger took her to the police station. Queenie was frightened, tired and hungry, and after being given something to eat she told the police officer her name and age and everything she knew about the lady and gentleman named "Patson": about their grand clothes; the furnished house at Gloucester Cottages; and about the lady who had waved them off in Bristol and told her she was her grandma.

❦

Mrs Barber, the landlady of Gloucester Cottages, also told the police everything she knew about the haughty young couple who had rented the cottage for a week. She said they had made a grand looking pair:

he so natty, his sharp features framed by a sandy moustache, fancy
looking in his long grey frock-coated suit, his black leather boots
polished to a shine, and a dark corduroy cap perched on his head. She,
in a pale and delicate dress and a flattering round-rimmed hat, trimmed
with brown fur: tall, trim, well-educated and perfectly poised; quite
the lady. She had sensed they were moneyed from the clothes they
wore; so much so that at first she hadn't been at all surprised when
Mr Patson explained that he was, in fact, a Scotland Yard Detective, *en
route* to Manchester where he was to deliver the child for some furtive
purpose known only to the Yard. He had looked and acted the part,
and she had found no reason to doubt his story.

But as the days went by, Mrs Barber's concerns about the Patsons
grew; specifically her concerns for the welfare of the child in their care.
She told the police of the couple's strange habits, how they would
leave Queenie alone in the house for hours on end. She told them also
that since the couple had left, mail-order companies had been sending
demands for the payment or return of a vast amount of goods which
had been delivered to the Patsons several times a day, from all over
the country.

DEVONPORT (Borough)
For abandoning a girl, age about 4, on 17th inst. – A PARSONS alias
PATSON, age 30 to 35 height 5ft 8in, complexion fair, sharp features,
hair and moustache sandy; dress grey suit, cord cap, black shoes.
Stated he was a detective from London and was going to Manchester.
Accompanied by a woman aged 30 to 35, height 5ft 6 or 7; dress light
colour dress, round rim hat, trimmed brown fur; of good address.
They received parcels on approval from all parts of the country, but
failed to return either goods or money.
Warrant issued
Information to Head Constable Matters, Devonport.
*Police Gazette*, 31 May 1895

Arthur and Polly passed a quiet ten days in Bristol after leaving
Devonport and, by the time the warrant was issued on 27 May for the
arrest of the man suspected of abandoning Queenie Baker, they were
already boarding a train to Cardiff.

# 32  Granny Smith

Amelia had needed to work hard to persuade the Guardians to grant her permission to leave the workhouse to wave off her daughter on 24 April. Once out, she had used her time profitably, planning her re-entry into ordinary society with methodical detail. There were advertisements to place; there was accommodation to seek. She had also to ponder the difficult question of how she would manage the day-to-day running of a house of confinement without Polly. She would need assistance; but such help was expensive.

Dyer had sensed a naiveté about Jane Smith. The old woman had made honesty a byword and found good in everyone. Dyer won her over with the promise that they would live as sisters for the rest of their days, thus avoiding the loneliness of old age. Together they would nurse infants, caring for those otherwise unloved and unwanted. She would be comfortable: well fed, well cared for, and paid a shilling a week to help out. It was a picture-perfect vision and one which Jane Smith had not dared wish could ever be hers again.

❧

TO CLERGYMEN & OTHERS – Wanted, someone to wholly adopt Twin Boys, aged three, who are well provided for – Apply, giving full particulars, to 838, Daily Press Office.

*Western Daily Press*, 18 June 1895

Amelia had convinced the workhouse Guardians that she was ready and able to quit the institution and face life on the outside once more. She had an address lined up in Channings Hill in Fishponds, where she proposed to sustain a living as a midwife. The day in mid-June when she finally walked out of the workhouse she was handed back her clothes which were by now fusty, moth-eaten and crumpled. Back in February, they had been 'stoved' (baked in a stove in order to kill off any infestations), parcelled up and shelved in a store room, where they had remained for four months. Their pitiful condition marked her out as a former workhouse inmate.

Jane Smith also walked out of the Barton Regis Workhouse that day, having sought permission for a few days' urgent absence. It would be a long and traumatic year before she would return.

Operating under the pseudonym of Annie Smith, Dyer immediately began adopting infants and toddlers as if she had never left off. Jane Smith, fifteen years her senior, was kept busy tending the infants who passed through the house. Dyer soon nicknamed her "Granny Smith".

INQUEST IN BEDMINSTER – The City Coroner held an Inquest yesterday, at the Bedminster police-station on the body of a newly-born male child, which was found on the 18th inst. in Bridge-Valley road. P.C. W Harper, 57 C, state that whilst on duty on the 18th inst., in Bridge-Valley road, he saw a parcel in the bush at the side of the road. On examination it proved to be the body of a child, wrapped in a newspaper.

*Bristol Times & Mirror*, 21 June 1895

INFANT FOUND DEAD IN A POOL AT WESTBURY
– On Wednesday evening in a pool in a field near Westbury on Trym, by a labourer named Robert Anstey, who at once gave information to the police. The body was in a very decomposed state.

*Bristol Times & Mirror*, 28 June 1895

Dyer took in babies faster than she had done at almost any other period; Granny, struggling to reacclimatize herself to life on the outside, was overwhelmed. Dyer told Granny to refer to her as Mother ("surely as grim a use of the word as history affords" – *Daily Courier*, 28 April 1896). She would set off many times a day to collect a baby; and many times a day would also leave the house with an infant in her arms. Of those who left, none was seen by Granny again. They went out as fast as they arrived and she hadn't even the time to learn their names. It seemed there was a lot more to Dyer's method of nursing children than she had imagined.

WANTED to place a Child, 12 months old, in country for change of air, 305 Stapleton Road.

*Western Daily Press*, 1 July 1895

WANTED someone to take Entire Charge of a healthy baby – Apply by post stating terms, to EJ, Letter Exchange, Christmas Steps.

*Western Daily Press*, 5 July 1895

WOULD Lady like to Adopt young Baby Girl, dark? – Apply by letter, B, Times & Mirror Office.

*Bristol Times & Mirror*, 15 July 1895

Granny was anxious about the strange routine in her new home. She could only trust that Mother was doing the right thing by these poor children. For it was an uneasy time in the city: stories were appearing in the Bristol press about the fate of the unfortunate unwanted. Bodies of abandoned infants were being found all over the city. It moved Granny to tears, that there could be such cruelty so close to home.

THE MYSTERIOUS CASE AT KINGSDOWN – The City Coroner held an Inquest yesterday in the Bedminster Police Station, on the body that was found in Somerset Street. The body, which was that of a child ... Mrs Quick, residing at 46, Dove Street, said she observed the parcel against the side and on investigating it she found it to contain the body of a young child. Medical evidence having been given, the jury returned a verdict that the body was found on a step in Dove Street, but whether the child was stillborn or not, owing to the decomposition of the body, it was not possible to say.

*Bristol Times & Mirror*, 10 July 1895

WANTED HOME with Respectable Person, no children, for child 2 years; country preferred; *HOME* Times & Mirror Office.

*Bristol Times & Mirror*, 1 July 1895

One day in early July, Mother brought a two-year-old boy to the house and named him Bertie Palmer. By now, however, three weeks of the constant traffic of infants had raised the suspicions of the neighbours, and soon after Bertie's arrival Granny opened the door one morning to a young man in his late twenties. He greeted her in a lilting Scottish accent and introduced himself as John Ottley, Inspector for the Bristol branch of the National Society for the Prevention of Cruelty to Children.

Jane Smith listened uneasily to Mr Ottley's explanation of what was permissible by law under the terms of the Infant Life Protection Act. Mr Ottley was satisfied at least that the old woman was genuine in her affection for the children in her care, but made an arrangement to return to visit Dyer a few days later.

Dyer's immediate response to Granny's account of Ottley's visit was startling: they were moving, and soon. She would secure new lodgings for them first thing in the morning, and Granny was to pack what few possessions they had. Two days later they left for Eastville, taking only Bertie with them.

# 33 One Step Ahead of the Law

At twenty-six, John Ottley's youth belied his experience. Throughout May and June of 1895 alone, he had given testimony at Police Courts and Coroners' Inquests on an almost weekly basis, and had been witness to such maltreatment, exploitation and abuse of children that he was able to recognize instantly the hallmarks of the baby farmer. He would have been familiar, too, with the young, single women who declared themselves too scared, too poor, or else too reluctant to raise their infants. The women who gave up their babies, abandoning them either to the streets or to the whim of individuals like "Annie Smith". The best of them were gullible and helpless; the worst guilty of murder. Many in between consoled themselves that their actions were laudable: they were angel makers.

So when Ottley returned after a few days to discover that the house at Channings Hill had been vacated, it confirmed his suspicions about the standard of care being offered by "Annie Smith". He alerted the Bristol police and began to make quiet enquiries as to Smith's whereabouts.

Inspector Robertson of the Bristol police had frequently worked alongside John Ottley. Robertson was also in possession of quite a sizeable file on a Bristol baby farmer named Amelia Dyer, one which stretched back sixteen years and took in many of her aliases. "Smith" had been favoured by Dyer back in 1879, in the "Totterdown Baby Farmer" case. Since then, the plight of the governess whose infant Dyer had adopted had been carefully tracked, until December 1894, when Dyer had once more slipped through the net. This latest alert by Ottley bore all the signs of a Dyer operation; the neighbours' descriptions of a tall, heavy woman in her fifties only added to Robertson's conviction that "Amelia Dyer" and "Annie Smith" were one and the same.

Robertson questioned the neighbours in Channings Hill, and learned that they had seen as many as six infants a day coming into the house over a three-week period, prompting them to raise the alarm with the NSPCC. Inside the house, Robertson found more than thirty telegrams relating to the adoption of unwanted infants from women all over the country, as well as numerous letters. Despite sustained efforts, however, none of the babies referred to in the correspondence could be traced.

Robertson, like Ottley, was a Scotsman; an Orcadian in his mid-forties and a father of four. He harboured grave concerns for the welfare of the two-year-old child reported by the neighbours to be in the care of this woman, said to be headed for Eastville. He concentrated his force's efforts upon tracing "Annie Smith".

❧

INQUESTS IN BRISTOL

MONDAY – Before the City Coroner

DISCOVERY OF AN ERRAND BOY – At the Hope and Anchor, Jacob's Wells, on the discovery of a newly-born child. George Glue, of 2, Chapel Hill, stated that he was going on an errand for his employer when he saw a parcel lying in Codrington Place. He opened it and found it contained the body of a child. PC Parkhouse ... said that on receiving a communication from the previous witness, he went to the spot named and found a child's body, which he conveyed to the police station.

*Western Daily Press*, 30 July 1895

The Smiths' Eastville neighbours turned out to be just as inquisitive as those in Channings Hill; one in particular took great interest in the two elderly Mrs Smiths and the little child in their care, Bertie. Mother wasn't at all happy with the attention the woman next door lavished on the child whenever she saw him. In a matter of days, she announced to Granny she was not to make herself comfortable in Eastville: they would be moving once more, this time to join her daughter Polly in Cardiff. She instructed her to begin to make her preparations to leave, and went out, taking Bertie with her.

Dyer returned to the house in Eastville some hours later, and the same neighbour reported that upon seeing the woman return she had been curious, peering inquisitively at the nine-month-old infant Annie

Smith was suddenly cradling, and enquiring as to Bertie's whereabouts. She knew the midwife was not one for idle chatter, but even so had been taken aback at the curt rebuttal: "That's my business", she had been told, Annie Smith conceding only that the baby was her daughter's child, and that they were on their way to Cardiff to visit her in the morning.

The following day, 13 July 1895, with Granny and Mother already on board a train to Cardiff, two-year-old Bertie Palmer was found abandoned, wandering alone on Durdham Downs in Bristol.

※

Mr Ottley of the NSPCC arrived a day too late to catch the woman Annie Smith in Eastville. A neighbour told him everything she knew: that the woman "Smith" left the house with young Bertie, but had returned without him, carrying instead an infant in her arms, who she had claimed to be her nine-month-old grandchild. She had said that she was on her way to Cardiff to return it to her daughter there.

Robertson issued a warrant for the arrest of the woman going by the name of "Annie Smith", for abandoning Bertie Palmer on Durdham Downs. Meanwhile, Ottely worked hard to establish the true parentage of the nine-month-child Smith had claimed to be her own grandchild, and traced it to a young girl from Clarence Road in St Philip's who had given it over to Smith for adoption, along with a £10 premium. Little Bertie Palmer was sent to the workhouse at Barton Regis.

Several years later, during renovation work, the skeletons of four infants were uncovered in the garden of a house in Fishponds formerly occupied by Amelia Dyer.

# 34 A Family Business

MARRIED Couple, in good position, wish to ADOPT CHILD; good home; small premium. – Mrs Cory, Post Office, Cardiff.
*Bristol Times & Mirror*, 15 June 1895

Polly and Arthur had enjoyed six undisturbed weeks alone in Cardiff. They had money in their pockets from a series of lucrative adoptions, although they had arrived unburdened by any of the children for whom they were ostensibly responsible. Arthur had even secured himself a job working as a commissions agent for a London grain merchant, as he had done previously.

Polly had boosted their income, too: she had adopted a five-year-old girl from Bristol for a handsome premium, and an infant, also for a premium. She was bringing up the baby the only way she knew: with an inadequate diet to keep costs down; a laudanum-based "quietener", for effortless childcare. By the time Polly and Arthur met Mother and her new companion on the platform of Cardiff Station in the middle of July, the infant in Polly's arms was already beginning to fail.

Granny was soon busy tending to two newly adopted infants of Mother's. Living in close quarters with the Palmers, and seeing the condition of Polly's infant, could only have added to the old woman's growing unease. During her brief, five-week stay in Cardiff, she watched the infant deteriorate: it rarely uttered a cry, ate little, and then only reluctantly, and slept for hours. And looking at its fragile limbs, Granny can have been in no doubt that the child's death was imminent. However, without the long experience of infant neglect that both Polly and her mother could boast, Granny may not have instantly attributed the infant's demise to any culpable action of Polly's.

The Palmers called in a local physician, Dr Parr, to certify the baby's death. Granny may have given the Palmers the benefit of the doubt, but the doctor was not so accommodating. The child had clearly wasted away; a lack of adequate nutrition was indisputable, though whether through neglect or disease was less easy to ascertain. The woman Palmer said the child was hers; that she had given birth to it in the house. Her mother was a midwife by profession, she said. They had moved to the city, and her mother was advertising her services for the accouchement locally in the press. They had done all they could but the infant had simply failed to thrive.

Dr Parr accepted that the child had been recently born to Mrs Palmer. He accepted, too, that the child had perished as a result of diarrhoea and convulsions, but added a codicil to the death certificate that he suspected a lack of attention at birth had contributed to its demise.

The nine-month-old child adopted by Mother in Bristol did not remain long in Cardiff. Mother got up early one morning and left the house with him, telling Granny that she had received word from the child's aunt in London, and was travelling by train into the metropolis that day to meet her and return the boy. Granny had therefore been surprised when Mother had returned to the house just three or four hours later. It seemed impossible that she could have travelled to London, handed over the boy and returned to Cardiff, all in such a short time. Nothing further was heard of the child.

The two other infants Mother had brought into the house at Cardiff went out again so quietly that Granny was barely aware of the moment of their departure.

Inspector Robertson of the Bristol Constabulary continued to hunt the woman responsible for abandoning Bertie Palmer on Durdham Downs. He followed her trail to Cardiff where he had no doubt she would still be adopting babies. The Metropolitan Police had long been accustomed to tracking down those who made a living from the sale and neglect of infants by following up small ads. Robertson probably followed their example.

Dyer was an astute woman with long experience of outwitting the law. Whether alerted by a suspicious response to her advertisements, or tipped off about the "quiet enquiries" of the local police, one thing was clear: she knew her time in Cardiff had come to an abrupt end. Taking with her the child Polly had adopted from Bristol, she left the house and boarded a train to London. Nothing more was seen of the six-year-old girl.

⛥

The Palmers did not remain long in Cardiff after Mother left. Early in August 1895, they adopted another infant and bided their time before making their next move.

# 35 A Healthy Place in the Country

In 1895 the village of Caversham was decidedly rural. Lying on the northern reaches of the Thames it presented a timeless scene of bucolic dwelling. The river meandered past meadows and orchards, floodplain pastures and the gentle chalk hills and sloping fringes of the lower Chilterns. The lives of the villagers of Caversham centred on the river; boat-builders, bargemen, local farmers and their families all depended upon its waters or the surrounding fertile meadows for their livelihoods. Even the village laundress was obliged to lug buckets of water from the river to fill her copper kettles.

Not so strange, then, that the woman who appeared in this quaint and sleepy village in the middle of August 1895 should also come to rely upon the river, but for a far more sinister purpose.

Amelia Dyer arrived alone, alighting from a train at Reading Station. As the billowing steam cleared from the platform, she found herself in a grandiose building, the mellow creaminess of the old Bath stone and the imposing clock tower creating an elegant gateway into Reading. Whether by accident or design, she made her way to the Clappers Temperance Hotel, a small establishment run by a Mrs Clark and only a short walk from the station terminus in Vastern Road, well within sight of the rickety old Clappers footbridge which led over the Thames and the weir to Caversham. Viewed in the light of a glorious summer's day, the river could not have appeared more enticing. A Temperance hotel was an odd choice of lodging for a woman who, by all accounts, "drank brandy to excess", but it may have been that Mrs Clark offered a sympathetic welcome to a lone female traveller and the Christian values of the Temperance Movement would have presented Amelia with a cloak of respectability behind which to hide.

Three days later she was back on the platform at Reading Station to meet the train from Cardiff carrying Granny Smith, the

Palmers and a three-month-old infant who was being "nursed" by Polly. Together once more, the family spent a night at the Clappers Hotel before taking their leave of Mrs Clark and moving to a small terraced house in Caversham, number six in a block of newly built houses situated along the Thames front named Elm Villas. The family was hard to ignore, being "a curious kind of neighbour and of that character likely to cause talk". Beyond a few boxes and portmanteaux, no furniture was moved into the house and the family was forced to sleep on the floor. They had undoubtedly left Cardiff in a hurry (Arthur Palmer later paid 7s.6d. for a mattress, before purchasing other items of furniture). They were a mystery to their neighbours, the indolent Palmer preferring to spend his days digging the garden and planting shrubs, rather than taking up any kind of paid occupation. Sometimes he claimed to be a ship's steward on leave; at others that he was in the process of buying a public house in Basingstoke. On the whole, though, they were regarded as fairly respectable, being pleasant and courteous; it was noted, however, that "Mrs Thomas", as Amelia Dyer referred to herself, dressed most grandly at times, as when she was on her way to the station, but at others was seen to be very "shabby and neglectful of appearance".

꜒꜖

The "Miscellaneous Wants" columns of the *Western Daily Press* were particularly full that August with advertisements seeking anything from horsehair couches, wicker bath chairs and chicken coops to foreign stamps, smith's bellows and good homes for beloved pets. Among the advertisements for these everyday items could also be found a number of apparently incongruous and simply worded advertisements dealing in the business of baby adoption.

Amelia Dyer was an avid reader of these columns, and would have noted the adoption advertisements and read them with interest. She would have paid no heed to the fact that such advertisements sat so comfortably together, as much – or as little – importance being attached to a child's life as to the needs of the furniture dealer wishing to purchase "good sideboards".

Even with so many children on offer that month, she nonetheless placed her own advertisement in the *Western Daily Press* and sat back to wait for a response.

Highly respectable married couple wish to **ADOPT** child; good home. Premium required £10. c/o Bates, Handy & Co; Valpy St. Reading.

*Western Daily Press*, 20 August 1895

It wasn't long before various children began to be seen and heard in the Dyer/Palmer household. One set of neighbours, Mr and Mrs Manning, often heard children's voices and the sound of babies fretting. Willie Thornton, a bright young lad of nine, was the first to be brought to Elm Villas. He was later to recount in court that he could not remember his "Papa" but had been living in London with a Mrs Henwood before going to boarding school. He had been taken away from there by his "Godma", who, he said, was his "real Mamma", to an address in London where a Mrs Dalton lived. From there he was handed over to Mother. Willie arrived in Caversham with only a battered old carpet bag containing a few items of clothing, the sole reminder of his former life. Willie was the inconvenient child of a socially unacceptable tryst, and was now paying for his parents' mistake by being shunted from one home to another, so that his existence should not bring shame upon the reputation of his natural family. Despite an unsettled and difficult life, Willie became a great favourite with the neighbours in Elm Villas, on account of his intelligence, polite manner and sunny disposition. Mother undoubtedly received a healthy weekly sum for the boy which boosted the family coffers.

Willie Thornton, *Weekly Dispatch*, 19 April 1896

Willie was soon joined by a little girl, about four or five months old. She was brought back from London by Mother and the Palmers. Mother always told Granny she went to London for the children. She had left early one morning to catch the nine o'clock train, and the Palmers had gone out shortly afterward. Later that night, Mother arrived home carrying a child in her arms; Polly bore a parcel. The baby was healthy with beautiful curly hair and the parcel contained the very best clothes, little plaid dresses and a prettily embroidered white frock with a cape and a matching hat. There was a red gown and a piece of black mackintosh which was later used to line the child's cradle. Mother took the clothes and locked them in a box in her bedroom. The baby's surname was Isaacs. Granny grew particularly fond of "dear little Ikey", as she named her.

※

Granny Smith was a simple, faithful soul who, since leaving the workhouse, had experienced a very different kind of life from the one of care and comfort that Mother had promised: in reality she was treated as little more than a servant; she cleaned the house, minded the children and fed them on whatever meagre rations she was provided with.

There was a distinction between the children Mother fetched and those Polly brought in; Granny was only ever told to look after Mother's. Granny didn't care too much for cats, but Mother did, gathering the neighbourhood strays to her hefty bosom and allowing the tamer ones to sleep in her bedroom. She loved her cats and bought them cat meat, while the rest of the family had to make do with bread and dripping all week. Mother would sometimes, on a Sunday, buy six pennyworth of pigs' liver which Granny would chop up into small pieces and stew for dinner. Mother never ate this; she would always buy herself something nice.

Granny would sit and watch – observing the daily comings and goings of Mother and the Palmers. Watching how Mother would don a decent dress with clean collar and a pair of good boots, pinning her ribboned poke bonnet firmly on her head and fastening her long, blue nurse's cloak at the throat with a black bow. Observing how Mother and the Palmers made almost daily excursions to the town, down toward the river, over the Clappers footbridge and on into Reading, the vaporous air by the weir dampening their clothing and smelling faintly of sewage, the roar of the water muffling the sound of their footsteps. It could be a desolate place, and Arthur in particular was afraid of crossing the bridge after dark. It was narrow and the handrails precarious and, with only the lock-keeper's gaslight glowing in the distance, it could be a hair-raising experience. Mother had no such fears and would laugh at his cowardice as she strode on confidently, her long, dark cloak flying behind her. They often left early in the morning and returned home at unusual hours; sometimes they brought back with them yet another new baby and were too exhausted by the length of their journey to take their supper.

-ᚢᚦ-

## A CHILD STRANGLED AND THROWN
## INTO THE CANAL

On Saturday afternoon a lad named Frederick Worrall, who had been playing football, went to the canal near the Ashton Old Road to wash the dirt off his boots. He was passing under the bridge when he noticed a child's leg sticking out of the water. He got the assistance of some companions and they together drew the body of the child on to the towing path. The police were at once informed and the corpse was taken by Police Constable Pointon to the Fairfield Street Mortuary. There Dr. Heslop divisional police surgeon made a post mortem examination of the body which was that of a child apparently 5 months old. It had on a white linen skip, white linen shirt and white flannel binder. There was a cord tied tightly around the neck, and fastened to the waist by a piece of string was a granite set weighing six or seven pounds. The body, which was that of a well developed female child, had in the opinion of the doctor been in the water from 1–4 days. The tongue was protruding and the cause of death was strangulation. A coroner's inquiry was opened yesterday morning at the City Coroners Court and adjourned until Wednesday 15th. It was stated that about a week ago two strange women were seen to throw something in the canal near where the body was found, but the police have no substantial clue to the perpetrators of what at present seems a very cold-blooded murder.

*Manchester Guardian*, 1896

-ᚢᚦ-

Granny continued to watch: the newspaper advertisements that were scoured daily, the mounds of letters that were written and wrapped up in pieces of brown paper so that no one in the house would see the address. Mother was adept at writing letters, filling pages with a curling script and a cunning imagination; glowing descriptions of her tender regard for "the dear little ones" in her charge. She painted a pleasant picture of a comfortable and homely situation, "most healthy, with a little orchard just outside the front door". Willie usually took the letters out to post; he was cautioned to put each package into the box separately and to listen out for the sound of it dropping to be certain that each was posted safely. Piles of letters were delivered back to the house and stored in a tin on the mantelpiece.

> Farmer wife having no children, would adopt one; premium small.
> Farmer c/o Mrs Thomas, 6, Elm Villas, Lower Caversham, Reading.
> *Bristol Times & Mirror*, 21 August 1895

Granny could only sit back and watch as the mound of unworn baby clothes grew larger; the napkins and bonnets, the frocks and cloaks, all parcelled up and taken to pawn, the tickets stuffed in a jar in the kitchen. But worst of all she had to watch the unkindness. Had to sit back and watch Mother strike dear little Ikey a blow to the head for fretting at the pain of cutting teeth.

# 36 Like Mother Like Daughter

On 9 September 1895, Polly travelled alone to Gloucester to meet a Miss Elizabeth Goulding and her aunt, Mrs Elizabeth Carter. The meeting was to take place in a solicitor's office. Polly had for some time been exchanging correspondence in response to an advertisement she had come across in the *Bristol Times & Mirror*.

> **Wanted** a respectable woman who has no children, to take charge of a baby; Apply stating terms to Bristol Times & Mirror Office.
>
> *Bristol Times & Mirror*, 21 August 1895

Elizabeth Goulding was an unmarried domestic servant from Gloucester who had fallen for the charms of a hotel landlord and had given birth to his illegitimate child. Chas Aldridge was a married man, and as such he could not accept the child as his own, or indeed do the honourable thing and marry the mother of his bastard child. The simplest solution was to adopt the child out. For a one-off payment, Chas could absolve himself from all future involvement and in the process save his marriage and his respectability. When a Mrs Palmer answered his advertisement, all seemed set for a swift resolution.

Elizabeth Goulding enlisted the help of her aunt, Mrs Carter. Elizabeth was an orphan, and, in light of her disgrace, Mrs Carter and her husband Cornelius had allowed her to make their house her home. At a pre-arranged time they travelled into Gloucester to the offices of Mr Treasure, taking with them baby Frances Jessie Goulding. Mr Treasure had drawn up an agreement stating that Mary Ann Palmer would agree to take the child from Elizabeth Goulding for the sum of £10 and bring it up as her own. Mrs Palmer had stated that she had no children of her own and that her husband was a well-to-do poultry farmer and pig breeder. Mr Treasure read out the agreement, both parties signed it and the money was paid. Mrs Carter suggested that Elizabeth should accompany Mrs Palmer back to Reading and stay a day or two until the baby had grown used to its new surroundings. It seemed a sensible and thoughtful suggestion, but Mrs Palmer would not oblige, making the excuse that for the time being she and her husband "were in lodgings".

At the railway station Miss Goulding held her child for one last time while Mrs Palmer purchased a ticket. She had given Mrs Palmer a box of clothes, all lovingly washed and mended. Inside the box were three pinafores, two shirts, two bibs, a napkin, a nightdress, two pairs of socks, a brush and a child's red wool hat. The box of clothes made it back to Elm Villas, but Frances Jessie Goulding never did.

For some months following the adoption, Polly kept up a correspondence between herself and Miss Goulding. The pining mother made regular enquiries as to the wellbeing of her child. Polly wrote back in enthusiastic and affectionate terms,

> I am delighted to tell you that dear baby was as good as gold all the way coming home. I gave her a nice warm bath, fed her and put her to bed at half past eight and we never heard a sound of her until half past four this morning. Then I gave her a little milk and she went to sleep again until eight o'clock. She is so good, she don't seem to mind one bit. Mr Palmer is delighted with her; I know she will be a regular spoilt child. She has taken to us wonderfully.

Another letter dated 20 September read:

> Just a few lines to let you know we received the little slippers alright this morning, and they fit baby nicely. Many thanks for them. Now I must tell you baby is getting on lovely. She is not a bit of trouble now, and she has got so fond of us both – we would not part with her now for the world. She is such a dear little thing. She has another tooth all but through.

Just before Christmas Miss Goulding received what would be her final letter from Caversham,

> We have got a nice pelisse for her, and she does like to go out in it. She will soon be able to walk. She will stand up by herself and then she will go down, and when she do she will say "Oh dee". She can't say "Oh dear."

Miss Goulding was told that the Palmers had bought a lovely carriage for baby and were going to Weston-super-Mare for Christmas, then to Wallingford to the wedding of Mr Palmer's cousin taking *"our own dear baby with us"*. The letter ended by wishing Miss Goulding and her aunt Mrs Carter a Merry Christmas and at the end was a row of crosses to represent kisses from *"baby to all"*.

Elizabeth Goulding continued writing her letters to the Palmers, desperate for any news of her daughter; they were all returned marked *"Gone away"*.

---

**A Lady**, married, wishes to adopt a child – girl preferred. Premium required. Full particulars write Times & Mirror Bristol.
*Bristol Times & Mirror*, 13 September 1895

Toward the end of the family's stay in Elm Villas the Palmers went out on their own for the day, and brought back with them a tiny female infant no more than two months old. The child had come from Swindon, and they had received it from its mother on the platform of Reading Station along with the usual £10.

The family, now larger than ever, changed its quarters to a house just around the corner in Piggotts Road. This street of tiny, slate-roofed, terraced cottages began at one end with a hardware shop spilling its wares – brushes, brooms, rolls of string – over the narrow pavement, and ended with a screen of trees whose lower branches dipped into the river which ran along the bottom. Number 26 was the size of a doll's house, the tiny frontage struggling to accommodate two windows and a narrow front door. With four adults and at least four children crammed into the house, it was no wonder that the baby's bassinet was often left out in the rain, or that Arthur Palmer spent his days sitting on a bench at the county cricket ground. His excursions were noted by the lock-keeper who nodded to him almost daily as he crossed the river, newspaper in hand, his trademark slouch hat perched on his head.

The cottage looked out on to unspoilt meadow land and small orchards. The rising hulk of the newly built mill, severe and utilitarian, sat solidly in this landscape and beckoned many of the occupants of Piggotts Road through its gates in the mornings. The centre of Caversham was just a short walk away with its bustling roads full of florists, butchers, fishmongers, drapers, corn, hay and straw merchants, and the occasional sheep wandering freely between the milk carts and the cyclists. It was a close-knit, hardworking community; a difficult place for anyone to keep themselves to themselves. Nevertheless it was as pleasant a situation as any family could hope to live in: wide-open, healthy spaces, pleasing scenery and fresh, clean air.

⸎

On 20 October 1895, a Dr Deane paid a visit to 26 Piggotts Road. The young baby from Swindon, whom the Palmers had fetched only a few weeks before, had died in the house. Only Polly had been present at the death, but in the cramped conditions of Piggotts Road, every occupant was witness to the cold, stiff body which lay in the bassinet in the kitchen. Even young Willie was not spared the scene, stating matter-of-factly, "I saw it dead."

The Palmers passed the child off as their own, naming her after Arthur's mother Clara. Their names appear on the death certificate as parents of the deceased, Emma Clara Palmer, and the cause of death is recorded, as so often in the past, as marasmus – "wasting away". Prior to her death little Emma Clara would have weighed less than 80 per cent of what was considered normal for her age. Her skin would have fallen in folds over wasted and withered muscles; she would have been fretful, irritable and voraciously hungry.

Dr Deane was forced to state that death was due to natural causes; being unable to prove that the child had been denied nourishment. The undertaker at the cemetery in Upper Caversham received hurried instructions from the Palmers for the burial, but as no one attended the funeral, not even the Palmers themselves, the customary service at the graveside was dispensed with.

> Highly respectable Married couple, having no family, wish to **ADOPT** child to bring up entirely as their own. Good country home. Premium required £10.
>
> *Western Daily Press*, 1 November 1895

It was not long before Polly replaced this child with another. She arrived back in Caversham late one evening with a small boy called Harold. He was almost a year old and she had received him along with £12.

It had been almost three months since little Ikey had been brought back to Caversham. Granny Smith had grown inordinately fond of the child and was often to be found sitting in a chair outside the front door with Ikey nestled in her ample lap. So when Mother announced one morning that she was taking the child back to London, Granny was distraught and ran sobbing down the road to kiss the baby one last time before Mother disappeared around the corner and down toward the river. Ikey was taken away from the house in her white frock with matching cape and hat. Her other clothes and napkins remained locked in a box in Mother's bedroom. Mother arrived home after dark that night and told Granny that she had met Ikey's mother on the platform at Paddington, along with another lady who was going to adopt the baby. Ikey had been quite well, she said, and had not been at all bothered by her cutting teeth. Granny never forgave Mother for taking away her dear little Ikey. The children were always taken away, even the baby that Polly had brought from Cardiff, but their bundles of clothes remained behind. Granny was always told that Mother was taking the children back to London; all she knew was that none of them ever came back.

At least seven children had passed through the hands of the Palmers and Mother during their stay in Caversham; only nine-year-old Willie and baby Harold were left when, shortly after Christmas 1895, they chose to move on. Perhaps the neighbours were asking too many awkward questions; perhaps anxious parents were bombarding Mother with letters, threatening to come and see how their little ones were thriving in the country air: perhaps there was a family quarrel. Or maybe it was simply a calculated business decision, and, by moving the short distance over the river to Reading, Mother was crossing the borough boundaries and moving from the jurisdiction of the county of Oxfordshire to the county of Berkshire where she was entirely unknown.

Whatever the reason, the family split at this point: the Palmers went to London with Harold; Mother, Granny and young Willie moved to Reading. It wasn't long, however, before Mother revisited the banks of the Thames and crossed the slippery planks of the Clappers foot-bridge to dispose of some ghastly packages under cover of darkness.

# 37 A Case at Willesden

In the middle of January 1896, Mrs Charlotte Culham, a chirpy, showily dressed Cockney, and her husband, Albert Charles Culham, a carriage cleaner on the Metropolitan Railway (and a keen rabbit breeder), were pleased to rent out rooms in their modest house to a young couple and their sickly looking baby son, Harold. The two furnished rooms either side of the front door were engaged for a weekly sum of seven shillings. Polly and Arthur Palmer paid a month in advance. They seemed to be a pleasant and respectable couple; Polly made an effort to make the most of her slightly common features, and Arthur took far more of an interest in his appearance than was usual for a man. He seemed fond of silk hats and frock coats and kept his sandy hair foppishly long and his moustache neatly trimmed. He had not the strongest features: he was weasel-like, with very pale eyelashes and prominent ears. Although he was without employment when they first took the rooms, he soon found a position as a salesman for the Singer Sewing Machine Company. Number 76 Mayo Road, Willesden, was a comfortable place to lodge. The young couple had their own bedroom and a sitting room with an armchair, a dining table, a small fireplace and an overstuffed couch that was worn to a shine.

---

While the Palmers made themselves comfortable in Willesden, Mother, Granny and Willie Thornton moved into 45 Kensington Road, Reading. The rows of regimented red-brick houses would have looked mournful in the January half-light; the gas lamp at the corner of the street reflecting weakly on to the wet pavements and the damp air hanging around the roof tops and seeping between layers of clothing. Granny and Mother would have pulled their shawls tight around their shoulders as they lit a fire in the cold grate of the parlour to try and chase the chill away. The house was silent without the sound of babies stirring in their sleep.

With the amount of money that had come into her possession over the last few months it is somewhat surprising that it was necessary for Mother to rent out the downstairs parlour to a woman called Mrs Chandler and her two little girls. It seemed not to concern her that another pair of eyes would now be witness to the steady traffic of children passing through the front door; perhaps the two little girls in Mrs Chandler's care were helping to pay her rent; and, after all, two people in the same line of business would most certainly turn a blind eye to one another's dealings.

With the Palmers far away in London, Mother took full advantage of the phenomenally efficient postal service of the time. At the end of the nineteenth century a half-ounce letter cost just one penny to be sent anywhere in the country and deliveries were made between six and twelve times a day. With such a fast service, Mother was able to keep communications with the Palmers wide open, and it wasn't long before she arranged her first visit to Willesden.

Mother arrived at Paddington Station and took an omnibus the length of the Edgware Road, alighting at the corner of Mayo Road. It was a convenient ride away; the omnibuses from Paddington ran regularly, with two horses being changed for a fresh pair at intervals throughout the day. The driver, perched up high, would have been well wrapped up in oilskins to protect him from the chill of the January fog. Although sitting on the open-top deck would have proved a more pleasant ride despite the cold, decorum would have forced Mother to accommodate herself in the crowded and sweaty atmosphere of the enclosed lower deck. It was considered improper for a woman to travel on the exposed upper decks, and even the stairs leading to the lower deck had vanity boards which hid the ankles of ascending female passengers. There were seats for twelve, but space was limited and any luggage had to be held on the lap or placed by the feet in the layer of dirty straw which was strewn on the wooden floors. It would not have been the most comfortable of rides, with the smell of wet woollen clothing mingling with the scent of damp straw; the men in the carriage trying their best to avoid being brushed with mud from the caked hems of the women's skirts.

Mother's object in coming to London was to fetch a child from Shepherd's Bush to nurse. The child was to be collected from Coningham Road, and as Arthur was familiar with the area (he had a customer who resided in that same road) he accompanied her and waited outside while Mother went in to conduct her business. The young lady (a Miss Brown), who was staying in the house at the time, was under the impression that the stout, middle-aged woman who had come to collect her illegitimate child was the wife of a well-to-do farmer living in a village just outside Reading. She had placed an advertisement in the *Weekly Dispatch* and had received a reply from a 'Mrs Stansfield'.

45 Kensington Road
Oxford Road, Reading
Berks.
Sunday Jany 12. 96

Dear Madam, Seeing an advertisement in the London W. Dispatch, Lady Wanted to take a New Born Baby, I beg to say we are well to do Farmers we have no child. I should be delighted to take your Little one. We have a nice home and every comfort but no Child. A Child with me would be well brought up under Church of England influence and would have a mother and a fathers love, and I must tell you my Husband as well as myself are dearly fond of children. I should never take a child for the sake of money. I do really want a nice baby. I don't mind Boy or Girl, I could love either. I don't mind how small a sum you will pay if you will kindly reply and tell me all particulars I feel we may come to an arrangement. And if at any future time you would like to come and see me I would make you welcome to stay for a few days, for it is lovely in the Country in the Summer time. Now my dear Madam will you kindly send a line by return and tell me all particulars and oblige

Yours Respectfully
A. Stansfield

Mrs Stansfield appeared to be somewhat older than Miss Brown had been expecting; but no matter – the woman had fervently expressed her and her husband's desire to adopt a dear little baby – for a premium of £10. When "Mrs Stansfield" was shown to the front door she introduced the young man standing on the doorstep as her nephew. Arthur stepped up and took the baby's feeding bottle out of her hand and put it in his pocket, then both he and Mother walked away down the road, another child gripped tightly in her arms and a £10 note tucked firmly in her pocket.

## A CASE AT WILLESDEN

A signalman residing at Railway Cottages, Willesden, discovered a parcel tied with string and tape about 3 ft. from his doorway. Upon being opened it was found to contain the dead body of a male child. He called a constable who conveyed it to the public mortuary, where it was examined by Dr. J.B. Gibson, who found that the nose was squeezed in and displaced and the mouth bruised, death being due to intentional suffocation by direct pressure. A verdict of "Wilful Murder" was returned by the jury. It has been ascertained that the place where the parcel was found was not a public road, and the parcel could not have been thrown there from the railway.

*Weekly Dispatch*, 4 February 1896

# 38  Granny's Misgivings

Mother chose never to live anywhere that was too far from a railway station. From her earliest years in Totterdown, she had only to walk a short distance to catch the unmistakable scent of grime, acetylene and burning, sulphurous oil from the clouds of steam, soot and ash pouring from the locomotives. The distinctive chocolate and cream livery of the GWR carriages with their comfortable interiors of upholstered seats and oil lamps to read by provided Mother with a cheap ride. She was easily able to expand her business network into the towns along the main line. Advertisements were soon appearing in the Bristol, Gloucester and London papers. On any given day a quick perusal under the "Miscellaneous Wants" column of the *Bristol Times & Mirror* would reveal a whole selection of innocently worded advertisements, "sticky honey traps" to lure in the desperate.

> Wanted, comfortable **HOME** for Child 6 months old; state terms and if other nurse children.

> Married Lady wishes to Adopt Lady's Child as own; superior home; premium required.

> Wanted, A **BABY** to nurse; any age.

> Wanted, a child to **NURSE**; will be well looked after.

The babies began to arrive; most were brought to the house after dark. Granny, coming downstairs in the morning to light the fire, would often find a new child lying in the cradle in the kitchen. She would just as often wake in the morning to find that the baby she had kissed goodnight the evening before was no longer in the house. The mother had come to collect it, she was told. But the strange thing was that they never took the clothes; they were left in little bundles which Mother would pawn.

Granny was growing increasingly uneasy. She didn't like the way Mother was to the children; she was rough at times and had no patience when the babies cried. She would often shake the poor little things in a most shocking manner. She'd told Mother what she thought, but it had just turned into an argument. She didn't like it when Mother got into one of her rages; you never knew what she would do.

Granny left the house late one afternoon. Mother had been busy sewing one of her quilts so hadn't noticed her sneak out of the front door. She walked up to Oxford Road and turned right toward town. The Reading Union Workhouse was just over the road and she joined the straggle of grey vagrants queuing alongside the railings, waiting for the porter to admit them through the gates. She hadn't minded the rough bath they'd given her, or the scratchy workhouse uniform she was made to wear when her own clothes were taken away to be washed, disinfected and put into storage. She slept that night in the receiving ward, the thin urine-stained mattress and the iron bedstead combining to make her old bones ache. It was better than worrying about Willie and the babies. But all the same she wondered all night how they were getting along without her.

Mother had been waiting there for her in the morning; she told the workhouse master there was no need for Granny to be admitted as she had a perfectly comfortable home already. She had promised Granny she would be kinder, had promised to look after her better. And so Granny collected her things and they both walked back to Kensington Road.

It wasn't long, though, before Granny's growing concerns over the children led her once more to sneak out of the door of Kensington Road. This time she walked passed the workhouse and its yawning gateway and continued on toward the bustle of Broad Street. She walked through the marketplace with its stalls piled high with potatoes and pot plants, the traders in waistcoats with shirt sleeves rolled up. Through the tangle of cycles and women pushing perambulators, past the India rubber merchants, the tailor's shop and the cabmen's shelter and over High Bridge crossing the River Kennet and on into London Street. She walked past the police station at 1 London Street, on past furniture dealers, watchmakers, pawnbrokers and wheelwrights; the road was wide with plenty of room for the horse-drawn trams to pass by either side of the row of gas lights running down the centre of the carriageway. She turned left into the grand expanse of the London Road and stopped outside number 11, an unpretentious dwelling that had once been a shop, but now, in place of fancy hats or leather-bound books displayed in its windows, there were photographs.

Granny stood and stared mournfully into the window at the terrible images of children and babies: naked, abused and near to death. She didn't notice the tears streaming down her own cheeks until the door of the former shop opened and a concerned looking lady ushered her inside for a calming cup of tea. Granny walked back home that day feeling lighter in her heart. She knew it wouldn't be long before the kind lady's husband called at Kensington Road. He was an NSPCC officer and she hoped he would put the frighteners on Mother.

❖

Wanted, in comfortable home, **CHILD** (girl preferred; aged six to ten); terms moderate every care; good school.

*Bristol Times & Mirror*, 11 January 1896

Nellie Oliver arrived in Kensington Road at the beginning of February. She was only eleven years old but had been put on a train at Plymouth and sent to Reading under the charge of a Great

Western guard. Her mother was a domestic servant in Looe, Cornwall, and had placed Nellie out with a woman in Plymouth. The identity of her father was a mystery, but he was a man of means who paid a decent yearly sum for his illegitimate daughter. Nellie was a valuable commodity and those in receipt of the annual payment felt free to pass the responsibility of the child on to any willing third party, paying them a lesser sum and pocketing the balance. Mother not only received a moderate weekly sum, but an extra pair of hands to help around the house. Most importantly, Nellie could

Nellie Oliver, *Weekly Dispatch*, 19 April 1896

be used as another decoy: both she and Willie were kept well scrubbed and nourished. To the outside world they presented an impressive example of Mother's maternal skills.

❦

An advertisement Mother had placed in the *Western Daily Press* under the name of Thornley soon caught the eye of a young domestic servant from Bristol.

> Married couple having no child would **ADOPT** one; small premium.
> Mrs Thornley, c/o Ships Letter Exchange, Stoke's Croft Bristol.
> *Western Daily Press*, 3 February 1896

Mary Fry had recently given birth to a girl whom she named Helena. She was a single woman; the father was a well-to-do merchant in the city. It was a common enough situation and it suited everyone that the child be adopted out. The father could afford to pay the terms stated in the advertisement, being only too happy to rid himself of any potential embarrassment, and the young mother was aware that adoption was her only option. Mother arranged to collect the child from the platform at Bristol Temple Meads Station, along with £10 and her rail fare; she promised to give the little one a good home. On the morning of 5 March Mother left the house telling Granny that she was going to London to see the Palmers.

When she arrived home that evening she brought with her a brown paper parcel, about two feet long, which she placed on the sewing machine in the corner of the room. She didn't volunteer what was in the parcel and, as she was not in the best of tempers, no one dared ask. The parcel lay untouched throughout supper and into the evening; in the morning it had disappeared.

❦

It was Granny who first noticed the nauseating smell emanating from the deep recesses of the cupboard in the kitchen. Mother was in the habit of buying scraps of meat for her beloved cats and Granny wondered if some had been left to rot on a shelf at the back. She didn't challenge Mother on the matter as her moods had become increasingly strange, and the little bottle of brown liquid which she

The cupboard in the kitchen, *Weekly Dispatch*, 19 April 1896

kept in the pocket of her apron, and from which she would take nips, was beginning to appear more frequently.

Willie had noticed the smell, too; it was growing stronger, putting him off his bread and jam. He was a bright boy and knew better than to complain out loud. On a day when Mother had gone to town he looked inside the cupboard to see for himself what was causing the nasty stink. As he opened the door, the stench of rotting meat assailed his nostrils, causing him to gag and cover his mouth. Before he banged the door closed on it, he noticed, sitting high on a shelf, a long brown paper parcel with both ends tucked neatly in.

The smell grew unbearable. It permeated the front room and Mrs Chandler began to complain to Mother. She wouldn't pay rent for a room in a house which smelled so unpleasant. Mother vehemently denied the existence of any smell, but on Monday 30 March she rose from her bed before the rest of the house had stirred and took herself downstairs where she filled the kitchen bucket with soapy water. She instructed young Willie to run upstairs and tell Granny that she needn't get up as "there was nothing for her to do". When Granny came downstairs about an hour later, she was very surprised to find Mother scrubbing out the cupboard; she did not usually involve herself in such dirty household tasks. Granny offered to finish off the cleaning, but Mother said she would do it herself as the cupboard was so filthy and went to empty the dirty water in the backyard. Later in the morning Mother put on her cloak and announced she was off to the pawn shop. She walked out of the house with a brown paper parcel tucked under her cloak, and returned empty handed later that evening. The stench in the house disappeared, although Willie could never bring himself to open the cupboard again; faint traces of the mysterious odour still lurked in the musty interior, lingering among the shelves piled high with baby clothes.

Mother was unaware that the stinking parcel she had tossed in the river had not only failed to sink but, by the end of the day, would be lying unwrapped in the police mortuary.

# 39 The Barmaid's Daughter

Charles Jeffrey, chief clerk for the *Bristol Times & Mirror*, had recently received an order for six insertions to be placed in the "Miscellaneous Wants" column of the paper. The order was signed by A. Harding.

> **MARRIED** couple with no family would adopt healthy child, nice country home. Terms, £10. – Harding, care of Ship's Letter Exchange, Stokes Croft, Bristol.

Appearing alongside this advertisement on 18, 19 and 20 March 1896 was another:

> **NURSE CHILD** – Wanted, respectable woman to take young child at home – State terms to Mrs. Scott, 23, Manchester Street, Cheltenham.

Mrs Scott was in fact a twenty-five-year-old barmaid called Evelina Edith Marmon who had given birth to a female child in January that year. Despite her feisty nature and the undoubted love she felt for her child, she knew she was not in a position to keep baby Doris.

Evelina had grown up in the Gloucestershire village of Hartpury, the youngest child of seven, living at the heart of a hardworking agricultural community. Her father James was a poulterer by trade and his farmstead was one of many clustered around the old manor house. The census of 1881 shows Evelina and her thirteen-year-old brother Ralph as scholars, while the remaining five siblings are listed as poulterer's assistants. By 1891 Evelina's mother, Mary, had died and Evelina was living with her older sister Isabella, then married to a local horse dealer in the neighbouring village of Maisemore, with four children of her own. Evelina was nineteen and, according to the census that year, seems to have had no particular occupation. Her brothers and sisters all married into the local farming community and continued to raise poultry and horses and to fish the local waters. It was a monotonous life. The days ticked by with a repetitive rhythm; children were born; marriages were made; one generation bleeding into the next.

Evelina was not content to lead the life of a farmer's wife, to breed a flock of children destined for the same thing, then to die early as her mother had done, worn down and worked to death like an old carthorse. She wanted something better out of life; she wanted excitement.

The Regency spa town of Cheltenham lay roughly ten miles east of Hartpury, and, although the popularity of its spas had waned by the end of the nineteenth century, it was still a tasteful town lined with cream and white terraced houses interspersed with genteel garden squares, the magnificent Royal Crescent and the cultivated tree-lined walk of The Promenade. It attracted a respectable class of wealthy visitors, drawn by the elegant architecture and the refined main street with its flourishing shops. To a girl brought up surrounded by chickens and dirt tracks it must have seemed a glittering city rich with possibilities.

Evelina found lodgings on Manchester Street with an old widow lady called Martha Pockett. Mrs Pockett and her late husband Charles had for many years run the bars of the Plough Hotel, an ancient coaching inn and the original stopover for Royal Mail post coaches. She was able, through her connection with the hotel, to secure for Evelina a position as barmaid. Evelina was a good-looking young woman with a fine, strong figure and striking blonde hair; she possessed all the qualities necessary to survive as a barmaid in the nineteenth century: stamina, a quick wit, thick skin and an independent nature. The Plough Hotel was a very respectable establishment, and advertised itself as such in the 1893 edition of *Burke's Peerage*.

Nevertheless, bar work was not a respectable occupation, falling mainly to abandoned women or the wives and daughters of publicans. But it was a job nonetheless, and Evelina desperately needed to earn some money. Victorian sensibilities did not allow barmaids in respectable establishments to work anywhere other than in the plush surroundings of the saloon or lounge bars where the exclusively male customers tended to be wealthy. Despite its classier nature the bar-room banter would have

# HELTENHAM
# PLOUGH HOTEL.

This old established County Hotel having recently undergone
extensive alterations and improvements is now replete with
every comfort for Families and Visitors.

Commodious and Handsome New Coffee Room,

AND

## LADIES' DRAWING ROOM.
## BILLIARD AND SMOKE ROOMS

Have been Re-decorated, Furnished, and fitted with all Modern Improvements.

* * * * * * * * * *

Telephone No. 46; Telegraphic Address, "PLOUGH," Cheltenham.

Table d'hôte at separate tables from 6 to 8.

### TARIFF STRICTLY MODERATE.

* * * * * * * * * *

## SPECIAL ARRANGEMENTS FOR RESIDENT BOARDERS.
## EXCELLENT CUISINE.
Cellars of Fine Old Vintage Wines.
### PERFECT SANITARY ARRANGEMENTS.

---

Livery ⬧ accommodation ⬧ unequalled ⬧ in ⬧ the ⬧ County.
*CARRIAGES OF EVERY DESCRIPTION.*

---

TARIFF ON APPLICATION TO THE MANAGERESS.

An advertisement from *Burke's Peerage*, 1893

been ribald and Evelina would have batted the bawdy comments away with practised detachment. The pay was low and the hours were long, for as well as serving customers there was the cleaning and preparation to be done before the tavern opened and the cleaning and tidying to do when the bar closed, often late into the night. Evelina would have spent hours on her hands and knees oiling and rubbing the woodwork of the bar, cleaning all the brasswork and polishing to a shine the decanters, wine glasses and tumblers arrayed on the shelves.

Unwanted pregnancies were an occupational hazard for barmaids, and an attractive girl like Evelina would have drawn the attention of many of the male customers.

Unusually for the time, Martha Pockett was a sympathetic landlady who allowed Evelina to keep her rooms even when her pregnant state became obvious and she was forced to leave her job. Martha was old, infirm and not in the best of health, so probably relied on Evelina more than she was prepared to admit. Baby Doris Marmon was born with a smattering of light brown hair and a healthy set of lungs on 21 January 1896. In the early, exhausting days of motherhood it perhaps crossed Evelina's mind to return to the bosom of her extended family in Hartpury; but she must have known deep down that in such a small community, where decency, hard work and Christian morals were valued above all else, her fall from grace and her illegitimate child would only bring shame and sorrow to her family.

Evelina realized that she could not rely on the charity of her landlady for long; she needed to go back to work. Finding another position as a barmaid would not be too difficult, but looking after her child at the same time would be impossible. Mrs Pockett was too old and ill to be left in charge of a young baby, so that left only one option.

Evelina placed her advertisement in the *Bristol Times & Mirror* hoping to find a loving and respectable woman to take care of Doris in exchange for a weekly fee. If and when her circumstances changed, she planned to reclaim her daughter and bring her home.

Evelina checked a copy of the *Bristol Times & Mirror* and saw alongside her own advertisement another placed by a childless couple named Harding, who described themselves as having a "nice country home". Not wishing to incur the couple's disapproval by admitting she was an unmarried mother, Evelina replied to the advertisement using the name of Mrs Scott; better to be thought of as an unfortunate widow than a fallen woman.

On 20 March she received the first of a number of communications from Mrs Harding.

To Mrs Scott,
Dear Madam, – In reference to your letter of Ashton's [*the name of the letter exchange used*] of a child, I beg to say I should be glad to have a dear little baby girl, one I could bring up and call my own. First I must tell you we are plain, homely people, in fairly good circumstances. We live in our own house. I have a good and comfortable home. We are out in the country and sometimes I am alone a great deal. I don't want a child for moneys sake, but for company and home comfort. Myself and my husband are dearly fond of children. I have no child of my own. A child with me will have a good home and a mothers love and care. We belong to the Church of England. Although I want to bring up the child as my own, I should not mind the mother or any person coming to see the child at any time. It would be a satisfaction to know and see the child was going on alright. I only hope we may come to terms. I should like to have baby as soon as you can. If I could come for her I don't mind paying my fare one way. I should break my journey at Gloucester. I have a friend in the asylum I should be so glad to call and see. Kindly let me have an early reply. I can give you good references, and any other particulars you may ask me I shall be pleased to answer.
I am yours respectfully, A. Harding

Evelina could not believe her luck; Mrs Harding sounded every bit the respectable and caring woman that she'd hoped to find for Doris and she wrote back at once begging her not to consider anyone else until they had met and reached an agreement

45 Kensington Road, Oxford Road Reading,
Sunday March 22, '96.

To Mrs Scott
Dear Madam, – Many thanks for your letter of this morning. I shall not answer anyone else until I hear from you again. I do hope we may come to terms. Rest assured I will do my duty by that dear child. I will be a mother, as far as possible lies in my power, and if I come for her, if you like to come and stay for a few days or a week later on I shall be pleased to make you welcome. It is just lovely here in the

summer. There is an orchard opposite our front door. You will say it is healthy and pleasant.

Hoping to hear soon

I am yours, A. Harding

I think Doris is a very pretty name. I am sure she ought to be a pretty child.

Evelina was certainly taken with the letters of Mrs Harding, but even so she wrote back seeking reassurance that she would be welcome to come and see her child any time she wished: all she wanted was for her daughter to be loved as much as she herself loved her.

45 Kensington Road, Oxford Road Reading,
Tuesday, March 24, 1896

My dear Madam, – your letter just to hand, and I shall be only too pleased for yourself, or any friends to come and see us sometimes. We don't have many visitors out here in the country. I assure you it would be as great a treat to us as the change would be to you. I shall really feel more comfortable to know the dear little soul had someone that really cared for her. I shall value her all the more. Rest assured, I promise you faithfully, I will do a mothers duty by her, and I will bring her up entirely just the same as my own child. Every care will be taken of her, and when you come you will soon see I do my duty. Dear child I shall be only too glad to have her, and I will take her entirely for the sum of £10. She shall be no further expense to her family. I will come on Monday next. If I shall I will let you know later on what time train. I have not a timetable, but I will find out and let you know.

I am yours faithfully, A. Harding

But if Tuesday will suit you better kindly let me know, as either day will suit me

45 Kensington Road, Reading.
Friday morning

My dear Mrs Scott, – Just a line to say that, as I have not heard from you to say I must not come on Monday, I take it for granted that I may come for baby on Monday next. I shall leave here at 9.50 in the morning, and get to Gloucester sometime about 12. I shall go straight to Wootton Asylum. I shall not be there long as it will be their

dinnertime. Then I will take the next train for Cheltenham. I fancy I can be at Manchester Street not later than 2 o'clock. I shall be glad if I can get an early train back; if I can get a fast train I shall not be so long on the road with baby. I hope it will be a fine day.
I am faithfully yours A. Harding

P.S. – My husband says if the mother would like an agreement would you kindly draw one out, and we will sign it

45 Kensington Road, Oxford Road, Reading,
March 29, 1896.

My Dear Madam, – Your letter safe this morning. Yes, I will come on Tuesday next by the 9.50 train. I will bring a good warm shawl to wrap round baby in the train. It is bitter cold here today.
I am yours faithfully A. Harding

Mother was glad of her heavy shawl and warm boots as she dressed to leave the house on the morning of Tuesday 31 March. She was going up to London, she said, to see Polly, and she was taking Willie's carpet bag with some clothes in it for baby Harold. She left the house early leaving only a shilling on the table for Granny to buy the children's food with.

"Mrs Harding" arrived at 23 Manchester Street at around half past twelve, having decided to forgo her visit to Wotton Asylum on account of the sharp winds and icy temperatures. Evelina was surprised to discover that the woman she had been corresponding with was rather more elderly than she had anticipated. But she seemed strong and capable and, more importantly, seemed to fall for the charms of baby Doris in an instant; and, as she had promised, she had brought a warm shawl to wrap the child up in against the cold.

Evelina had prepared well for Doris's departure; she had sewn a dozen and a half little napkins and had, four days previously, taken the baby to be vaccinated. Her little arm was still swollen and sore. A smallpox epidemic was sweeping through the neighbouring town of Gloucester and many people were realizing their folly in evading the vaccination laws. The virus was spreading fast with one house after another becoming infected. The young were hugely susceptible and the consequences of catching the disease were usually fatal for any child less than twelve months old. The Gloucester authorities were desperately trying to contain the epidemic, issuing quarantine orders and sending a medical officer to every house to vaccinate, without charge, any man, woman or child who had not hitherto been vaccinated.

Even the local postal service adopted precautionary measures lest the virus should spread to other parts of the country via letters and packages. The local papers reported:

> Instructions have been given for the use of disinfectants at the Gloucester Post Office with the view to reducing as far as practicable the risk of infection during the prevailing epidemic. All letters, packets, newspapers etc. are collected in a large basket for the purposes of disinfection. This is accomplished by means of the vapour arising from crude carbolic acid, which is contained in metal bowls placed underneath the letter basket; the acid being kept continually steaming by the aid of lamps under them. The contents of the basket are thus permeated by the fumes arising from the powerful disinfectant and in addition the mail bags are thoroughly sprinkled both inside and out with the carbolic before they are dispatched. It is satisfactory to know there has not been a case of smallpox in the established postal and telegraphic staff at Gloucester which numbers nearly 300.
>
> *Gloucester Journal*, 18 April 1896

Evelina gave Doris's vaccination certificate to Mrs Harding; she had also packed up a cardboard box of clothes – chemises, petticoats, frocks, nightgowns and a powder box – enough to last a good few months. Mrs Harding could not be persuaded to take a weekly sum for Doris as she wanted to bring the child up as her own, and did not want the worry that it might be fetched away at any time. But, she assured Evelina, she would be only too glad for her to visit the baby in her comfortable country home whenever she wished. The agreement was signed and £10 promptly disappeared into the layers of Mrs Harding's skirts. Evelina comforted herself with the thought that at least her baby would be safe in the country, out of reach of the devastating effects of smallpox.

I, Annie Harding, of 45, Kensington Road, Reading, in consideration of the sum of ten pounds paid to me by Evelina Edith Marmon, do hereby agree to adopt Doris, the child of the said Evelina Edith

Marmon; and do bring up the said child as my own, without any further compensation over and above the aforementioned sum of ten pounds. As witness herewith we have this day the 31st day of March in the year of our lord one thousand eight hundred and ninety six, subscribed our names, Annie Harding, Evelina Edith Marmon, in the presence of Martha Pockett, widow of 23, Manchester Street Cheltenham.

Doris was dressed in her best fawn-coloured pelisse and Evelina carried her to the railway station. Mrs Harding fussed all the way as to whether baby was warm enough, urging Evelina to keep baby's head well covered from the biting chill of the cold March day. To gain some extra time with her child, Evelina accompanied Mrs Harding from Cheltenham Station to Gloucester Station, from where the connecting train to Reading was to leave. Mrs Harding fetched a tatty looking carpet bag from the cloakroom at Cheltenham, telling Evelina that it contained some eggs and clothing for a friend. Evelina stood on the platform, straining for a last glimpse of her daughter as the choking steam enveloped the windows of the 5.20 train to Reading. She returned to her lodgings a broken woman.

Mrs Harding had said she would let her know of their safe arrival in Reading, and a couple of days later Evelina received the promised letter.

Views Road, Kensal Rise,
Dear Mrs Scott, – When I got home last night a wire was waiting for me. My sister dangerously ill; so this morning came up. My dear little girl is a traveller and no mistake. She was so good last night, and did not mind the journey. She slept all the way. I shall stop now till Saturday. Sunday I will write again if not before.
In great haste I am, yours, with love. A. Harding
A longer one next time.

Evelina wrote back at once, enquiring as to when they would be back in Reading and wanting to know how the vaccination mark on Doris's arm was faring. She was anxious, as it had been bothering Doris greatly, and she hoped Mrs Harding was taking good care of it.

She never received a reply.

-❧❧-

It was nine o'clock in the evening by the time Mother alighted from the train at Paddington, struggling to carry the carpet bag, a cardboard box, a small baby and a black and white checked shawl which had unravelled itself from around the infant. It was a dull, wet night and the broad pavements of the Edgware Road would have been slick and greasy, the heavy, lazy mist of rain made visible by the feeble glow of gaslight. A typical evening in the metropolis; the air a dingy yellow, and the rain only serving to enhance the stale, foul odours which swam in the layer of coal smoke and fog which hovered over nineteenth-century London. Pavements were lit here and there by squares of light thrown out by shop windows and public houses, and street vendors with their newspapers, hot potatoes and steaming kidney pies shouting over the rumbling of hackney cabs and carriages churning up the mud as they conveyed their passengers to theatres and parties.

Mother made her way through the throngs toward the omnibus terminus where the London General Omnibus Company ran a regular though ponderous service to Willesden. With a baby squirming in her lap and the cloying smell of stale ale and unwashed bodies adding to the unpleasantness of the journey, Mother would have been relieved to pay her fivepence fare when the omnibus finally stopped near Mayo Road.

Mrs Mary Ann Beattie, a sallow-faced woman who lived at number 11 Mayo Road, had also been travelling on the omnibus, on her way home from an evening out. She alighted behind Mother, and seeing that she was heavily laden, asked how far she was going. Learning she was making her way to 76 Mayo Road, Mrs Beattie offered to carry the older woman's bag. The bag was scuffed and worn, obviously well used; it weighed a great deal and before long Mrs Beattie's fingers began to ache. The baby was wearing a fawn-coloured cape, but it was not wrapped up in it tightly and its little limbs and face were exposed to the air and the cold, thin rain that was still falling. It was whimpering from the chill and Mrs Beattie, walking beside Mother, tried to shield it with her umbrella and to pull the cape over its face. With three young children of her own at home she knew such a young baby should not be exposed to the dangers of the night air.

It was the last act of kindness baby Doris Marmon was ever to experience.

There was a young woman standing at the door of 76 Mayo Road, and Mrs Beattie placed the bag against the step explaining that she had carried it for the lady with the baby. As she set off toward her own home, she saw both women go into number 76, the older one carrying the infant. The door was shut behind them.

※※

Inside 76 Mayo Road, a work basket was opened and rifled through. From the tangle of threads, bobbins, pincushions and thimbles, a quantity of white tape was removed. It was of the type commonly used to bind and edge hems and was of a good length: enough to be wrapped twice around the soft folds of Doris's neck. The tape was pulled tight, held for a second, and then tied in a knot. Too young to comprehend, to fight back or resist, Doris would have struggled for her last breath until her limbs went limp and she lost all consciousness. For a few short minutes her chest continued to heave in an involuntary attempt to fill her lungs and her mouth opened and closed like a baby bird in a last, silent bid for life. Before the warmth had left her tiny body, she was wrapped from head to toe in a napkin and placed out of sight.

※※

Mother and Polly opened the box of clothes that had been sent with Doris. There were a few good items and Polly sorted out those that would do for Harold. All children up to a certain age wore the same type of clothing, little boys as well as girls being dressed in frocks. There were a number of garments which Polly took a fancy to, in particular the fawn-coloured pelisse in which Doris Marmon had left home. The rest of the clothes were put to one side for the pawnbroker.

Charlotte Culham, the landlady of 76 Mayo Road, was not surprised to find Mrs Thomas in the Palmers' sitting room on the morning of Wednesday 1 April. Since the Palmers had moved in at the beginning of January, the woman had been a regular visitor. She had arrived late the night before, she said, and had slept all night in the chair. She gave Mrs Culham a pair of child's button-up boots, saying she thought they might be useful for her little girl, Ethel. When

Mr Culham came in from his nightly carriage cleaning duties at the railway depot, Mrs Thomas went through to him in the kitchen and paid him the Palmers' overdue rent.

The Culhams saw no more of Mrs Thomas or the Palmers until later that evening, when Arthur Palmer came home and asked Mrs Culham not to bolt the front door that night as they were going out and would not be back until late.

# 40 *The Undertaker's Wife*

In the middle of March 1896 the manager of the *Weekly Dispatch* in London had received the following letter:

> Sir, – kindly let the enclosed advertisement be in the above mentioned paper this week, and oblige
> Yours
> Mrs A. Harding

> **MARRIED** couple with no family would adopt healthy child, nice country home. Terms, £10. – Harding, care of Ship's Letter Exchange, Stokes Croft, Bristol.

Mrs Amelia Hannah Sargeant seemed to be a thoroughly respectable woman. Married in her early twenties to Alfred Sargeant, the son of a parish clerk, she had, by the time of the 1891 census, given birth like clockwork every other year to six children. Alfred was an industrious husband who had begun his working life as a carpenter and joiner, honing his woodworking skills making coffins; by the end of the 1890s he was running his own undertaking business, supplying those buried in the nearby South Ealing cemetery with their mahogany caskets as well as finely carved tombstones.

In March 1896, Amelia Sargeant found herself with a young child she wished to adopt out. She was later to maintain that the thirteen-month-old boy, Harry Simmons, was the child of an old friend of hers called Rizzy Simmons who had been widowed shortly after giving birth. Despite having six children of her own, Mrs Sargeant had agreed to take in the child for the sum of six shillings a week. With little room in the Sargeant household, Harry Simmons was sent to a Mrs Sharp in Brentford and, thinking that she would be receiving the promised six shillings a week, Amelia Sargeant in turn paid this sum to Mrs Sharp. This arrangement continued for almost a year, with Amelia Sargeant visiting the boy every week or so and continuing to pay out the six shillings a week without ever hearing a word from the mother. It was eventually decided that young Harry should be removed from the care of Mrs Sharp and adopted out permanently.

The advertisement which appeared in the *Weekly Dispatch* on 18 March, from a Mrs Harding, seemed to hold the promise that a loving and permanent home could be found for the boy. Amelia Sargeant replied to it immediately, and a couple of days later received the following reply:

45 Kensington Road, Oxford Road, Reading, Berks.
Friday, March 20th, 1896

My Dear Madam, – In reply to your letter just at hand, I beg to say I should be pleased to have a dear little boy. I have no child of my own. I do not want a child for money's sake. We live in the country and I am alone a great deal sometimes. I want a child for company and home comfort's sake. I may say we are in fairly good circumstances. We live in our own house. I have a good and comfortable home. We belong to the Church of England. A child with me would be well brought up and have a mother's love and care. I should like to take him entirely as my own child. But at the same time if the mother or any friends would like to come and see him sometimes I should be pleased to see them, and no doubt it would give them more satisfaction to see and know the child was going on all right. I can give you good references if you wish, and any further particulars you may wish I shall be pleased to send you.
I am, yours,
A. HARDING

Amelia Sargeant was impressed with the letter, but was not prepared to take the reassuring words at face value. She wrote back requesting a visit and the reply from Mrs Harding was swift and welcoming.

45 Kensington Road, Oxford Road, Reading.
Sunday, March 22nd, 1896.

To Mrs Sargeant,
My Dear Madam, – Your letter to hand too late to reply last night. I beg to say I shall be very pleased indeed to see you if you will come.

Will Wednesday next suit you, March 25th? If so I will be glad. Tuesday is my washing day, I cannot well put off. I think it only right you should have an interview. Will you kindly let me know what time I may expect you? I am glad he is a nice strong child. When you come I am sure you will say it is a nice open healthy place. We have an orchard opposite our front door, and in summer time it is just lovely. I won't stop to say more now. Hoping to see you soon.

I am, Madam, yours

ANNIE HARDING

I forgot to say you can take the tram in Broad Street. The fare is 2d. It will bring you to Kensington Road.

Amelia Sargeant travelled to Reading on Wednesday 25 March. She walked from the railway station to the tram stop in Broad Street and paid her twopence to travel the length of Oxford Road, alighting near the top end of Kensington Road. Although the area was far from the rural idyll she had been expecting from the descriptions in Mrs Harding's letters, once she'd left the noise and dust of Oxford Road and the rattling of the tram disappearing into the distance, Kensington Road did seem a pleasant and open street. The rows of terraced houses stretched the length of the left-hand side of the road, but on the right-hand side they stopped short of the cricket ground and an area of land belonging to Elm Lodge. There were indeed some clumps of elm trees which she supposed could constitute the orchard mentioned in the letters. Arriving at number 45 at two o'clock in the afternoon she was greeted at the door by the imposing figure of Mrs Harding. She seemed to be a kind person, a homely and motherly woman. The house seemed clean and comfortable enough, and the two women spent just over an hour in pleasant conversation.

Mother had risen early that morning to prepare the house in readiness for her visitor. All sign of the children had been hidden away: Nellie and Willie were sent off to school and Granny was dispatched into town with the remaining babies.

Mrs Harding confessed to her visitor that her true name was Mrs Thomas, and that she only advertised in the name of Harding because she had lived in Reading with her husband for twenty-two years and they were very much respected in the town. They were so well known that she did not wish to advertise under her own name. She said her husband was a goods guard on the Great Eastern

Railway, and that she was not in the habit of taking in "nurse" children. She professed to have a great fondness for children, and was reluctant to have to live without them. Mrs Sargeant left Kensington Road that day having arranged to hand over little Harry Simmons for the sum of £10 to the woman she now knew as Mrs Thomas. She was satisfied that she would be kind to Harry and saw no need to make further enquiries or to ask for references. It was only a question of arranging a suitable date.

45 Kensington Road, Oxford Road, Reading.
Friday morning

My Dear Mrs Sargeant, I hope you arrived home safe. I could not write yesterday as promised, some friends dropped in and when they left it was too late for the post. My husband says I shall be in town on Monday, you had better send a line and say the time most suitable for you to get to Paddington. I can be there at time in the morning, say between ten and one o'clock in the morning, so if you will kindly drop me a line and say what time you can get there, I will be there to meet you. If the mother requires an agreement kindly let your husband draw one out, and myself and husband will sign it.
I remain, yours faithfully,
ANNIE THOMAS
Kindly address Thomas.

45 Kensington Road.
Sunday afternoon.

My Dear Mrs Sargeant, – Many thanks for your letter of this morning. I cannot wire from here today, Sunday. The General is closed until eight o'clock at night, so I have just sent down to the station. I do hope you will get it all right. Of course I will have the dear little soul. I should have liked the money paid down, but I will trust you. You can send it in a registered letter. That will be all right. If you pay me five pound, the other five in April, as you say, that will do. I don't want you to come down again before Whitsuntide. By that time the person in my house will be gone away and then I should like you to come. Bring your husband and some of the children if you like, and by that time my little boy will be getting used to me. I find I can't come up now on Monday. I shall be up on Tuesday middle day. Will you come on Wednesday morning? I will be there on the down platform, under the clock, at eleven o'clock on Wednesday morning. I should come Monday, but my husband wants me to go somewhere very important with him, so I hope you won't be put to any inconvenience.

I am, truly yours,

A. THOMAS

I hope the dear little boy is all right. Yes, thanks, my cold is better.

In this letter there was an enclosure:

My Dear Mrs Sargeant, – My husband is just returned from the station. He went down to send off your telegram. They was closed, and, like the General Post Office, won't be open until tonight; so he says a letter will reach you quite as soon. I do hope you won't be put about.

Mother and Polly left Mayo Road at mid-morning on Wednesday 1 April. Polly took Harold with her, dressed in his newly acquired white flannel frock and fawn-coloured pelisse. They were to meet Mrs Sargeant under the clock on the down platform at Paddington Station at around eleven o'clock. The interior of the station, with its great glazed roof and wrought-iron arches, would have echoed to the sounds of hurrying feet, guards' whistles and the clank of hand carts trundling along with their loads of leather-strapped trunks and cases.

Mrs Sargeant and her husband Albert arrived at Paddington Station at almost a quarter to twelve. They found their way to the clock on the down platform and standing underneath it was Mrs Thomas and a young woman she introduced as her niece. She had a very sickly looking child in her arms who she said was her own. It was a little boy and he was wrapped in a fawn-coloured pelisse. By contrast, Harry Simmons was a fine, healthy looking little fellow with a good helping of fine brown hair and clear blue eyes. He, too, was dressed in a little cloak, dark brown and of plush velvet.

The station's refreshment rooms were nearby, elegantly furnished with lace-covered tables; huge steaming urns replenished delicate cups of tea and coffee and hungry passengers tucked into hard-boiled eggs, cold sausages and ancient ham sandwiches. In a corner of this room, with mop-capped waitresses bobbing from table to table and the excited chatter of travellers rising over the steam of their beverages, Harry Simmons's fate was sealed.

Amelia Sargeant handed over £5 to Mrs Thomas along with an IOU for the remaining £5 which was to be paid on 11 April. The receipt was written on one of Albert Sargeant's memorandum forms and bore a penny stamp.

A. Sargeant
Funeral Furniture,
Monumental Mason,
50 Ealing Road South,
Ealing, W.
Received of Mrs A. Sargeant the sum of Five Pounds on account.
April 1st, 1896
ANNIE THOMAS

Amelia Sargeant also handed over a parcel of clothes; a couple of red frocks and a number of flannel petticoats were among the articles done up in brown paper and tied with string. Mrs Thomas promised always to be good and kind to the child and invited Mrs Sargeant to come down to Reading any time she liked, "to see if the child was going on all right".

Mrs Thomas said she would write immediately on arriving back in Reading, and after kissing the baby goodbye Amelia Sargeant watched as Mrs Thomas and her niece climbed aboard an omnibus which lurched down the road taking Harry toward his new life.

Circumstances which have transpired recently go to show that Reading has for some time been suspected as a refuge of those anxious to dispose of children. It is roughly estimated that thirty or forty bodies were found last year in the London district of the Thames, and it was quite possible that they had been disposed of up the river and had floated down with the stream. An inspector of the Thames police points out that the bodies were nearly all those of infants and in the majority of cases, the organs were fully developed, proving that the infants had lived for some time. As long ago as August it was believed that the bodies were all disposed of by one person, and curiously enough suspicion rested on a woman rather than a man as the murderess.

*Reading Standard*, 17 April 1896

Polly and Mother arrived back at Mayo Road at two in the afternoon. The new baby had by now started to cry, hunger pains clutching at his little stomach. An India rubber "titty" was plugged in his mouth to silence his wails, but no bottle or food was offered. He was picked up and shaken.

*"Little Devil, if it keeps this up I shan't stick it for long."*

The work basket was searched, but there was no more white tape to be found. So the napkin was unwrapped from around the cold, still body of Doris Marmon, the knot in the tape around her neck was picked undone, and the length of it removed. She had gone a funny colour and the tape had left deep marks around the circumference of her neck.

Harry Simmons went off quietly. He was also too young and unco-ordinated to grasp at the tape being pulled tightly around his neck, and his feeble struggles were over within a minute. When the final, fruitless heaving of his chest had stilled, he was wrapped in a shawl and left on the couch, for all the world as if in a deep slumber.

# 41 The Carpet Bag

Polly put Harold to bed at about six o'clock. Not long after, Arthur came home and enquired if they had fetched the "little nipper". He was nodded toward the crumpled mound at the head of the couch, Mother sitting calmly at the other end. After supper, Arthur, Polly and Mother all went out. They had been looking forward to visiting the Sporting and Military Show which was currently being staged at Olympia. They locked the sitting-room door leaving the three babies alone in their rooms, only one of them still alive.

The halls at Olympia were brightly lit, and a sea of top hats and pretty bonnets poured through the doors. It is not certain exactly what the Palmers and Mother saw that evening, but it would have been very similar to the sights on display at the Royal Military Exhibition held a few years earlier in Chelsea. Here there were displayed a variety of historical artefacts including such items as a helmet worn by Oliver Cromwell, the cloak and sword worn by Wellington and a snuff box fashioned from the breastplates of officers killed at Waterloo. The musical talents of the military bands were shown to their best advantage and the expertise and pageantry of the British Empire were demonstrated by spectacular displays of horsemanship, field exercises, drill parades and military tattoos. It was a stimulating evening and Mother enjoyed herself enough to purchase a programme to take back with her to Reading.

Back in Mayo Road, the Palmers took themselves off to bed while Mother made herself comfortable on the couch with a pillow and blanket which Polly had given her. She slept soundly that night, waking only once in the early hours when she fancied she heard the sound of a baby crying. But on checking underneath the couch she saw that the two bundles were quite still.

Charlotte Culham saw the Palmers and Mrs Thomas the following day, Thursday 2 April, at about noon. Mrs Thomas was in the sitting room relaxing in the armchair. There was a carpet bag lying on the floor; it was placed there carelessly, open and obviously empty.

Albert Culham had recently rebuilt the fire grate in the kitchen, and as a consequence the unused bricks had been placed in a heap in the backyard, piled haphazardly under the rabbit hutch. During the late afternoon this pile of bricks was disturbed; a whole one and a second one with the end broken off were removed and taken into the house. The dead bodies of Doris Marmon and Harry Simmons were squeezed into the empty carpet bag. They had to be pushed down to make room for the bricks, and even then the bag would not close. It nonetheless seemed the most convenient way to carry the babies, so a piece of brown paper was laid over the top of the bag to hide them from view and it was tied around the middle with string.

Arthur and Polly accompanied Mother to Paddington Station. They left Mayo Road at about twenty past seven, with Mother carrying the bulging carpet bag. At the omnibus stop, Arthur held the bag for her while she went into a cookshop to purchase a pastry for the journey. The cookshops of London were manned by white-sleeved assistants who spent their days turning currant rolls and thick slabs of spotted dog on to sheets of greaseproof paper. Mother spent twopence on a package of warm spiced dough.

At Paddington, Arthur bought her a ticket and he and Polly stood on the platform while Mother climbed into an empty carriage. A young lady, being seen off from the station by a rather dapper looking gentleman, climbed into the carriage with her and took a seat by the window. After an awkward moment, Mother climbed back out of the carriage with her bag and made her way down the platform until she found another empty carriage in which she settled, storing her carpet bag under the seat.

It was a fast train, leaving Paddington at 9.15 and arriving in Reading at 10.05. There would nevertheless have been plenty of time for Mother to sit back and enjoy her pastry, plenty of time for her to lick every last greasy crumb from her fingers. Part way through the journey Mother undid the string around the bag and moved the bricks to the "other side" so that the bag would not "look so large".

Witnesses were later to report that the night of Thursday 2 April 1896 was particularly dark. Swollen clouds hung low over a wet and miserable Reading, blackening the skies and obscuring any moonlight.

The fast train from Paddington had pulled into Reading station on time, 10.05, and Mother had carried her weighty bag out into the wet, dark streets and down toward the river and the Clappers foot-bridge. There was someone lurking in the shadows near the bridge and this made Mother feel uneasy: she was obliged to wait in the steadily pouring rain for fifteen minutes until she was quite alone. She pushed the carpet bag through the railings of the bridge and was perturbed that the loud smack as it hit the water could be heard over the surging currents of the fast-flowing river. She turned to hurry for home and was startled to hear a "Goodnight" from a man she passed near the railway arches.

John Toller was a well-built man in his early thirties. He was not local to Reading, but had moved in recent years from Wales to take up a position as an engineer at Reading Gaol. He was a man in mourning: he had recently lost his five-year-old son Bertie. On this particular evening he had been to the theatre in a bid, perhaps, to ease the raw pain of his bereavement. The Royal County Theatre on Friar Street had been built the previous year to replace the Princess Theatre which had been destroyed in a fire. It was reputedly an exotic place with a luxurious interior which lifted the spirits of all who stepped inside.

John Toller's journey home to Forbury Road took him past the railway arch near the Rising Sun public house. He noticed a woman coming toward him through the arch from the direction of the river. The windows of the Rising Sun cast a light into the otherwise dark night, and at the point where the woman passed him a gas lamp at the side of the road lit up her features. She was middle-aged and heavily built, wearing a dark, floor-length cloak which blew open in the wind to reveal a homely apron underneath. John Toller thought he recognized her, so wished her a goodnight as they passed. She did not reply and, as he turned back to look at her, he noticed she was empty handed and walking back in the direction of the railway station and the town.

A few days were to pass before John Toller realized the significance of his encounter.

Mother arrived back in Kensington Road at gone eleven o'clock. She had a strange look about her and seemed somewhat agitated. Granny was used to these moods. No doubt Mother had been taking her brandy, alternating nips of burning alcohol with little sips from the brown sticky bottle of laudanum she kept in her pocket. She told Granny that the reason she was so late home was on account of missing two trains. The platforms had been crowded with holiday travellers and if it hadn't been for a "special" train being put on, she never would have got home at all. She'd left the carpet bag in London with Polly, she'd said. Polly didn't have a bag and she needed one to pack up a few things in to take to Bridgwater. They were all moving to Bridgwater on Sunday, she said. Polly, Arthur, herself and Granny. No mention was made of the children.

# 42 Good Friday

When the police arrived at 45 Kensington Road on the evening of Friday 3 April, only four days had passed since the discovery of the baby's body in the Thames. The address on the sodden parcel paper and its subsequent connection to Mrs Thomas of Kensington Road, and the results of the "sting" operation, had both served to confirm the suspicions of the police regarding the identity of the child murderer.

But they had little idea that the woman they had come to question had enacted the most abominable of atrocities over and over again. They had little idea that the woman whose overlarge hands gently caressed her precious cats and sewed neat stitches into the worn fabric of her family's clothes had the previous evening consigned to a watery grave the bodies of two infants who had been in her care only a matter of hours.

It was only when they began to search the few small rooms of the comfortless house that they realized the sheer scale of the case they had uncovered, the grisly details of which would horrify a nation for months to come. From the backs of shelves and from fusty cupboards and dented tins they ferreted out bundles of telegrams arranging adoptions, quantities of child vaccination certificates, pawn tickets relating to children's clothing, newspaper office receipts for advertisements, and ink-stained letters from anxious mothers enquiring after their little ones.

From the dates and contents of the letters, and the sums of money mentioned, it seemed that the suspect had enjoyed a long and profitable career as a baby farmer of the worst kind, and had undergone several aliases, among them Thomas, Weymouth, Harding, Smith, Stansfield, Thornley and Wathen. In the last few months at least twenty children had been entrusted into the care of the woman now revealed as Mrs Amelia Elizabeth Dyer.

※

Since leaving the Barton Regis Workhouse, Mother had never stayed anywhere longer than three months and she had already made arrangements for herself and the Palmers to move to the Somerset town of Bridgwater. Granny was aware of these plans but it seemed that Amelia's true intentions were to abandon her and the children in Reading, leaving them to call upon the mercies of the workhouse. The police had caught up with Mother just in time.

※

It was five o'clock in the evening when Amelia Dyer was escorted into the shadowy interior of a police cab. The neighbours, drawn outside by the rumble of carriage wheels and the sound of horses (incongruous in the narrow terraced street), would have stood gossiping in knots. They may well have wondered what crime the quiet and respectable woman at number 45 could possibly have committed, but their imaginations could never have conjured up the horrors they would hear about in the weeks to come.

※

The very serious part of the business is the fact that certain letters, found in the woman's rooms, clearly show that many of the parents who have entrusted their children to the woman, knew the fate in store for them.
*Gloucester Journal*, 18 April 1896

You'll remember I gave you £5 in order to get rid of my child, and although it is now five years ago, I will see you in hell before I own the child or pay anymore. You can do what you like with it for all I care. I washed my hands of it the day I left it with you, and you can do exactly as you please. You can't find me out, and I never intend to let you know where I am. I have got clear of all now, and I shall not get myself into another muddle. Do as you like, and whether little Georgie goes into the workhouse or not I don't mean to worry. I have suffered enough.

You can do your best and do your worst. I don't care what you do with Jessie. She is yours now, not mine. It is quite true I have not the feelings of a mother, but when I read your advertisement I was only too glad to see a chance of getting rid of what would prove a drag on me all my lifetime.

> Letters found at 45 Kensington Road, and published
> in the *Weekly Dispatch*, 21 June 1896

⊰⊱

From other letters found at Kensington Road, the police obtained their first clues as to the identity of the female infant found strangled in the Thames. They believed that she might have been a baby from Bristol named Helena Fry, but as the body was so badly decomposed they could not be certain and therefore the child's name was kept out of the newspapers. The police also found information that would lead them to pay a visit to the Palmers in Willesden.

⊰⊱

It took just half an hour for the police van to convey its passenger to the police station in London Street. The original charge sheet written out that evening is held at the Thames Valley Police Museum, Sulhamstead, and reads:

Annie Dyer, alias Thomas and Harding,
45, Kensington Road, Oxford Road
Occupation: Nurse
Did, on 30th March 1896, feloniously, wilfully and of her malice aforethought kill and murder a certain female infant, Helena Fry daughter of one Mary Fry.

The Reading police notes from the case of Amelia Dyer have been lost to time. But the ghastly events which unfolded throughout the late spring of 1896 were reported at great length and in grim detail in the provincial and London newspapers, each new development seized upon and retold with salacious relish.

The man in charge of investigations was Chief Superintendent George Tewsley; a portly gentleman with a commanding presence, the obligatory handlebar moustache and neatly trimmed fair hair tucked under a well-brushed bowler. From the speed with which the case was unravelled, it is clear that he was a man of formidable talent and indefatigable energy.

Several papers of the day reported the sensational details of Amelia Dyer's attempted suicide while being held in the charge room at Reading police station. The bootlace around her neck was found knotted below her left ear, in the same position as the tape that was found tied around the neck of the baby in the parcel. But it was a pathetic endeavour – just like many of her previous attempts at suicide – and she was soon divested of any article likely to pose a danger to herself.

### NURSE CHARGED WITH HOMICIDE

At Reading yesterday Amelia Dyer, alias Thomas, an elderly woman, described as a nurse, was charged with having murdered a child, name unknown. Superintendent Tewsley stated that on Monday last a parcel was found in the river Thames at Reading and when opened was found to contain the body of a female child. They had evidence to prove that the accused left home on that day with a parcel similar to the one found, and that the string securing it was identical with some she had borrowed, whilst the tape by which it was suggested the child had been strangled corresponded with that found at her house. Accused, who in answer to the Bench said: "I do not know anything about it; it's a mystery to me", was remanded for a week and taken to HM Prison Reading.

*Weekly Dispatch*, Sunday 5 April 1896

# 43 Dyer on Remand

Reading Gaol was built in 1844 on the site of the former county prison alongside the banks of the River Kennet. Built from red Tilehurst bricks with keystones of honey-coloured Bath stone and ornate turrets and crenellations, it created an imposing backdrop to the town dubbed "The Capital of Berkshire".

It was one of a number of "New Model" prisons built in England at the time, based on the design of London's Pentonville. Its innovative cruciform shape enabled the four radiating wings to be visible to the prison staff stationed at the centre, the wings being galleried with separate cells on open landings, which allowed the enforcement of the "separate system". Inmates were kept isolated for twenty-three hours a day in dark, badly ventilated, ill-smelling cells, with only an hour a day being spent in the chapel and the dreary, damp exercise yard.

Amelia Dyer was to spend the next four weeks of her life here, locked inside one of thirty-one cells arranged over the three galleries of E-wing, home to female drunks, thieves and syphilitic prostitutes. The cells were dismal, dimly lit and measured only thirteen by seven feet with a tiny slit of a window to frame a sliver of sky. The meagre furnishings which graced each interior consisted of a roughly made three-legged stool, a stained table nailed to the floor, a crude set of shelves and a narrow plank bed. A dented copper hand-wash basin and a fetid earthenware WC lurking in a corner of the whitewashed room were the only concessions to feminine hygiene. The iron-studded wooden doors which hung heavy in their frames kept prisoners apart and muffled the moans and cries which all too often reverberated around the landings.

This harsh regime, unrelenting and soul destroying, was immortalized by Oscar Wilde in *The Ballad of Reading Gaol*. Wilde had been incarcerated in cell three, floor three, block C, since May 1895 and by the time Amelia Dyer arrived in April the following year he was already a broken man. Sentenced to two years' first-class hard labour for the crime of sodomy, Wilde was compelled to spend six hours a day on the treadmill; ascending the wheel step by painful step for twenty minutes at a time, interspersed by only five minutes' rest. It was exhausting and wholly unproductive work. With breakfast and supper consisting of only bread and a thin gruel, and a dinner of 8oz of potatoes and 4oz of bread, Wilde suffered from chronic diarrhoea and his health was irreparably damaged. When not employed on the treadmill, Wilde would be locked up in his cell to sew endless pieces of rough sacking into post bags or to pick loose the hard and tarred fibres of old rope until his fingers grew slippery with blood.

But Amelia was not to experience these hardships. As a prisoner on remand she would enjoy privileges and luxuries other inmates could only dream of. Still able to wear her own clothes, Amelia avoided the indignities of the heavy, ill-fitting female prisoner's dress and the circular badge other inmates were obliged to wear which bore the wing, floor and number of their cells. With money in her pocket, she could eschew the appalling tins of foul-smelling gruel and indigestible bread, and instead order in her own food from the tradespeople who supplied prisoners on remand. Mindful of every creature comfort, she ordered in fish, pork and fowl, and insisted upon her full allowance of alcohol, which every prisoner was able to claim under prison rules. She was even able to send out a written order to Messrs Farrer and Sons, newsagents of Reading, to supply her with copies of the popular paper, the *Weekly Dispatch*.

Sunday

My Dear Granny

I want on Monday some clean clothes. All I have here are so dirty. There are some clean that Mrs Clark washed. Pair of stockings in Nellie's box, all my clean collars and brooch, all my clean aprons, also the last two new white ones I made; one is in the box upstairs. I can finish it out. My clean flannelette petticoat is in the brown box beside my bed. In Nellie's tin box there is a piece of new diaper; I want that and the pinafore Mrs Clark washed, you know the one Mrs Chandler gave to Harold. I also want the patchwork counterpane of my dear Willie's, and the dark blue bag with the patchwork in too, as well as the new Holland sheet I made. I left it on the machine, and the large

scissors; don't forget them. I want to cut out some pinafores of it, also that blue print I had for more bodices; I want that as well. Put all that in one parcel and put the strap round it; Willie can carry it down for you. The new work basket I bought the other day I want; you can put my cotton box in it, and there are some reels of white cotton in the under white box on the shelf. I shall want all the white cotton. There are some of my stockings that want mending, put them in as well as a card of mending cotton. See there are some pins in the cotton box and in the small basket I keep my crochet in; I think there is a small tin box I keep needles in; send it. Be sure and see there is a fine darning needle in it. Now, there are three books I want, 'Old St. Pauls,' 'East Lynne,' 'Barnaby Rudge,' 'Barnaby,' I think, is upstairs in one of the boxes. I have a thimble in my pocket. The books and cotton box can all go in the work basket. Be sure you don't forget my brooch, collars all aprons, they will last me till I take my trial; and if you bring all I tell you now you won't have another journey with it. Same time put in my dear boy's smallest photo, just as he is in the frame. Willie can have it again. I am allowed to read or sew, so bring it down as early Monday afternoon as convenient and then I shall have something to do
With love to all
A.Dyer

I find this large shawl almost too warm, could you manage the little fawn coloured one. I mean the one with the pale blue border, and you can have this one. Don't forget the print; I can do my bodices here.
Amelia Dyer

Amelia spent her time in Reading Gaol in relative comfort, surrounded by personal belongings, provided with good food and able to lose herself in the popular literature of the day. One of Amelia's favourite books, *East Lynne*, was a romping novel and a classic Victorian melodrama. Published in 1861 it was a phenomenal success, earning the author Mrs Henry Wood as much fame in her lifetime as the celebrated Charles Dickens himself. With illegitimacy and fallen women as central themes, it tells the story of the aristocratic Lady Isobel Vane and her eventual ostracism from society. The death of her only child, Little Willie, is played out in a tragic scene. According to a letter Amelia wrote to Granny Smith while in custody it was "a beautiful book. I cried my eyes out over the death of Little Willie."

# 44 The Arrest of Arthur Palmer

On the Monday following Amelia Dyer's arrest, Sergeant James and DC Anderson travelled to London to search the premises of 76 Mayo Road, Willesden. They turned up unannounced and asked Arthur Palmer if he had any objection to them looking through his rooms. "None whatsoever" was the reply. The two officers found an unusual amount of infant clothing (far more than would have been necessary for the Palmers' adopted child Harold) and a large number of pawn tickets relating to infant clothing from pawn shops all over London and as far away as Cardiff. Arthur Palmer told the police that all the clothing had been given to his wife Polly by his mother-in-law. Polly confirmed that the brown plush cloak that Harold was wearing had been brought to the house by Mother only the other day.

※

The police had found a letter at Kensington Road addressed to a "Mrs Stansfield". After making further enquiries it was discovered that "Mrs Stansfield" had, a couple of months earlier, been to a house in Coningham Road, Shepherd's Bush, to collect a baby. A man fitting Arthur's description had been seen waiting for her outside the house. When questioned on this matter Arthur denied all knowledge:

> No. I will not go so far as to say that I did not call at Coningham Road but I can't remember it. I know there is a road of that name in Shepherds Bush, because I have a customer there.

He was shown the letter from "Mrs Stansfield" and asked if the handwriting was that of Amelia Dyer.

"Yes, but I know nothing at all about it," he replied. "My wife's mother has not brought any children with her here on any occasion."

Sergeant James and DC Anderson strongly suspected that Arthur Palmer was lying. The baby apparel and pawn tickets all seemed to suggest the Palmers' complicit involvement in Mother's baby business, and the Shepherd's Bush baby was now missing, after having clearly been passed into the care of "Mrs Stansfield", alias Amelia Dyer.

The elegant houses on Coningham Road provided a sharp contrast to the lowly terraced establishments of Mayo Road. They were five-storey affairs with basements below street level and elegant stone steps leading to smart front doors with well-polished brasses. Arthur Palmer could well have had customers here among the well-to-do barristers, high-class tailors and independent businessmen who resided in these properties with their wives and families, cooks and housemaids. Mrs Martha Smith lived at number 7 and had been closely involved in arranging the adoption of a female child belonging to a Miss Brown. The exact nature of her relationship with Miss Brown is unclear; perhaps Mrs Smith had simply been helping a servant girl in trouble; or perhaps, as is more likely, she was running a discreet house of confinement.

Sergeant James and DC Anderson escorted the Palmers to the house in Shepherd's Bush where they met Martha Smith. She immediately recognized Palmer as the gentleman she had noticed walking up and down in front of her house on the afternoon of Saturday 27 January while a Mrs Stansfield was in the house "fetching Miss Brown's baby away".

"When I let Mrs Stansfield out of the front door, you came up the steps and took the baby's feeding bottle and put it in your pocket. Mrs Stansfield said, 'This is my nephew and he is going away abroad soon.' Then you both walked away in the direction of Uxbridge railway station together."

Arthur Palmer could only reply, "Very good if you say so; I suppose it's true."

He was then arrested on suspicion of being concerned with Amelia Dyer and of causing the death of a child sometime between 25 January and 30 March 1896.

"Very good; I know I am innocent of it."

Two days later the police returned to Mayo Road to find Polly

Palmer in the process of packing a cradle with baby clothes. They took away with them many items which were later to be identified by grieving mothers.

# 45 Bodies and Bricks

With one tiny body having already been recovered from the Thames and with an astonishing number of infants still to be accounted for, the police lost no time in overseeing the dragging of the wandering stretch of river which ran from the Clappers footbridge to the mouth of the River Kennet.

A number of local labourers were employed in this most gruesome of tasks. Henry Smithwaite was one such, and at around five thirty on the evening of Wednesday 8 April he brought up on the end of his hooks a parcel of what looked like linen rags. As the bundle broke through the surface of the water it split open and Smithwaite watched aghast as first a brick and then what looked like the shrivelled head of a tiny infant fell from inside the wrappings. The brick immediately sank from view, but the head, caught up in the current of the river, floated obscenely upon the surface before being whisked away and lost over the frothing waters of the weir.

The remains of the parcel were eventually recovered from the river and sent to the mortuary to be examined by Dr Maurice. The parcel consisted of a white linen wrapper tied together with cord. Wrapped up inside was the badly decomposed body of a male infant only a few weeks old. The infant was dressed in a chemise with a flannel band swathing its middle and two napkins fastened by a safety pin. Around the remains of his neck was a length of white tape, tied tight and buried deep in the flesh. As the body was in such an advanced state of decomposition, it was impossible for Dr Maurice to ascertain whether the child had been already dead when consigned to the depths of its cold grave. The jury at the inquest returned a verdict of "Found dead in the River Thames".

*Friday 10 April 1896*

The dragging operations continued. The unusual amount of activity on the river attracted the attentions of many curious passers-by who dallied by the towpath and voiced their theories in hushed and melodramatic whispers. By now rumours had spread and gossip was rife and the people of Reading were hearing, with horror, stories of missing children and of a woman being held at Reading Gaol who had used the river as a dumping ground for the murdered bodies of scores of innocent young victims.

Dragging for bodies near Caversham weir, *Weekly Dispatch*, 19 April 1896

At midday, a third body was hauled from the cold clutches of the water, wrapped in old sacking and tied up with thick cord. There was a brick in the parcel, tied tight to the chest of the nine-month-old baby boy curled up inside. There were two pieces of tape bound tightly around his neck and in his mouth was crammed a pocket handkerchief. What was left of the infant had been wrapped in an old white woollen shawl and a piece of twilled sheeting with patches on it. The baby looked as if it had been a fine one, with a crown of soft brown hair and enough teeth to enable Dr Maurice to establish its age.

The jury at the inquest held the next day was to return a verdict of "Found dead in the River Thames the presumable cause of death being suffocation".

At about twenty to five in the afternoon, the team of draggers were to make their second macabre discovery of the day. Halfway across the Clappers footbridge at Caversham, on the left-hand side, a battered carpet bag with brown leather handles was caught on a hook and drawn up from the waters. It was tied around with string with about three inches left gaping open at the top and a piece of brown paper laid over the contents. Sergeant James, who had been superintending the dragging of this particular stretch of the river, cut the string from around the bag and prepared himself to examine inside. Although fairly certain of what he would find, he cannot have expected the pitiful reality of the sight that met his eyes. Wedged tightly into the bag, face down and one on top of the other, were the stiffened little bodies of two infants, one male, one female. There were also two bricks, a whole one and a broken one, both blackened by soot.

Up to Saturday five bodies have been taken from the Thames, all having met their death in a similar manner by strangulation with a piece of tape, the bodies then being placed in a parcel with a brick in it and deposited in the Thames. It is said that some thirty or forty infants were found drowned in the Thames within the London district last year, and that the bodies had been in the water six days or more, so that they must have been placed in the river some distance from London. Some of our London contemporaries hint at a gang of baby farmers, and that the Reading horrors are only a part of the doings of members of the gang.

*Berkshire Chronicle*, Saturday 18 April 1896

*Saturday 11 April 1896*

Saturday 11 April dawned warm and balmy. The bitterly cold days of late March had at last rolled away and spring had well and truly arrived. It was a day for throwing open windows and hanging stale bedding over sills to air; a day for pegging starched and dripping sheets out to dry and beating the dirt and dust from stuffy carpets. The residents of Reading would have hurried with their chores in order to join the throngs of people already gathered in the centre of Reading.

At an early hour the roads surrounding the courthouse were dense with onlookers, all anxious to catch a glimpse of the two prisoners due to appear before the magistrates. When a cab being driven at a brisk speed pulled up outside, its horses agitated by the noise and press of bodies, women, children, tradesmen and clerks all rushed forward, making it almost impossible for the occupants to step down. The crowd held its collective breath as a uniformed prison warder emerged from the dim interior of the cab, followed by a handcuffed Arthur Ernest Palmer. The prisoner affected an appearance of lofty indifference as he was escorted down the cemented walkway into the entrance of the courthouse, the jeers of men and the screeches of angry women following at his heels. Dressed in silk top hat and long frock coat, he did not flinch at the indignation of the crowds.

The crowd mobbing Mrs Dyer, *Weekly Dispatch*, 3 May 1896

Before long another cab appeared in the distance being pursued by a mob of swift-footed boys. As it pulled up outside the courthouse the noise of the crowds abated to a murmur as the substantial figure of Amelia Dyer stepped heavily out on to the pavement. Accompanied by a female warder, she stumbled slowly and hesitantly down the walkway toward the doors of the courthouse, whereupon the crowds remembered their outrage and gave voice to it vociferously as she disappeared from view.

Arthur Palmer was the first to be ushered into the dock in the prickling silence of the courtroom. Carrying his silk hat under his arm, he looked the image of respectability, with perfectly trimmed whiskers and a dapper black and white checked tie contrasting with his colourless complexion. He stood poised and calm, watching for the doors to open and for his mother-in-law to enter the room. She appeared with a constable supporting her by the elbow and proceeded to walk with painfully slow steps toward her seat in the dock. Her face was devoid of emotion; her mouth set in grim determination. As she spotted Arthur standing waiting, she was heard to mutter to a court official, "What's Arthur here for? He's done nothing."

Standing before the magistrates, Amelia Elizabeth Dyer was charged with "having on or about March 20th in the Parish of St Mary, Reading, feloniously killed and murdered a female child unknown". Arthur Ernest Palmer was charged with being an "accessory after the fact that he on March 30th did knowingly conceal the murder of a female child name unknown with intent to enable Dyer to elude the pursuit of justice".

As the identity of the first body found was still in question, and as certain other matters had since come to the knowledge of the police, not least the discovery of more murdered infants, it was recommended that the case be adjourned to the following week.

❧❧

Certain letters found in Kensington Road had led the police to contact Evelina Marmon, the barmaid from Cheltenham, and Amelia Sargeant, the married woman from Ealing, and on the morning of Saturday 11 April both women were brought from their homes to Reading.

Evelina had been informed by the police that she had placed her child in the custody of a woman who "could not be depended upon to properly act by it"; she left Cheltenham fully expecting to be able to bring her daughter home.

Instead she was escorted to a collection of grim buildings situated on Lock Island in Reading. Surrounded by the grey waters of the River Kennet, Lock Island was home to the Reading Corporation Isolation Hospital, and the mortuary. The cold stone room with bare brick walls and a sour smell contained the bodies of two dead babies lying on slabs with rough woollen blankets pulled up to their chins and with their heads resting on sheets of brown paper.

Evelina Marmon could not contain her grief upon recognizing one of the babies as her own Doris. It had been a mere eleven days since Evelina had given her child up into the care of a Mrs Harding. She did not at first understand the full implications of the horror that had taken place, exclaiming through her tears, "She was in perfect health when I sent her away."

Amelia Sargeant was equally distressed upon recognizing the body of the second child as that of Harry Simmons, a child she had last seen only ten days earlier when she, too, had given him up into the care of a woman called Mrs Harding.

⁂

Until the mid-nineteenth century it was a requirement for Coroners' Inquests not only to be held in public, but specifically in public houses. Southampton Street, Reading, was home to a number of such inns. Set a short distance away from the main hub of the town, the tall spire of St Giles Church towered over the street's assorted buildings, casting its long shadow over the roofs of Lord Clyde's Beerhouse, the Little Crown Inn, and the Reindeer Inn with its advertisement for Hewett & Sons' ales and stouts set solidly above dusty wooden doors. Across the street from the Reindeer Inn was a neat, well-maintained building with a polished glass-panelled frontage, bearing the name "St. Giles Coffee House". Although it did on occasion provide its customers with steaming jugs of bitter coffee, it was in every respect an ordinary ale house.

On the evening of Saturday 11 April, within the cramped but comfortable confines of this particular public house, Mr William Weedon, local solicitor and acting coroner, held the inquests on the bodies of Doris Marmon and Harry Simmons.

Mrs Amelia Sargeant was the first witness called to give evidence.

She was dressed entirely in black and was visibly distraught, having identified the body of Harry Simmons only a few hours earlier. She told the story of his short life and related the events which had led her to hand him over to a stranger at Paddington railway station. She had acted in good faith; she had been sure that "Mrs Harding" would be good to the boy.

"I have seen some of the clothing at the police station which I sent with the child. I made it all myself. I do not think the clothing has been worn since I sent it to her. My husband came with me when I handed the child to the prisoner at Paddington."

Henry Smithwaite was next to give evidence and confirmed that he had found the carpet bag containing the bodies of the two children. DC Anderson and Sergeant James told how they had conveyed the bag to the police station, where, in the presence of Dr Maurice, the two bodies were taken out and photographed.

Young Willie Thornton proved to be a first-class witness. He gave his evidence in a "very intelligent manner" and earned the commendation of the coroner, who told him he was "the best witness he had had in a long time". Willie proved that the carpet bag had belonged to him. He had brought it with him when he had come to live with Mother six months earlier. He knew the carpet bag was his by the pattern and the torn state of the inside. It was kept in a cupboard upstairs. The last time he had seen it was on the Tuesday before Good Friday. Mother had gone up to London and taken the bag with her.

Evelina Marmon confirmed that the body of the female child she had seen that morning at the mortuary was that of her daughter Doris. She was certain of the identity. She had had the baby vaccinated four days before she parted with her. She recounted how a Mrs Harding had come to Cheltenham to fetch the child. Evelina had handed over £10 and Harding had promised to provide Doris with a happy home.

"All for £10," the coroner interjected, "an easy way of getting rid of a child. I don't know how you could expect it to be done."

"I wanted to pay her so much a week, but she said she wanted the child as her own, so that I could not fetch it away at any time." Evelina sensed the coroner's reproachful tone and added defensively, "I gave her a lot of clothes."

The inquest was adjourned, pending further evidence, until the following week.

# 46 Mrs Dyer Confesses

Mother had plenty of time to ponder on the course events had taken. With Arthur now in the dock beside her, it was likely that the police would soon catch up with Polly, and she couldn't have that. As unlikely as it seems, this woman, who thought nothing of wrapping up the bodies of dead babies as though they were little more than joints of meat, had strong maternal feelings. She was determined to protect her daughter at all costs.

Miss Ellen Gibbs was one of three matrons employed at Her Majesty's Prison Reading. Nearing retirement, she was the longest serving and most experienced of all the women employed at the gaol, and as such was responsible for attending to Reading's most notorious woman prisoner. She was well used to the sounds of crying and singing and foul-mouthed obscenity which penetrated the doors of the women's cells and out on to the landings. There was nothing unusual in hearing the prisoners mutter and rant to themselves. Dyer was no different; she spent a good deal of her time singing hymns and talking aloud to herself.

Rumours had been circulating that since her incarceration Mrs Dyer had become "scarcely accountable for her actions" and Miss Gibbs was unable to leave her unattended night or day. Amelia was becoming increasingly afraid and panicky and after seeing her son-in-law in the dock she had become more anxious than usual, saying over and over again that he should be cleared, that Arthur Palmer should be set at liberty.

It is tempting to assume that Amelia was beginning to experience the effects of laudanum withdrawal, but this is unlikely as while her money lasted she would have been able to order in a supply along with her meat and newspapers. It is more likely that, after more than two decades of laudanum abuse, she was simply displaying her usual pattern of behaviour when under stress and was succumbing to another "episode".

On 16 April she did a most extraordinary thing. After requesting a pen and some notepaper she wrote two letters: one to Arthur, and one which she asked to be passed to Chief Inspector Tewsley to be presented to the magistrates at her next hearing.

"Now I have eased my mind," she said as she gave the letters to the matron.

To the Chief Superintendent of the Police
Sir, Will you kindly grant me the favour of presenting this to the magistrates on Saturday the 18th inst. I have made this statement now as I may not have an opportunity then. I must relieve my mind. I do know and feel my days are numbered on this earth, but I do feel it is an awful thing to draw innocent people into trouble. I do know I shall have to answer before my Maker in Heaven for these awful crimes I have committed, and as God Almighty is my judge in Heaven as on earth, neither my daughter, nor her husband, and I do most solemnly declare that neither of them had anything to do with it. They never knew I contemplated doing anything until it was too late. I am speaking the truth and nothing but the truth, as I hope to be forgiven. I myself, I alone shall have to stand before my Maker in Heaven to answer for it.
Witness my hand, AMELIA DYER.

It was a remarkable admission, causing Miss Gibbs to remind her charge that she was only on remand and yet had just pleaded guilty to everything.

"I wish to; they can't charge me with anything more than I have done. That's all."

My poor dear Arthur, Oh how my heart aches for you and my dear Polly. I am sending this to tell you I have eased my mind and made a full statement. I have told them the truth and nothing but the whole truth, as I hope to be forgiven. God Almighty is my judge. I dare not go into his presence with a lie. I do hope and pray God will forgive me. I had a letter from Polly. She is coming down. You will have a lawyer, but for myself it is only throwing away money. I know I have done this dreadful crime and I know that I alone have to answer for it. I have just wrote a long letter to Willie and another to father. Also I have wrote out a true and faithful statement of everything. I hope

God will give you both grace and strength to bear this awful trial. God bless you my dear boy.

Your broken hearted mother A. DYER

Let me have just one line Friday morning.

The letters were handed to the governor of the prison, Colonel H. B. Isaacson, who in turn passed them on to Chief Superintendent Tewsley. From here on, Amelia Dyer seems to have cared little about saving her own skin, and these letters were only the first of her efforts to exculpate her daughter and son-in-law.

# 47 A Murderess Identified

The unseasonably warm weather in Reading continued through to the following week; the sun beat down on to a town now entirely caught up in the horror unfolding within its midst. The hordes of sensation seekers who traipsed the length of Kensington Road to stare with delicious expectation through the windows of number 45 were delighted to find Granny Smith sitting outside basking in the heat. An extra shiver of pleasure ran down their backs when they spotted the baby nestled comfortably against the old lady's bosom; a baby who had undoubtedly escaped the dire consequences of Mother's special care.

> Publicity given to the case has caused many anxious enquiries to be made to the Reading police by persons who have entrusted children to Mrs Dyers care. Four women who had given her children and premiums have been to the Borough to claim the children. They could not, however, be found, but pieces of clothing found in a box in Dyers house have been recognised as parts of the outfits of these children.
>
> *Reading Observer*, Friday 17 April 1896

Across town, in the backyard of the police station, Mother was placed in a line along with four other women and made to stand in the uncomfortable glare of the morning sun. The heat had warmed the concrete ground and the little yard had become still, hot and airless.

Evelina Marmon was first to be led from the relative coolness of the police station to stand in front of the line of five middle-aged women. Upon seeing Mrs Dyer standing blinking in the harsh light, she immediately burst into tears and exclaimed, "That is the dreadful woman to whom I handed Doris."

Amelia Sargeant was carrying an umbrella to protect her from the sun. She too recognized Mrs Dyer and pointing toward her with her umbrella said in a broken voice, "That's the vile creature who had the little fellow."

Both Evelina Marmon and Amelia Sargeant were much affected by coming face-to-face with the woman in whom they had placed so much trust, but their positive identification provided the police with a much needed link in their growing case against the "Reading Baby Farmer".

⚏

Although the weather outside was more like summer than spring, a tremendous fire was blazing in the huge grate of the courtroom as Amelia Dyer and Arthur Palmer stood for the second time in front of the magistrates. When Sergeant James walked into the courtroom, his arms full of brown paper parcels containing the redeemed clothing of a dozen or more infants, many of the women present were moved to tears.

The "formidable" carpet bag with its brown leather handles and somewhat ragged bottom was placed in close proximity to the witness box and a collective shudder passed through the courtroom as Sergeant James withdrew two bricks and a quantity of white tape from its interior. Amelia Dyer stared at the floor as she was charged with the murders of Helena Fry, Doris Marmon and Harry Simmons. Arthur Palmer nonchalantly stroked his whiskers as he was charged with being an accessory after the fact.

As the circumstances of the case were so grave, it was proposed that the prisoners should be remanded in custody for a further week in order that information received in recent days could be "sifted and tested". The nature of the evidence in relation to the case of Doris Marmon was outlined and the prisoners were removed from the courtroom.

# 48 An Interview with Palmer

Before being taken back to his cell, Arthur Palmer requested permission to speak to a representative of the *Weekly Dispatch*. It was an unusual occurrence but his request was granted and the interview took place in an empty cell in the presence of Chief Inspector Tewsley and DC Anderson. Arthur Palmer's sole objective in speaking to the press was to protest his innocence; and this he did most vehemently.

I want you to correct all the wicked things the papers have said about me. It is true I am the husband of Mrs Dyer's daughter, and it is true that I have lived with her, but at the same time I know nothing about her business. There has never been a single child that I knew anything about. She did come to my house with Doris, but beyond seeing it I know nothing about it.

I swear I know nothing. I do know that occasionally she had money, that she had a lot of money, but before God I can swear that I never knew how she got it or when she got it.

I know that she did have Miss Marmon's baby, but when she came to my house she told my wife that she had got a baby, but she did not intend to keep it. She had got someone to take it, and turning to my wife she said, "I don't want fifteen shillings a week; it's no good to me, they won't pay." And then the police say they have found "lots" of clothing ... but what do I know about the clothing? If she says I have had one penny of her money – if she says I helped her – she is a liar, and I can prove it.

Don't let them think that I am so wicked. I'm only a man, and I can say before my Maker that until I got home that night I knew no more than you did about the baby. My wife told me that Mother was going to take it to a home, that she knew a dear, good, old soul that wanted it. Me – a murderer. Me – knowing anything about the matter, why it's rubbish; she knows it.

I tell you sir; I know nothing about the babies. I never touched a penny of the money, and if I have the rope round my neck tomorrow, I am innocent.

At this, Mrs Dyer, who was housed in a cell close by, was heard to shout, "That's right!" The interview was halted and the Special Crime Investigator from the *Weekly Dispatch* was asked to leave.

# 49 Further Developments at Reading

Chief Superintendent Tewsley was convinced there were still the remains of a number of children lying strewn about the bed of the river, so Henry Smithwaite and a number of other labourers continued to drag the Thames. Every day, from dawn to dusk, the men dropped their hooks into the swirling waters and closely inspected every scrap of paper, canvas and linen caught up by the large metal claws. Large crowds of ghoulish onlookers gathered every day along the banks of the river, their numbers swelling to many thousands when the dinner bell of the Huntley & Palmers biscuit factory sounded and the workers were released for an hour from the heat of the steaming ovens and the monotony of the packing department.

On the afternoon of Thursday 23 April, only two or three yards from where the carpet bag had been found, the draggers' hooks lifted another parcel to the surface. DC Anderson was close by at the time and took charge of the package which was wrapped in a piece of canvas and tied tightly with a length of clothes line. A brick had been attached to the clothes line but had been dislodged by the hooks and had dropped back into the water. When the clothes line was untied and the canvas pulled open the body of an infant, in a worse state of decomposition than any of the other bodies so far recovered, was revealed.

Dr Maurice was able to ascertain that it was a female child of around twelve months old. She had light brown hair and was dressed in a napkin, a red flannel gown and a long white nightdress. The initials J.D. or J.G. – it was hard to discern exactly what the letters were – were embroidered on a corner of the gown, heartbreaking evidence of a mother's attention to a child who was now beyond

Amelia Dyer in the dock

identification. A piece of black mackintosh had been wrapped around the body before it had been parcelled up in canvas. Around the child's neck was the now familiar piece of tightly tied white tape, and a pocket handkerchief had been thrust into her mouth. The body had been in the water for some four to six months and was in such bad condition that Dr Maurice was unable to state the precise cause of death; but his opinion was that the child had been strangled before being placed in the water.

*Saturday 25 April 1896*

Amelia Dyer's and Arthur Palmer's third appearance in front of the magistrates saw the courtroom overflowing with representatives of the press, legal luminaries, witnesses and a few privileged members of the public who had been granted admittance. There were artists from the illustrated newspapers busily sketching in their pads, telegraph messengers and young boys acting as runners for the local news-papers.

All eyes turned to the doors leading to the cells as Arthur Palmer was escorted in to take his place in the dock. He sat with one arm leaning casually on the darkly varnished woodwork, his true feelings only discernible by the paleness of his already wan complexion.

Apart from looking more haggard than usual, Amelia Dyer appeared unchanged and kept her eyes directed, as usual, toward the floor.

Mrs Mary Ann Beattie was the first witness to be called. She told of how, on the evening of 31 March, she had helped to carry a carpet bag belonging to a woman she had met coming off an omnibus near to Mayo Road in Willesden. The woman had been carrying a young baby and had entered number 76 Mayo Road after being greeted at the door by a young woman. Mrs Beattie identified Amelia Dyer as the woman she had seen carrying the baby and the carpet bag.

Mrs Charlotte Culham, landlady of 76 Mayo Road, then gave evidence that she had seen Amelia Dyer at her house with the Palmers on the morning of 1 April and at noon on 2 April. She had seen no babies, but had noticed the carpet bag lying empty on the floor of the Palmers' room. Her husband Charles was able to identify the two bricks found in the carpet bag alongside the bodies of Doris Marmon and Harry Simmons as having come from Mayo Road. He had recently moved a fire grate in the kitchen and the loose bricks, many of which bore scorch marks, had been stored under a rabbit hutch in his backyard.

John Toller, an engineer at Reading Gaol, told how, on the way home from the theatre on the evening of 2 April, he had passed a woman he could now identify as Mrs Dyer, walking away from the direction of the river and the Clappers footbridge.

Granny Smith was able to confirm that Mother had arrived home in a queer mood late that same evening without the infamous carpet bag.

As the police still had evidence forthcoming and other witnesses to call, the case was remanded for the third time and the prisoners were taken back into custody.

*Monday 27 April 1896*

The Reading Borough Police Station was the venue for the final inquests into the deaths of the first baby found in the Thames on

30 March and Doris Marmon and Harry Simmons, found dead in a carpet bag in the Thames on 10 April.

Although the police had been unable to prove conclusively the parentage of the first child (as the coroner remarked, "It is not everyone who will come forward on such occasions as this"), they had evidence from Granny Smith to prove that the brick found in the parcel had been one she had used to rest her flat iron on. It was distinguishable by the line of mortar on one side which prevented it from standing level. Granny also identified the clothes on the body as having at one time belonged to a child named "little Ikey" who had lived with them at Caversham for a while before Mother took it away, and she also remembered Mother bringing home a parcel one evening some time before her arrest. It had been a strangely shaped parcel, about two feet long by one foot wide. The parcel had disappeared by the next morning, and a foul smell had begun to seep from the cupboard in the kitchen. The smell had abated on the morning of 30 March when Mother had left the house with a parcel to take to the pawn shop.

On this same day Mother had been seen walking by the river by a local man named William Povey. She had been acting very strangely, he said, and had been carrying a brown paper parcel under her arm. DC Anderson gave evidence that he had found some macramé string in a tin box in Mrs Dyer's bedroom which was identical to that which had been wrapped around the parcel found in the river. He also provided evidence of finding a quantity of white tape in the house, identical to the tape that had been used to strangle the baby girl.

Unable to prove conclusively that Amelia Dyer had strangled the child, the jury returned a verdict of "Wilful murder against some person or persons unknown" but added a rider that Annie Dyer, alias Thomas alias Harding, disposed of the body afterward.

Evelina Marmon and Amelia Sargeant were called upon to state that they had now identified Mrs Dyer as the woman they had handed their children to, having picked her out among four other women. They were also able to identify certain articles of clothing; Mrs Sargeant recognizing a brown plush cloak as the one Harry had been wearing when she passed him into the care of Mrs Dyer. Mr Weedon, the coroner, asked what reason there could be for Mrs Dyer to adopt children in this way for £10 unless it was purely for gain: "From her surroundings there is no reason why she should adopt children in the sense we meant by adoption. She is a woman of considerable age and rather badly off, for they sometimes sleep on the floor." There was, he said, "ample evidence to arrive at a conclusion. We are not required to go so minutely into the case as is necessary before the magistrates. There is a little difficulty as to where the children were murdered, but that we must leave for others to settle."

It took the jury of twelve men only a matter of minutes to return verdicts of "Wilful murder" against Mrs Dyer in the cases of both Doris Marmon and Harry Simmons.

# 50 Trial by Newspaper

The letter of confession which Amelia Dyer had written to Chief Superintendent Tewsley had been kept secret so as not to prejudice her case; the letter written to Arthur had also not reached its intended destination.

Amelia was not happy.

Allowed to order in the newspapers and read all that was being written about her case, she was dismayed to find no mention of her letter and no mention either that Polly and Arthur were now free from all blame. In her letter written to Arthur on 16 April from Reading Gaol, Amelia had reassured him that he would have a lawyer, but for her she had said, "It is only throwing money away." It seems she must have had a change of heart for on 23 April she wrote another letter, this time addressed to her solicitor with whom she had been communicating with regard to a possible defence plea. On 24 April the solicitor's managing clerk and a shorthand writer met Amelia in her cell. She handed over to them some confidential notes she had been making about her case, and among the papers was her second letter of confession.

This one was made public, appearing on the front page of the *Daily Courier* on Tuesday 28 April. It caused a public sensation.

From Amelia Dyer,
H.M. Prison Reading
April 23, 1896

Sir,
In reply to Telegram in reference to plead in my defence, I must tell you I am afraid there is not any chance of saving my life, unless you plead upon the cause of insanity, and if you do that I may be spared, during her Majesty's Pleasure. My reason for saying this is a very good

one. 6 years ago I was an inmate of Gloucester Asylum 2 years after that I was sent to Wells Asylum I got better since then I was sent up to Gloucester Asylum I had not my only discharge out a month on trial I was only home 2 weeks when I had to be taken back again. Finally I had my discharge a twelve month last February all the time I have been here I have not been well, I have not been accountable for my actions they have not left me unattended night or day one moment. 2 years ago now this time I tried to drown myself but I was rescued and taken to the General Hospital at Bristol and my mother died at Dr. Fox Asylum at the early age of 45 years.

One day last week I sent a written statement to the Chief Superintendent of the police stating my Son-in-Law had nothing at all to do in the matter that I alone was guilty. Now I look back the most insane part of it is I had invited all the Friends of those Children to come and spend Whitsuntide Holiday with me and they accepted the invitation and was coming. Mrs Dean the attendant who have charge of me or any or all of the officials here will tell you my mind have been quite unhinged. In fact I have been bad in my head all the time. Some days not so bad as others I do know this I should certainly kill myself if only had the opportunity but I must tell you honest and truthfully my daughter Mary Ann Palmer or her Husband Arthur Palmer they never knew but that I meant to do right by those Children they never knew contemplated doing what I did.

The Home Office was horrified that such a letter had been made public, and an inquiry was launched to investigate the breach in procedures at Reading Gaol. The prison authorities were to place the blame on Amelia's solicitors, remarking, "She handed over to them some confidential notes she had been making about her case ... Probably this was the news printed in the *Daily Courier*." Whatever the truth of the matter, not only had Amelia Dyer succeeded in placing in the public consciousness the possibility that her son-in-law was innocent, and so too her daughter, she had also managed to raise the question of her own sanity and culpability.

So much horror has been created by the discovery of the Reading baby murders that an alleged "confession" had a sensationalist interest, eagerly snapped at by the enterprising journalist. The Daily Courier today reproduces by eager permission of The Weekly Dispatch, a letter purporting to have been written by the accused woman, Mrs

Dyer, in prison and handed to a representative of the press. This letter contains a confession of guilt and a plea of insanity ... We ask in all seriousness whether prison authorities are not to be gravely blamed for allowing such letters to be communicated by prisoners to the press. Mrs Dyer is now in custody on the charge of murder. It is for the law to pronounce whether she is guilty, whether she is insane. Trial by newspaper in the *interim* is contrary to all decent precedent or principle.

*St James's Gazette*, 28 April 1896

# 51  A Body in the Reeds

Police Constable Frederic Vince lived in the village of Sonning. Part of his duties as a constable was to walk a beat which took him along the towpath from Sonning toward the Dreadnought public house. Nestled into the bank of the Thames, the Dreadnought was a popular stopping off point for many of the boatmen who worked on the river and on any given day a collection of punts, rowing boats and barges could be seen moored alongside the towpath in front of its peeling façade. PC Vince would have enjoyed his gentle stroll along the river despite feeling hot in his heavy helmet and close-fitting jacket.

Thursday 30 April was a glorious spring day, the sun filtering through the trees on to the dusty pathway. PC Vince may have been looking forward to a jug of ale upon reaching the inn, but with three-quarters of a mile to go he spotted among the reeds, about six feet from the bank, another miserable parcel with some linen protruding from its wrappings. Knowing at once what the parcel would contain, he fashioned a drag from some string and a stick and managed to bring the bundle to shore. He then made his way to the Dreadnought where, instead of a cooling jar of ale, he procured a boat and a piece of floor cloth, which he placed under the fragile parcel, before towing the boat back along the river to the police station.

The body inside the parcel was that of a baby boy of about nine or ten months. He was wrapped in a piece of white flannel and although there was no brick in the parcel there was a gaping hole through which, it was conjectured, a brick might well have fallen. The head of the boy was wrapped in pink flannel, the ends of which were twisted and formed like a rope. These were crossed at the back of the head and brought around to the front where they were tied tightly under the child's chin. A pocket handkerchief was stuffed underneath the fabric.

A Body in the Reeds

Dr Maurice found the body to be extremely decomposed, having been in the water between three and four months. There was nothing left by which the body could be identified. He was of the opinion that the flannel, being tied in such a way, would have been sufficient to cause death by strangulation, although there was not enough evidence to say positively. The jury at the inquest had no choice but to return a verdict of "Found drowned".

From information in the possession of the police, they are confident that the body was thrown into the water not far from the "Dreadnought," and the landlord of the "Dreadnought" has stated that he saw a man with a parcel near the towing-path about the time the child is said to have been drowned. It was in order to find this child that the dragging operations were carried on near the "Dreadnought" last week. It is stated that the child was one which Mrs Dyer received at Caversham and whose whereabouts could not be traced.

*Berkshire Chronicle*, Saturday 2 May 1896

# 52  Polly and the Actress

Since the arrest of her husband, Polly Palmer had been kept under constant supervision by the Reading police and officers from Scotland Yard, both parties anxious to discover all they could about the movements of Mother and Arthur Palmer. She was called on in particular to give a detailed account of the circumstances surrounding the murder of Doris Marmon and Harry Simmons in the sitting room of her house at Willesden, and the packing of the bodies in Willie Thornton's carpet bag.

During questioning she unwittingly revealed details of her own involvement in what was clearly the family business, and this prompted the policemen to place her under house arrest.

—※—

The adjourned inquest into the death of the sixth baby found dead in the Thames was due to take place at the Reading Borough Police Court on the afternoon of Friday 1 May and Polly was to be called as a witness.

When the time came for her to travel to Reading under police escort, her adopted son Harold had to be left in Willesden, possibly under the temporary care of her landlady, Charlotte Culham. He had been with Polly for less than six months and his health was deteriorating rapidly.

The police and the public at the time were never to learn what became of young Harold Palmer; his fate was no concern of theirs. Indeed, they were never aware that his young life had ever been in danger. But a death certificate written out in July 1896 reveals a sinister and tragic truth.

Not long after Polly was taken to Reading, Harold Palmer was passed over into the care of Mr C. W. Wright, the master of Hendon

Union Workhouse. He was already seriously ill and on 11 July, aged just two years, he died of a condition known as *stomatitis*, or *cancrum oris*. The gums and linings of his cheeks would have been severely inflamed and ulcerated, the infection spreading until his lips and cheeks were slowly eaten away by the gangrenous disease. The most common cause of *cancrum oris* is severe malnutrition and very low levels of hygiene. Polly, it seems, had perfected the art of slow starvation and neglect.

⟩⟨

At the Reading Borough Police Court all eyes were on Polly as she entered the room in the company of a Scotland Yard detective.

Miss Elizabeth Goulding, a rather shabbily dressed thirty-year-old spinster, had contacted the police after reading about the Reading baby murders in her local paper. In November 1894, she had given birth to an illegitimate child, a little girl she had named Frances Jessie. The father was a married man whose wife insisted that the baby be adopted out to save them all from shame and gossip. Elizabeth Goulding had little choice in the matter, being unable to support the child herself. The following September, when Frances Jessie was almost ten months old, a woman had been contacted through an advertisement in a newspaper and it was arranged that Elizabeth should meet her at a solicitor's office to hand over her daughter.

Elizabeth Goulding was able to identify Polly Palmer as the woman she had handed her child to on 9 September 1895, along with the sum of £10. She had later received a number of letters from Mrs Palmer describing the progress of her daughter, but since just before Christmas last she had heard nothing and her own letters of enquiry had been returned to her marked "Gone away". The body in the mortuary could have been her Jessie; her facial features had rotted away but the little scrap of hair looked familiar. Frances Jessie's hair had been a similar colour, although maybe not quite as dark.

Polly seemed calm as she stood in front of the coroner and the jury of twelve men. Dressed in a stylish outfit with her hair neatly arranged beneath her bonnet, her manner and composure set her apart from the distressed and dishevelled woman who had just given evidence.

She agreed that she had indeed adopted the child Frances Jessie Goulding, but she had not meant to have the child herself. She explained that she had been authorized by Mother to get a baby for a young actress called Miss Robb who lived in Birmingham. Miss Robb had had her own illegitimate child and was receiving an annuity from the father. When this child died she wanted to replace it with another so she would continue to get the money.

"I took the child the next day and handed it to Miss Robb."

"How came you to write to Miss Goulding and describe the progress of the child?" the coroner asked.

"Because Miss Robb wrote to Mrs Dyer that the child was getting on well and I told her what Miss Robb had told me about the child."

"How is it you say that you and your husband were both very fond of it? You could not hear that from a letter from Miss Robb."

Polly did not reply.

"Cannot you account for that?"

"Miss Goulding was loath to part with the child and seemed fidgety. I thought if I said that she would be more satisfied."

Polly claimed that Miss Robb had been confined to Mother's house in Fishponds for three months before giving birth to her baby. She was sure she would be able to produce the child if she could find Miss Robb. But she did not know her by any other name, or what theatre she worked in.

Granny Smith, who was fast becoming a fixture on the witness stand, ended the inquest by stating that Polly had not been correct in saying that she had brought a child home one night and then taken it the next day to Birmingham. Granny Smith could not recall the child being brought back to Elm Villas at all.

The coroner reminded the jury that if they thought Mrs Dyer had murdered this child and that Mrs Palmer was an accessory before the fact, they must be satisfied that she was an accessory not only to bringing the child to Reading, but that she was an accessory to the death of the child. It was clear Mrs Palmer brought a child to Reading, but there was a doubt whether this was the child for which they were holding the inquest. No doubt the child had been murdered. It was for the jury to say whether Mrs Palmer had told untruths. She had certainly given her answers with hesitation and some of them seemed insufficient.

The jury did not take long to reach a verdict of "Wilful murder" against Mrs Dyer with Mrs Palmer being an accessory before the fact.

Superintendent Tewsley immediately placed Polly under arrest and she was led from the police station into a waiting cab and taken to prison. For most of the way a large crowd of people followed behind, anxious to see the daughter of the "Reading Baby Farmer". More and more people joined the throng as the horses pulled their passengers through the streets of Reading. The angry mob continued to yell out their anger and hatred long after the black cab disappeared through the prison gates.

# 53 A Damning Testimony

Amelia Dyer was distraught to discover that, despite all her best efforts, her daughter Polly had been committed to prison on the coroner's warrant. She was desperate to be allowed contact, but the prison authorities refused her requests; the next time she would see her daughter would be in the dock.

The final episode of "The Reading Horrors" to be played out in the Magistrate's Court drew as large a crowd as on previous occasions, the object of interest this time being the rumoured appearance of the murderess's daughter. Mother, looking forward to seeing Polly, had made an effort with her appearance and added to her usual dark cloak and bonnet was a large fur boa and brown kid gloves. The fur had the effect of softening her features and she looked every inch an ordinary and homely mother. Superintendent Tewsley escorted her to the ante-room at the back of the dock and she looked around expecting to see Polly.

"Where is she – isn't she here? Has she gone already?"

When Tewsley informed her that Polly was still in Reading Gaol awaiting permission from the Home Office to be released to give evidence that day, Amelia was heard to mutter darkly, "If you had told them what I had written you, they never would have touched her."

Since Amelia's last appearance in front of the magistrates, her solicitors, Messrs Lindus and Bicknell of Cheapside, London, had instructed Mr Raymond Linford and Mr Ardeshir Kapadia as her barristers. Mr Kapadia was the only son of a wealthy tea merchant from Shanghai and had conducted many important cases. He had medical and legal degrees so was qualified to practise as either a doctor or a barrister. Mr A. T. Lawrence appeared for the Treasury to prosecute.

The first surprise of the day came as Mr Lawrence rose to address the court and stated that, after considering the case of Arthur Palmer, he had come to the conclusion that the evidence was not sufficient to justify him asking for the committal of Palmer upon the charge by which he was arrested. To the bewilderment of the press and spectators, and to the obvious relief of the defendant, Arthur was discharged and ordered to leave the dock.

His triumph did not last long. As he walked out of the courtroom with his head held high and his hat in his hand, he was immediately arrested by Chief Superintendent Tewsley on another charge.

Two days later, at the courts in Devonport, Arthur Palmer was found guilty of abandoning a four-year-old girl named Queenie Baker in the streets of that town in May 1895. He was sentenced to three months' imprisonment with hard labour.

-=⊟⊡=-

Amelia Dyer had removed her fur boa with a flourish and was sitting at her place in the dock with her eyes downcast; only a slight twitching of her mouth and some nervous movements of her hands betrayed her true demeanour. Her behaviour of late had become erratic, punctuated by periods of depression and bouts of anxiety as she worried over what was to become of "poor Polly". As a consequence the police had removed from the courtroom anything that Amelia might have used to harm herself, including the iron spikes which guarded the central bar.

The court was informed that Mr Lawrence proposed to call some additional evidence in the cases of Doris Marmon and Harry Simmons and was hoping to produce Mrs Mary Ann Palmer as a witness.

The publication of Dyer's confession in the national press (in which she had exonerated her daughter and son-in-law of all blame and hinted at her own insanity) had created an unprecedented public furore. Until now, the court had avoided addressing the question of Dyer's admission of guilt for fear of prejudicing the case, but because of the excessive press coverage the magistrate clearly felt this issue could no longer be ignored. The prosecution wanted to submit as evidence Mrs Dyer's letters of confession that she had first written to Chief Superintendent Tewsley and Arthur Palmer. Mr Kapadia objected, arguing that he had "no doubt the magistrates would commit her to take her trial for the present charge", and adding, "it seems to me that it would be like bringing down a hammer to crush a fly to have the letters read in court".

His objections were overruled and the court fell silent as the clerk read out the passages in which the accused woman admitted her guilt. For the first time Amelia Dyer reacted, burying her face in her hands and breaking into a flood of tears. Miss Gibbs, the prison matron, was called to give evidence that Mrs Dyer had written the letters of her own volition and had been of sound mind when she had done so. The court was then adjourned to await the expected attendance of Mrs Palmer.

At twenty to two the cry of "Call Mrs Palmer" echoed around the courtroom and caused a great shuffling and stirring of bodies. The doors leading to the cells were thrown open and Polly appeared dressed in a smart, light grey coat and a black satin bonnet. The appearance of her daughter induced Amelia to burst into a fresh flood of tears.

If Mother was intent on saving her daughter from the gallows, the same degree of loyalty did not extend from Polly. Her testimony was riddled with misinformation and half-truths as she did her best to absolve herself from any blame. Polly's impact on Mother's case was devastating, as she told

Polly Palmer, *Weekly Dispatch*, 3 May 1896

her version of the events leading up to the murder of the carpet bag babies, Doris Marmon and Harry Simmons.

On the evening of 31 March 1896, she said, Mother had arrived at Mayo Road carrying a baby in her arms. Polly claimed that Mother did not come into the house immediately, telling Polly that she was holding the baby for a Mrs Harris, who was just at the grocer's shop at the end of the road and would be following shortly to take the baby. Polly said that she left Mother on the doorstep and went back into the house to fill the coal scuttle, put the kettle on and wash her hands. Ten minutes later she went into the sitting room and found Mother with her back to the door putting a carpet bag under the couch.

Mrs Beattie, who had helped Mother off the omnibus at Mayo Road, had already testified that she had seen Amelia Dyer and Polly Palmer walk into the house together and shut the door behind them. If Beattie's evidence was correct, Polly was lying. Furthermore, Polly must have known what happened to Doris Marmon.

Polly said Mother had brought a box with her, inside which was a quantity of infants' clothing. She said Mother had told her she had made them for Harold. One of the items was a fawn-coloured pelisse.

At this point the court was reminded that Evelina Marmon had already identified the fawn-coloured pelisse as the one she had sent to Mrs Dyer. Mrs Sargeant had also testified that she had seen Polly's child, Harold, wearing the pelisse the next day when she met her and Mrs Dyer at Paddington Station to hand over Harry Simmons.

Polly said she had seen nothing more of the baby Mother had brought to the house.

The next day Polly had accompanied Mother to Paddington Station where they had met Mrs Sargeant. Mother had been handed some money and the child Harry Simmons. (The brown plush cloak that Harry had been wearing at the time had been found by the police in Mayo Road and subsequently identified by Mrs Sargeant.) On the way back to Mayo Road the child had grown fretful and Polly claimed that Mother had been cross with it, calling it a "little Devil" and saying that if it carried on like that she would not "stick" it long.

They got back to Mayo Road at about two o'clock and Polly went to put Harold to bed at about six o'clock. As she left the room she heard Mother remark, "Don't be many minutes", or "Don't come in for a few minutes". When Polly returned to the sitting room Mother was sitting on the couch and the boy was lying at the head, covered in a shawl. Mother had said the child was asleep and pushed Polly away, saying she would wake him if she came any nearer. When Arthur returned home he enquired after "the little nipper" and Mother would not let him look either, saying again that he would wake if anyone came near.

After supper, Mother, Polly and Arthur all went out. Mother had wanted to go to the Sporting and Military Show at Olympia but Polly had objected as it would have meant leaving the babies for too long and they would get fidgety. Instead, said Polly, they went for an evening walk and Mother insisted on locking the sitting-room door before they left.

Polly had lied again: they had all gone to Olympia after all. In fact, Mother had enjoyed it so much that she brought a programme back for Granny as a souvenir. (In the 1970s the programme was handed to the Crime Museum, now at New Scotland Yard, by the grandson of NSPCC officer Charles Bennett. Bennett had been given it by Granny Smith.)

Mother slept on the couch again that night telling Polly that she didn't mind the baby being there. But when Polly entered the sitting room at eight o'clock the next morning the little boy was gone and Mother was sitting fully dressed on the end of the couch. When she asked where the child was Mother replied, "The baby's all right, don't worry about him."

Later that morning as Polly was sweeping the sitting-room floor she noticed a parcel shoved under the couch. It was tied up in a napkin and resembled the shape of a child's head. Again she asked Mother what had become of the child and again was told, "The baby's all right."

At around dinner time, Mother asked if Arthur would get her a brick.

"No, not unless he knows what you want it for," Polly had said to her.

"All right, I can get one myself," Mother had replied. Polly saw her in the backyard with a brick in her hand which she brought into the house and put under the couch next to the carpet bag and the parcel.

Polly insisted that she saw the carpet bag and an oddly shaped parcel *under* the couch, and that she knew nothing of the two dead babies. But her landlady, Charlotte Culham, had already testified to seeing the carpet bag lying empty just inside the door to the sitting room at noon that same day. Again, Polly had lied.

Later on Mother asked Polly and Arthur to accompany her to Paddington Station to see her off on the train back to Reading. Polly went to get herself ready and when she returned to the sitting room she noticed that the parcel and the brick were gone and the carpet bag was packed. Polly had then asked Mother what the neighbours would think if they saw her coming in with a baby and going away without it. Mother had replied, "You can very well make some excuse about that."

Mother was also taking a parcel of linen away with her and asked Polly if she would carry the carpet bag. Polly refused, but offered instead to carry the parcel.

"No, I will carry it," Mother had said.

Arthur had held the carpet bag for Mother while she went into a cookshop to buy something for the journey, and he had continued to carry it until they boarded the omnibus to the station. They saw Mother into a carriage of the 9.15 express to Reading. A young lady entered the carriage after Mother, so Mother changed to an empty carriage and Polly saw her put the carpet bag under her seat.

The discrepancies in Polly's testimony were hardly questioned but everyone in the courtroom recognized the impact of her words. Polly did not look at her mother as the chairman asked the weeping Mrs Dyer to stand as he formally charged her with the murder of Doris Marmon and Harry Simmons at Willesden.

"You are committed to take your trial at the next Sessions of the Central Criminal Court in London" were the last words to echo around the courtroom that day.

※

Amelia Dyer was transported to Holloway on the 6.30 train to Paddington. As the train drew out of Reading Station the picturesque scene of the Thames and the weir at Caversham and the Clappers footbridge came into view. Mrs Dyer dissolved into tears and stared out of the window until the river disappeared from sight.

The streets surrounding Paddington Station were dotted with newspaper vendors, many of whom were holding placards loudly proclaiming "Mrs Dyer's Full Confession" and "Is She Mad?" As Mrs Dyer and her police escort left the station in a cab bound for Holloway she was heard to mutter to herself, "There you are again, it's all over London."

## ACTIVITIES OF THE LONDON POLICE

In the event of any flaw occurring in the evidence of the Reading cases, whereby Mrs Dyer should be released, the London police are said to have now seven cases fully prepared, the evidence of which would be sufficient to justify re-arrest. One of the most important cases in London is that of the body deposited in a parcel in Raynes Court, Shadwell. This is the only case known where the person depositing the body was seen. Two girls actually saw a woman place this parcel, and both of them now are prepared to go into the witness box to identify Dyer as the woman they saw. Another case is that of a child found at Paddington station some few months ago. Another case which is also connected with the prisoner is that of a child at Highbury Avenue which is almost proved by the marks on the linen which the body was wrapped in. The four other cases are those of bodies found in the Thames and each one has a chain of circumstantial evidence which would justify an arrest. It is now stated that since June last Dyer has received no fewer than 50 children, whose ages range from a few weeks old to 10 years.

*Reading Standard*, 8 May 1896

# 54 Holloway

### PROBABLE PLEA OF INSANITY

Mr Ford, managing clerk of Messrs. Lindus and Bicknell, solicitors, had an interview on Wednesday in Holloway Gaol with Mrs Dyer and found the prisoner quite broken down in health and spirits. The interview was a prolonged one and Mrs Dyer wept the whole of the time. It is understood that it has been finally decided to raise the plea of insanity on behalf of Mrs Dyer.

*Reading Standard*, Friday 8 May 1896

As her mother languished in a cell in Holloway, singing her hymns and growing increasingly morose, Polly, back in Reading Gaol, had at last realized the seriousness of her own predicament and wrote a long letter to Mother begging, "get me out of it".

In response to this appeal Mother wrote a detailed confession exonerating her daughter from all involvement in the murder of the Goulding child. She sent a copy to Polly and another to the Special Crime Investigator of the *Weekly Dispatch*. Both letters went first to the governor of Holloway, who, seeing the nature of their contents, handed them to Scotland Yard. The letters were leaked to the press and the *Weekly Dispatch* of Sunday 10 May printed the details of Dyer's admissions in all their "sickening minuteness". Mother wrote to her "Darling Polly" that she would "tell them all about the dear little children that I have put away". She told of how grieved she was when she heard that Polly was in custody and how she could not get "a wink of sleep during the whole of last Friday night". She described the murder of one of the babies and how she forced a handkerchief into the child's mouth to stifle the death cries. She could not remember how many she had put in the weir, but said, "You will know all mine by the tape around their necks."

Polly did not receive Amelia's letter and was not to know until much later how hard Mother had tried to save her.

Dr Forbes Winslow, doctor for the defence and physician to the British Hospital for Mental Disorders and Lecturer on Mental Diseases at Charing Cross Hospital, visited Amelia on two occasions while she was in Holloway and both times found her to be suffering from delusions and hallucinations. She claimed to have no memory of her crimes and complained of pains in the head, giddiness and weakness; voices were speaking to her telling her to take her own life; she was sleeping badly and dreaming of terrible things.

> My poor boy! My poor mother! I had fearful scenes last night. I fancied I handled my mother's bones, picking them out of the coffin. When my poor boy went away and enlisted I never slept for three weeks. I beat the rats off. Everything seemed to fly to my head, and I feel I want to fly to my boy.

The sudden cessation of a considerable laudanum habit would induce the same physical and psychological symptoms exhibited by Dyer at Holloway. Although opium withdrawal was not considered by Dr Forbes Winslow, he was adamant that Amelia Dyer was a person of unsound mind and not responsible for her actions.

Dr James Scott was a Bachelor of Medicine and the medical officer at Holloway. He was acting on behalf of the prosecution and, since Mrs Dyer's admittance to Holloway, had observed her on a daily basis. Beyond her desire to commit suicide and her loss of recent memory he could find nothing in her behaviour that was consistent with insanity. His report stated:

> Mrs. Dyer has been quiet and orderly and free from excitement. She has not been melancholic although occasionally depressed. Her memory has been good. She has eaten and slept well. She understands what is said to her and converses coherently and rationally. Insane delusions have not been detected, but she has stated that occasionally she felt as if she could destroy her own life. She has not however attempted to do so, and the opinion is expressed that Mrs. Dyer is not insane, and has not been since her transference to London.

Dr George Savage, also acting on behalf of the prosecution, was a man of impeccable credentials. He had been a physician at St

Bartholomew's Hospital for seventeen years, a Lecturer on Mental Diseases at Guy's Hospital for twenty and had published many books on the subject of insanity. After spending an hour with Amelia Dyer, he, too, came to the conclusion that although she suffered "symptoms of a transient nature" she did not suffer from homicidal mania and was "not mentally unsound".

# 55 The Old Bailey

The Old Bailey in 1896 was situated a few hundred yards north-west of St Paul's Cathedral and was named after the street which ran alongside it. Newgate Gaol stood next door and this close proximity allowed prisoners to be easily transported to the courtrooms for their trials.

The trial of Amelia Dyer, indicted for the wilful murder of Doris Marmon and Harry Simmons, took place in the Old Court on 21 and 22 May 1896 in front of Mr Justice Hawkins, with her daughter Mary Ann Palmer standing as the main witness against her.

Sir Henry Hawkins was known on the court circuit to be a harsh judge but with an eccentric side to his nature. His dog accompanied him everywhere and sat hidden in his robes during trial. It was well known that "m'lud's dog" was a fine companion who conducted himself with "judicial gravity".

The accused woman, who had confessed to the killings but was pleading insanity, looked a good deal older and thinner than she had appeared at Reading. Standing in the dock in a plain black dress and without bonnet, her hair scraped back into a knot, Amelia Dyer listened as Evelina Marmon and Mary Ann Beattie gave their evidence. She was subdued and pale, only looking up once and flushing momentarily when her daughter appeared, taking her place in a witness box hung with various items of infant apparel connected to the case.

Polly had changed considerably since being taken into custody, her cool demeanour replaced by a harassed look.. "She was a good deal paler than at her previous appearance," reported the *Weekly Dispatch* on 24 May 1896, "and the absence of toilet requisites in H.M. prisons interfered a good deal with her attractiveness." She retold the story of Mother's visit to Mayo Road in a quiet but clear and distinct voice. She was asked to explain how the items of clothing that had once belonged to Doris Marmon and Harry Simmons had ended up at her own house and she told of how Mother had brought them, saying she had made them for Polly's own nurse child, Harold. She had received £12 when she had adopted little Harold.

Justice Hawkins asked her if she had really wanted to adopt a child.

"Yes," she replied.

"Then why not take it without any money?"

Polly had no answer to this question.

The prosecution asked Polly to repeat what her mother had said about the child Harry Simmons after they had collected him from Paddington Station. With a degree of reluctance she told how Mother had called it a "little Devil", shook it because it was fretful and said she "shouldn't keep it".

Cross-examined by Mr Kapadia, Polly ended the day by telling how Mother had been confined in the Gloucester and Wells Asylums and how she often suffered from delusions.

When the trial resumed the following day, Polly was once again called to the witness box and told the court of the many children her mother had taken in to nurse throughout the years and the many changes of address. She told of how her mother had gone into an asylum on two occasions when pressure was being put upon her by the parents of a child she had "adopted". She was rigorously questioned as to the number of children Mother had at her different residences, but could give no satisfactory answer.

Mrs Sargeant, Mr and Mrs Culham, John Toller, Granny Smith, Dr Maurice, DC Anderson and Miss Gibbs, the prison matron, were all called to repeat the evidence already given at Reading. The prosecution closed their case by suggesting that Amelia Dyer had carried on a business of "trafficking in infants", for which she received premiums, and that afterward she strangled the infants and disposed of the bodies in the Thames.

It was down to Mr Kapadia to prove that Amelia Dyer had been "unaccountable for her actions" at the time of the murders. But it was an impossible task. The evidence of Dr Forbes Winslow was flimsy and two doctors who had attended to Amelia during her time in the asylums were unable to lend weight to her cause.

Dr Scott of Holloway Prison and the eminent specialist Dr Savage rebutted the evidence for the defence. Both had examined Amelia Dyer and both were of the opinion that she was perfectly sane at the time of the murders.

Mr Kapadia attempted to strengthen Amelia Dyer's plea of insanity by telling the court that her own mother, Sarah Hobley, had died a lunatic. When Amelia was eleven her mother had died of typhus and in her final days had suffered a complete mental collapse. Amelia remembered only the madness and not the typhus which had caused it. The prosecution then called Dyer's brother, James Hobley. He was the last witness to stand in the box and told the court he had been estranged from Dyer for thirty-five years and requested that his name be kept out of the press. He told the court, "My mother was never insane – there was never a case of insanity in our family, so far as I have heard our family history."

Dyer stands for the verdict, *Famous Crimes*, 1905

The trial of the "Reading Baby Farmer" had finally come to an end and the lights of the court were lowered as the jury exited to consider their verdict. The only sound to be heard was the ticking of the court-room clock reverberating around the walls of the sombre room. Dr Forbes Winslow would later claim that the damning press coverage coupled with the "severity" of Justice Hawkins' remarks throughout the trial "no doubt influenced the minds of the jury". He claimed to have overheard a juror remarking that Dyer's visions of having been eaten by worms would, "soon be a reality". In any event, after only four and a half minutes the jury returned with a verdict of "Guilty".

Justice Hawkins pronouncing the death sentence,
*Famous Crimes*, 1905

The colour drained from Amelia Dyer's face as Justice Hawkins donned the black cap and in solemn and measured tones pronounced the death sentence. The muscles of her face twitched and she began to rock backwards and forwards on her feet before being assisted from the dock and led out of court.

# 56 Newgate

I want to keep myself cool and quiet because they are going to let me see Polly. My poor child has been brought from Reading to Holloway and she is there now … I want you to tell the world that whatever my daughter has said about me in the witness box, I forgive her from the bottom of my heart. She told them all she knew poor dear … What makes them so cruel to me that they won't let me live to see Polly out of her trouble? … I wish the world could understand what it is to have someone saying to you 'Get rid of them, get rid of them'. I don't feel mad now, it's so nice and quiet here … I used to like to watch them with the tape around their neck, but it was soon all over with them; though when I had thrown them in the water I felt better and easier like in my mind … Before I die I want you to tell the mothers of the little babies that I pray for them every night to forgive me in their hearts.

Extract from an interview with Amelia Dyer by a journalist
from the *Weekly Dispatch* from Newgate Gaol

Amelia was taken to Newgate Gaol to await her execution and on the morning of Friday 5 June she received her long-wished-for visit from her daughter. Polly had been transferred temporarily from Reading Gaol to Holloway for the sole purpose of visiting her mother in Newgate. A wire grille separated the two women and their conversation was witnessed by a number of attendants. There is no surviving record as to what they talked of that day, but with Polly's trial at Reading due to take place on the 16th of the month it is safe to assume that some mention was made of the possible outcome. Amelia's Newgate file reveals that Polly had written to her mother on several occasions, her prime concern being that her mother's memory and credibility as a sane witness would not hamper her own case in any way. It is telling that on the very afternoon of the visit Amelia wrote another letter to the authorities proclaiming her daughter's innocence once again.

June 5th

I am thankful to say I have seen my dear child now this morning. The parting is more than I can bear. I was glad to see her looking so well dear child. God only knows how grieved I am to know she is suffering for no fault of her own. She did nothing, she knew nothing. I am speaking truthfully the girl is innocent of the charge against her.

The following day the governor of Newgate Gaol was served with a subpoena ordering Amelia Dyer to appear as witness at her daughter's forthcoming trial. It was a unique occurrence in the history of criminal procedure: Amelia's execution was due to take place a week *before* her daughter's trial. But there was to be no respite for Amelia as it was deemed that a prisoner under sentence of death was considered already legally dead and therefore any evidence she could offer at her daughter's trial would be inadmissible.

Amelia never gave up protesting her daughter's innocence and it was only on the eve of her execution that she was to learn that the charges against Polly had been dropped. Polly was still ordered to appear before the Berkshire Assizes but, as the Treasury offered no evidence against her, the case was dismissed and she was set free.

# 57 The End

The morning of 10 June 1896 dawned dark and gloomy. The almost tropical temperatures of the past weeks had finally eased and a warm, heavy rain fell on the streets outside Newgate Gaol, turning the hard-baked ground into wet sludge. Amelia Dyer had spent the night thrashing about on her hard bed, muttering and quietly sobbing. She was barely able to touch the bread and butter, eggs and tea which were offered to her for breakfast. She had been brought her own clothes to dress in and her hair had been scraped up into a knot on the crown of her head so as to leave her neck bare.

The condemned cell at Newgate Gaol, *Weekly Dispatch*, 7 June 1896

# The End

After requesting pen and paper Mother wrote what was to be her very last letter.

My Child, my dear Child,
May God Almighty Bless you and keep you. It is a great relief to me to know you will not be prosecuted. I knew it yesterday. Now my child for Willies and Annie's sakes don't go abroad no doubt you will have a letter from our Chaplain. I myself can say no more only God Bless and keep you both. Mother
My hope is built on nothing less than Jesus blood and righteousness.

⊰⊱

James Billington was born to be a hangman. From an early age he had constructed model scaffolds in his backyard and played at executions. When not performing his duties for the prison authorities he worked as a barber in his home town of Bolton. Just before nine o'clock he entered Amelia Dyer's cell and swiftly pinioned her arms. Supported on both sides and barely able to walk, the condemned woman was virtually carried to the scaffold shed where she was asked to make a final statement.

"I have nothing to say" was the reply.

James Billington placed the bag over her head and adjusted the noose. At nine o'clock precisely the lever was pulled and Amelia Elizabeth Dyer dropped to her death.

On account of her weight and the softness of the textures, rather a short drop was given. It proved to be quite sufficient.
Extract from Prison Commission File: Record of Execution.

# 58 The Auction

SENSATIONAL SALE
WEDNESDAY 10 JUNE, AT 3 0'CLOCK
45, KENSINGTON ROAD, OXFORD ROAD
READING
BABY FARM

*Reading Standard*, 12 June 1896

By the morning of Amelia Dyer's execution, 45 Kensington Road stood empty. Nellie Oliver, Willie Thornton and the last remaining baby had all been rehoused. Granny Smith returned to Barton Regis Workhouse in Bristol where she remained until her death in 1901.

Mr Henry Hutt, local auctioneer, was charged with selling the contents of the Dyer household, "occupied till her arrest as a murderer". The proceeds of the sale would no doubt have satisfied a landlord whose rent had not been paid for some weeks. The paucity of items listed in the auctioneer's catalogue revealed that any money Mrs Dyer had made from her "Massacre of the Innocents" had either already been spent or hidden away. Despite the poor quality of goods on offer, Mr Hutt found himself besieged with applications from those who wished to view the interior of the infamous house, no doubt to gloat over the many ordinary items that had been touched by the murderess's hands. Mr Hutt, being a man of principle, tried not to pander to morbid curiosity, but nevertheless, as the time for the sale approached almost a thousand people had congregated down the length of Kensington Road. Carts, wagons and bicycles jammed together as men, women and children gathered – "all eager to see and secure some fragment of the goods which had such a horrible story attached to them". The crowds remained in the road and Mr Hutt set up his rostrum behind the front railings while his clerk set himself up in the front parlour.

The skies over Reading had been growing darker by the hour, black clouds rolling and merging and blocking out the light. As the sale was about to commence, an angry growl of thunder heralded the start of a fierce storm. It was a surreal scene and those in the crowd of a superstitious nature were somewhat alarmed. The sale was halted four times before the storm eventually drifted its way south.

Among the items up for sale was a rudimentary armchair made by Arthur Palmer. Its four legs were enclosed at the bottom by rough boarding with the seat made from a lid. Closer inspection revealed it to be no more than a sugar box with a back and a basic pair of arms. The lid would have been hidden when the seat was covered by a cushion. The purpose of this strange piece of furniture seemed all too clear to the bidders. "If the murderess was interrupted she could deposit a body or other incriminating evidence in the box without delay."

There were plenty of showmen in the crowd and bidding was brisk with the grisly object eventually fetching twenty-nine shillings from a man named Pocock. There was keen competition among the bidders, particularly when a bedstead and bedding upon which the murderess had slept and a child's cradle were offered up for sale. A photograph of Dyer's son Willie caused much excitement and protestation from the crowd. Many were against the photograph being put up for sale, shouting, "Don't show the boy up, he can't help what his mother did!" A battle of wills ensued between those who wished to save the photograph for the boy and those who wanted to secure it for other purposes. It was eventually sold for five shillings to a kind-natured person who promised to hold on to the photograph and hand it back to Willie Dyer when he returned home from sea.

The entire contents of Amelia Dyer's home realized a paltry £7.15s.3d.

※※

Two weeks after Amelia Dyer's execution the *Weekly Dispatch* filled its front page with a statement made by Mary Ann Palmer. The daughter of the "Reading Baby Farmer" painted a scandalous and distressing picture of her life with the murderess. Recounting her mother's crimes in vivid and shocking detail, she ended her story with an extraordinary claim that she had in fact been a nurse child herself, taken in by Amelia when she was only three weeks old. She claimed only to have learned the truth of her parentage shortly before her wedding to Arthur Palmer when Mother had revealed that her real parents were a gentleman farmer and his wife, close relations of William Dyer's. The statement ended with a solemn affirmation that all she had said was true in substance and detail and the *Weekly Dispatch* reproduced her signature at the end of it.

# 59  Legal Repercussions

In July 1896, the unprecedented furore caused by the Amelia Dyer case was too great to be ignored by the Home Office. In a series of memos from Whitehall, the Secretary of State made clear his feeling that "the recent case of Elizabeth Dyer in which a series of infant murders extending over a period of years was brought to light, have convinced Sir Matthew Ridley that the [Infant Life Protection] Act of 1872 has not secured the results which were expected by Parliament". His first step was to urge all borough and district councils to routinely pursue "the advertisements of baby-farmers (such as those by means of which Elizabeth Dyer seems chiefly to have obtained the children entrusted to her)".

Secondly, he admitted that the case highlighted that there were "important limitations in the Act itself"; that it was essentially "defective"; and announced that its improvement was to be put "under the consideration of a Select Committee of the House of Lords".

The second Infant Life Protection Act came about as a result of the findings of that Select Committee. The new act accounted for the shortcomings of its predecessor and provided authorities across the country with the remit to identify and supervise the nursing and adoption of infants under their jurisdiction, along with power to enforce it.

Every authority was to appoint inspectors who would implement and maintain the terms of the Act: they were to make frequent inspections of any residences they had reason to suspect were houses of confinement or baby farms. They had the authority to remove any children found to be abused. It also stipulated that any newspaper advertisements "relating to establishments for taking in infants are to be submitted to the Commissioner, with a report of any circumstances connected therewith known to the Police".

⌐⊨⊨⌐

Three more baby farmers would hang for infanticide during the ten years that followed the execution of Amelia Dyer.

# 60 A Brown Paper Parcel

The thirteenth of September 1898, two years and three months after the execution of Amelia Dyer, was one of the hottest days recorded over the past half-century. Fred Dennis, carriage and wagon examiner for the GWR, was enjoying the relative cool of the early morning as he began his shift at Newton Abbot railway station. At about 7.15, as he passed by a carriage which had been shunted into a siding the night before, he heard a child's cry. He searched under the carriage before realizing that the sound came from within the locked ladies' compartment. Calling to his foreman, Thomas Wills, to bring the carriage key, the two men unlocked the door and entered the compartment.

Under the seat was a brown paper parcel tied up with string, a second bundle containing infant clothing and a bottle of milk. Thomas Wills untied the string from the parcel and pulled aside the brown paper. Inside was a baby girl, about three weeks old; she was cold and her clothing was soaked through, but she was very much alive.

GWR Inspector James Tucker had been on duty the evening before when the 9.13 train from Plymouth had arrived at Newton Abbot. As the train was terminating, he walked the length of the plat-form shouting "All Change!" in the usual way. As he reached the last compartment a female passenger put her head out of the window and asked if she needed to change for Bath. Inspector Tucker informed her that she did and he opened the door of the carriage to help her out, locking it behind her. The woman was in her early twenties and was dressed in a fawn-coloured skirt, a lace-trimmed blue blouse and a white sailor hat. Over her arm she had been carrying a dark blue cloak. The carriage she had been in was shunted into the sidings.

From information given them by the two GWR employees the police were able to trace the woman to Bath and then on to Brize Norton where, on 14 September, she was arrested along with her husband. Letters found at the couple's home revealed they had advertised for a baby to adopt and that the wife, "Mrs Stewart", had travelled to Plymouth to collect the newborn child of a widow lady called Jane Hill.

Dear Madam,

Your letter just to hand. I beg to say I should be pleased to take the little one referred to. I will do so for £12 instead of £15 if the mother will pay my railway expenses. The little one with us would have a good home, would be brought up well and have a parents love and care. My husband is a farmer here and it is a very healthy place. If we took the child and the mother wished to see it, we should be pleased for her to do so at any time. Hoping to hear from you by return

Believe me to remain

Yours very truly

Mrs A Stewart

The couple in question were identified as Polly Palmer and her husband, Arthur Ernest Palmer.

# Acknowledgements

We are indebted to Ken Wells, Curator of the Thames Valley Police Museum, and to Alan McCormick, Curator of the Crime Museum, New Scotland Yard, for their time and generosity in allowing us access to their archives. Thanks also to Dr Allen M. Anscombe, forensic pathologist, who patiently and painstakingly talked us through our many medical queries; Michael Lubieszko, forensic anthropologist, for his gruesome but invaluable assistance; and Francis Disney for his knowledge of Shepton Mallet Gaol. If we have misinterpreted or misrepresented any information they have shared with us, the fault is entirely ours.

This book could not have been written without the help of the staff at Bristol Records Office, Bristol Central Reference Library, Berkshire Records Office, Gloucester Records Office, London Metropolitan Archives, Devon Records Office, Newton Abbot Library, Somerset Records Office, Wells Library, Cardiff Records Office, the National Archives at Kew, the British Library, the British Newspaper Library and Reading Central Reference Library. Thanks to Dawn Bishop at Reading City Museum and to Jenny Lister, Curator of Fashion and Textiles at the V&A. Also to Julius Herrstein, Curator, and John Pimm, of the Glenside Hospital Museum, Bristol, for their enthusiasm, access to their archives and their vast knowledge of the history of psychiatric nursing.

Thank you to Jack Holmes, Alex Southam, James Deary, retired Metropolitan Police Inspector Malcolm Cotton, and map-reader extraordinaire Barry Boulton, for helping us in their own individual ways.

A big thank you to Mike: for tolerating an eight-month-long Dyer obsession; for his unstinting confidence in this project; and for editing in the face of great adversity. Thanks to Bob and Jeannette Vale and Claire and Chris Pap for their childcare, spare rooms, tea and sympathy.

# Acknowledgements

Huge thanks to Paul for his technical support and for learning how to cook. Also to Sheila Whitehead for braving the London Underground system in her capacity as assistant researcher; to Jason and Nicola for Indian takeaways and a free London pad; and to Daisy, Ella and Riley for putting up with Dad's cooking.

And, finally, thanks to Penny Phillips at André Deutsch for her belief in us and her enthusiasm for this book.

This book has been extensively based upon primary sources, but the following titles have also been consulted:

Francis J. Disney, *Heritage of a Prison HMP Shepton Mallet*, 1986.

Francis J. Disney, *380 Years of Prison Regimes*, 1992.

Madge Dresser and Philip Ollernshaw, *The Making of Modern Bristol*, Redcliffe Press, 1996.

Douglas Duncan, *The Mendip Hospital*, 2000.

Donal F. Early, *The Lunatic Pauper Palace; Glenside Hospital, Bristol, 1861–1994*, Friends of Glenside Hospital Museum, 2003.

Simon Fowler, *Workhouse*, The National Archives, 2007.

Julius Herrstein, *Glenside Hospital*, produced and printed by the author, nd.

Ian M. C. Hollingsbee, *Gloucester's Asylums, 1794–2002*, 2002.

Barry Horton, *West Country Weather Book*, 1995.

Helen Reid, *Life in Victorian Bristol*, Redcliffe Press, 2005.

George R. Sims, *Among My Autographs*, Chatto & Windus, 1904.

W. Wood (editor), *Survivors' Tales of Famous Crimes*, Cassell & Co., 1916.

# Index